DAVID CRONENBERG
CLINICAL TRIALS

DAVID CRONENBERG
CLINICAL TRIALS

VIOLET LUCCA

Foreword *by* Viggo Mortensen

Contents

FOREWORD — *page 9*

Part I

INDIVIDUATION

Introduction — *page 17*
i. The Persona — *page 26*
   i.i   Part A
   i.ii   Part B
ii. The Shadow — *page 82*
   Stereo
   Crimes of the Future (1970)
   Scanners
iii. Animus/Anima/Animum — *page 92*
   Dead Ringers
   Naked Lunch
   M. Butterfly
   Crash
iv. The Self — *page 114*
   Shivers
   Rabid
   The Brood
   The Fly

Part II

PSYCHOTHERAPY

Introduction — *page 129*
v. Confession — *page 132*
   A History of Violence
   Eastern Promises
vi. Elucidation — *page 140*
   Cosmopolis
   Maps to the Stars
vii. Education — *page 150*
   A Dangerous Method
   The Dead Zone
   Spider
   Crimes of the Future (2022)
viii. Transformation — *page 168*
   Videodrome
   eXistenZ

INTERVIEWS — *page 185*
FILMOGRAPHY — *page 264*
AFTERWORD — *page 274*

ACKNOWLEDGMENTS *page 277*
IMAGE CREDITS *page 280*
INDEX *page 281*
BIBLIOGRAPHY *page 284*

DAVID CRONENBERG: CLINICAL TRIALS

6

7

DAVID CRONENBERG: CLINICAL TRIALS

8

Foreword
CRONENBERG IN REFLECTION
BY VIGGO MORTENSEN

When I met David Cronenberg in Los Angeles in early 2004 in connection with the next movie he was planning to make—*A History of Violence*—I was already, like many others, an admirer of his work. I did not know what kind of man I'd be meeting. Although I'd seen his movies and seen photographs of him in magazines, I'd not yet seen or heard many interviews he'd given. Based on his movies and the photographs of him, I wondered if he'd be a brooding or intimidating presence. In any case, although I'd found some moments in his movies darkly humorous, I did not expect to be laughing much during our encounter. To my surprise, he was extremely gentle and affable, and had me laughing within minutes of sitting down to have breakfast with him.

Of course, that morning I had no idea I'd eventually have the good fortune to work for him on that movie and, so far, three others (*Eastern Promises*, *A Dangerous Method*, and *Crimes of the Future*). More importantly, there was no way to know we'd become more than creative collaborators—that we'd be good friends and continue to communicate regularly over the next twenty years. Nor could I have imagined that I would actually have the temerity to offer him a role in my directorial debut, which he accepted and, unsurprisingly, did a wonderful job with.

As to what this introduction ought to be about… there is a lot I could say about him as a director and writer. Where to start, how to organize my thoughts about such a singular storyteller? There is a Spanish saying that translates roughly as: "What is good, if brief, is twice as good." Brevity is not often a strength of mine, however, except in some poems I've written. I'll just go with the first thing that comes to mind at this particular moment when I think of David, and take it from there.

In 2006 I wrote an essay on a connection between David Cronenberg's work and that of Carl Dreyer. After reading it at a Palm Springs awards ceremony early that year, at which I'd been asked to present a large and unwieldy career achievement trophy to David, I have not been able to find the text. Unfortunately I only had the one handwritten copy of the essay, and probably lost it that night in the California desert, or put it somewhere for safekeeping that I now cannot recall. Maybe it will turn up someday.

Because reading that sort of essay at a star-studded gala event to an audience enjoying their steaks and consuming copious amounts of alcohol had turned out to be a poor choice on my part—people talked a lot during my somewhat academic speech, and not many people other than David paid the slightest attention to it—I skipped the post-awards party in the hotel's impressive garden area and went to my room. Although I'd already had a few consoling drinks at the ceremony after the presentation debacle, I proceeded to consume the alcoholic contents of the room's mini-bar and lay down in bed to watch an old western playing on the TV.

David had invited me to accompany him to the party, but I'd been too embarrassed to attend after reading my serious-minded essay to that boisterous celebrity crowd. After about three-quarters of an hour and several drinks, however, I suddenly thought: "Fuck it. David is my friend; I shouldn't abandon him." I got dressed and went down to the garden, where I eventually spotted his signature spiky pompadour coiffure among the many bobbing heads. As I approached it, I saw that he was standing talking with a few people, including director Paul Haggis, whose movie *Crash* would go on to win the Best Picture Oscar that year.

Perhaps because I was a bit drunk, I walked straight up to them and said to Paul Haggis: "Oh, you're the Canadian director who directed *Crash*!" Then I turned to David and said: "And so are you!" This got a variety of laughs, some less comfortable than others. I may risk being indiscreet by telling you about that moment, but then it did not seem to me very discreet at the time, nor does it now, that Mr. Haggis had taken the title of David's relatively recent and quite memorable movie adaptation of J.G. Ballard's novel for his movie. But I digress.

I don't remember any details of the text I wrote for presenting David with his award that night, or even what my overall argument was. Perhaps that is for the best, as I am not sure what I'd think of it eighteen years later. However, it may be as good a place as any to finally start this introduction in earnest. Dreyer and Cronenberg. Why not?

In 2001 Armond White wrote that Dreyer was arguably "the first great film artist to pursue the ineffable in cinema...," and that he "gave depth to what early silent filmmakers innately understood yet took for granted: that cinema's ability to record reality also provided a view that transcended everyday reality." I do not take his statement as a reference to any cosmic or inherently religious content in Dreyer's movies, although many have claimed to perceive such ethereal qualities in his work. Rather, I see it as an acknowledgment that Dreyer was able to lead audiences to understand that anything can and will sometimes happen in life. It does not matter to me whether Dreyer believed in God or in life after death. That is irrelevant to appreciating his work as far as I'm concerned. What he shows us in his movies is grounded in physical and emotional immediacy. Flesh is flesh, death is death (even when "Inger" appears to wake from the dead at the end of *Ordet*), and life is mostly mysterious and unpredictable. Few directors—certainly in his lifetime—came closer than Dreyer to examining the passing of a moment in time on a human face as unpretentiously and devastatingly as he repeatedly did.

As Dreyer once said in reference to his *The Passion of Joan of Arc* and movies in general, "there must be harmony between the genuineness of feelings and the genuineness of things." No matter how expressionistic the look of that movie is, what I recall most vividly, after having seen it numerous times over the years, are the intimate and emotionally raw portrayals of "Jeanne" and the other characters in that story—mesmerizingly present, striving for an absolute personal truth.

In David's movies, which, like Dreyer's, always invite you into a very particular but consistently realized universe of the director's making, an unvarnished presentation of physicality and emotion is always at their core, regardless of genre. In a sense, both Dreyer and Cronenberg can be considered to be exacting surgeons in their meticulous exploration of human bodies, behaviors, and thought processes.

A quote from Danish author Karen Blixen related to this very sort of fearless reckoning with life, decomposition, and death comes to mind:

> *"I don't believe in evil, I believe only in horror.*
> *In nature there is no evil, only an abundance*
> *of horror: the plagues and the blights and*
> *the ants and the maggots."*

Aside from the superficial differences between Dreyer's and Cronenberg's movies—and their personalities, as far as I can tell—I believe that they have many things in common. Even the way they seem to be perceived by their peers, critics, and audiences—and their similar determination to ignore any constraints that those perceptions might put on their approach to the work they've chosen—strike me as congruent. Perhaps as a result of both directors' insistence on exploring whatever subject has attracted them at any given time, regardless of how "unmarketable" it might have seemed or how much it diverged from anything in their previous work that audiences had connected with, both have had to be quite stubborn to get their movies made.

Although David has been able to make more movies than Dreyer did, it has often been as difficult for him to find financial backing for his productions as it was for Dreyer. They are both greatly respected, but their approach to storytelling provokes as much wariness as anticipation in critics and audiences, and perhaps especially in potential producers. Perhaps this extends to actors as well, who sometimes decline David's invitation to play because of the perceived risk of taking part in something that might turn out to be a bit too grotesque or undecipherable. Many—if not most—actors do not want to make fools of themselves.

I can also be quite wary about taking on a new role. It takes a good deal of time and effort to properly prepare for, perform in, and then promote a movie. Consequently, I prefer, if possible and affordable, to wait until I've found a role—or it has found me—that is worth the personal investment required to do a good job of it. Even with David I have hesitated a couple of times—not to be in his movies when asked, but regarding which role to play in them. This happened initially with the third and fourth movies I played in for him. I trust him more than I trust most other directors, however, and I eventually jumped in and played the characters he wanted me to play. He knows what he wants, but you are always welcome to bring as much to the process of building a character as you like.

He is genuinely collaborative, and will carefully consider your ideas and your doubts before accepting or dismissing them. Working with him is not like working with anyone else. I recommend it, if you are lucky enough to be invited.

Another important thing that Cronenberg and Dreyer movies have in common, as I see them, is the representation of metamorphosis. The principal characters in their stories usually undergo significant changes, evolve physically and/or mentally in ways that can be surprising, disturbing, transgressive, self-sacrificing, and even redemptive. These conscious or unconscious transformations can be quite subtle or they can be obvious to the point of beggaring the audiences' belief in them. Rising from the dead, growing new internal organs, entirely changing identities, fusing with the unthinkable or unknowable, wreaking havoc or surrendering to immolation, sometimes destroying themselves or flirting with doing so in recognition of the ultimate end that awaits us all.

Characters in Dreyer and Cronenberg stories tend to reveal, unwittingly or not, the best and worst in themselves as they interact with other humans and with their environments. They are unmasked in the process, stripped down to their essential flesh and fear. They can change from the sublime to the ridiculous, from being empowered and at ease in the world to being utterly lost and vulnerable.

Cronenberg and Dreyer are equally existential in the sense that something always has to give, even break, in their stories. That tension, the pressure to surrender to metamorphosis and eventual decay, seems essential to the dramatic power of their movies. As the X song says: "This is a game that moves as you play." If you don't move, don't evolve and transform, you can't play.

DAVID CRONENBERG: CLINICAL TRIALS

DAVID CRONENBERG: CLINICAL TRIALS

PART I

INDIVIDUATION

In September of 2022, I attended Morbid Anatomy's virtual seminar "Protocols of Extreme Creativity," taught by Diana Pasulka. I had always hoped to make my own films, but time, money, exhaustion from my day job(s), and fear always got in the way. Over the course of the seminar's three sessions, Carl Jung came up repeatedly—active imagination, the collective unconscious, and his writing on UFOs, which neither argued for their existence or nonexistence, but saw them as a modern manifestation of angels or God in an uncertain, mechanized world. I was vaguely familiar with Jung, mostly through David Cronenberg's 2011 film *A Dangerous Method*, but this encounter left me wanting more. What I discovered was far more fascinating than what a certain Canadian psychologist who uses Jung's explicitly mystical, gnostic principles to interpret the Bible (and hate trans people) had led me to believe.

In particular, I found myself drawn to Jung's approach to schizophrenia. Unlike his contemporaries—and the overwhelming majority of mental health professionals working today—Jung actually listened to these patients' delusions and hallucinations and spent time analyzing them. He found patterns across them, which eventually led him to his theories of the collective unconscious; he also argued that schizophrenics were individuals who were stuck in the rawness and strangeness of the unconscious. I was struck by how humane this line of thought was, one that seemed to recognize difference without othering.

The intensity of my reaction comes from personal experience: my mother was a schizophrenic who was in and out of mental institutions throughout my childhood, and was eventually placed in an assisted living apartment, where she resided alone until her death at fifty-eight. (I was raised by two of her siblings and her father.) Like many who suffer from schizophrenia, she was often resistant to treatment.

As a child, I didn't understand why she was ill, and why she didn't want to be well. Her sudden, premature death (along with other things that I had previously accepted as merely part of her condition) led me to question the quality of her care. It was entirely public-funded—funding that, over the years, had been drastically cut by a series of Republican governors, and it was hard not to view her precipitous decline as the result of this. But there was also the medication she was given, which blunted her personality—it was impossible to sustain a conversation with her for longer than a few minutes at a time. My dutiful phone calls back home after moving to New York in 2007 were difficult. I suppose I could list other things. She went to bed extremely early every night, though glimpses of who she was (and her energy) would peek through as the time to her next dose approached, for example. For the sake of time—and for my aunt, who sadly outlived her younger sister—I will leave it at that. I reserve the right not to confess all.

I became enraged after her death, a feeling I return to every time I stop and think that her life ended the way it did, on a dirty kitchen floor. Had she simply slipped through the cracks, or was that always her ultimate destination? The approach to her treatment was shutting her away from public view, and forcibly fitting her into docility, a state of consciousness that was more socially acceptable in a world supposedly guided by rationality. I'm certainly not advocating for the end of all psychiatric medication in favor of herbal tinctures or some other woo-woo bullshit, as there are plenty of people who benefit from them and get to live their lives. But she didn't. I continue to wonder why this was the best-case scenario for a woman from a lower-middle-class family in Cedar Rapids, Iowa, who simply wanted to have children and care for them. She was unable to do that.

Schizophrenia is one of the least-understood forms of mental illness because it is so complex. This is no doubt why the fundamental approach to her care was, on the surface, not much different from those who were sent to Burghölzli, the Swiss clinic where Jung worked, more than a century ago. The lack of innovation and the widespread disinterest in non-biomedical research (such as efficacious treatments like the Hearing Voices movement or avatar therapy) strikes me as profoundly cruel. It's a market decision, not one driven by the sense of salvation that Jung possessed.

Schizophrenics terrify people for a lot of reasons, often under the misconception that they're actively dangerous. (They are actually less likely than other individuals to commit crimes.) Perhaps, as Jung viewed it, this fear comes from being confronted with the unfiltered unconscious. Whatever it is, it leads to a malicious dehumanization. Consider Jordan Neely, another person who "slipped through the cracks," and was strangled to death in a New York City subway car—in front of onlookers, or others who shamefully cast their gaze away—after he shouted something and (might've) thrown a few bits of trash around. He was sentenced to death for simply existing in a public space, by another man who had no right to hand down such a brutal punishment. The celebratory or indifferent reactions to Neely's murder—online, by the media, by public officials—chills me like little else. He, like my mother, had a family who loved him but couldn't help him. There are many injustices that transpire in the richest country in the world that could be ameliorated by allocating more funding to fix them. Yet money, which is treated as so precious and finite, which lies only in the hands of society's worthiest citizens, is spent elsewhere. Consider Elon Musk, a man who spent $44 billion on a bad website and harbors a strange desire to escape to another planet. Those delusions, though often critiqued, are socially acceptable. I find them far more menacing than a homeless person on a train.

The films of David Cronenberg frequently explore what happens when other forms of socially acceptable madness—which arise from conforming to a hyper-rational and science-centric worldview—go too far. There's Dr. Stringfellow in *Stereo* (who mutilates and isolates a group of college students in order to study telepathy), Dr. Rouge in the first *Crimes of the Future* (who causes an epidemic that kills all post-pubescent females), Dr. Hobbes in *Shivers* (who creates a parasite that causes its victims to become mindless sex maniacs), Dr. Keloid in *Rabid* (whose novel skin graft technique leads to another zombie-like epidemic), Dr. Raglan in *The Brood* (whose new therapy, psychoplasmics, leads to the violent deaths of multiple people by mutant children), Dr. Ruth in *Scanners* (who intentionally creates an army of half-schizophrenic, half-telekinetic people, including his own sons), Seth Brundle (who accidentally splices his DNA with a housefly's and attempts to fuse himself with his girlfriend to cure it), and the Mantle twins in *Dead Ringers* (who screw their patients and deal with their worsening drug addictions by syncopating their pill intake).

Yet they're also far more than this critique. They're darkly comic, beautiful, sad, frightening, entrancing, ominous, and profoundly philosophical. Their multifaceted nature brings me to another one of Jung's ideas: that of the numinous. This concept, either borrowed from religious scholar Rudolf Otto, the Latin root, or some combination of the two, is used to describe ineffable experiences that contain such conflicting feelings, but also impart a sense of the divine. The numinous gives us a taste of the infinite, of the mystery we struggle to comprehend in our human form; in Jung's words, they feed the "hunger of the soul." Cronenberg's films lend themselves to such wonder and terror, as they tend to linger. It's useful to think of the numinous when pondering the end of *Videodrome*, which can either be seen as softcore smut-peddler Max Renn (James Woods) dying by suicide or transcending to some other unknowable place, perhaps the "video arena." The reality-bending conclusion of 1999's *eXistenZ* (where a man anxiously wonders, "Is this still the game?") or the moment of grace (a man in near-constant physical agony blissfully smiling after he eats a bar of plastic) that marks the end of 2022's *Crimes of the Future* also feels numinous. Or, at least it does to me.

My goal, as always with my criticism, is to prompt new thoughts about a film—which, even if you strongly disagree with what I've written, hopefully leads to something novel in your own mind. You don't need to have suffered the same shame and indignities that have resulted from my mother's illness, my gender, my class, or any other part of me that is me to understand why Cronenberg's films are so captivating. They're well worth spending time with, regardless of what I put down. I just happen to be here with you.

Auteur theory has many flaws, too many to mention here. I certainly don't believe it to be universally true, so instead I'm treating the work itself as an individual: one that grows up, goes through a deeper reckoning of who they are, and then maybe seeks out a shrink. Thus, I've divided this book into two parts: Individuation and Pyschotherapy.

The first pairs Cronenberg films with the different stages of individuation, which is a process of self-discovery Jung outlined. (It's most easily understood as taking off a series of masks until you finally reach your inner, true self.) I thought that moving through this process parallels the journey of an artist: slowly, their work becomes more distinctively their own, truer to their own vision. The first chapter in this section, "The Persona," functions as a production history—the persona is the face you show to the world, so how someone behaves on set and what they say during interviews seems to fit this pretty well. The other chapters in Individuation pair a group of films with other parts of the psyche that must be integrated and are therefore more critical analysis than "cool trivia stuff." (There is a little bit of the latter thrown in there though, don't worry.)

The second half is divided into the different stages a patient progresses through in Jungian therapy. Rather helpfully, this half of the book is called Psychotherapy. Again, the films' connection to these various stages are conceptual or thematic. The only sequential treatment of Cronenberg's work will appear in the persona chapters. However, I hope you do read this sequentially, as that's how I thought of it. But if you don't, and just hop around between your favorites, that's fine too. Like I said, I'm just glad you're here.

DAVID CRONENBERG: CLINICAL TRIALS

24

25

PART I. INDIVIDUATION

i.i
THE PERSONA

PART A

WHAT IS THE PERSONA?

The process of individuation is akin to removing a series of masks, gradually revealing one's true self. The persona—the version of ourselves we present to the world—is the first to go. While the idea that "we all wear masks" is generally regarded as something so basic that it would only blow the mind of a twelve-year-old, it's nevertheless true and worthy of further examination. The image one presents to the world is entirely dependent on social and historical context: an individual is not the same person with their friends as with their family or with their coworkers or with their lover. This isn't a mark of insincerity, but rather being mindful of other people's expectations. If these images are scrambled, serious tensions arise. We can put on and remove these masks without becoming identified with them.

Except, of course, people do just that without realizing it. Someone with a prestigious job—be it a general or an editor at a legacy magazine—is particularly prone to this problem. The general barks orders at their family; the editor snobbishly dissects light conversation with their friends. Recent social changes have led this particular complex to proliferate, not least because of the aphorism "Do what you love and you'll never work a day in your life," and the advent of "hustle culture." As it becomes increasingly difficult to support oneself as an artist in any medium, and we are asked to use time after our day job to do what we really care about, we lose time to simply be rather than performing a role. The need for an online presence—to promote your work, yourself as a commodity, or to parasocially socialize—requires the creation of another persona and the strict maintenance of it. The validation that accompanies an online persona (which boils down to another adult clicking a cartoon heart on something you posted) can cause confusion about what is and is not real about ourselves. Reactions have also become a commodity.

At the very start of his career, David Cronenberg courted a public persona as a maniac, proclaiming to *The Herald* in 1969 that *Crimes of the Future* would be the most "controversial" film in Canada. (He admitted that he didn't have a script for it yet.) Over the next two decades, he would assert his unrelenting serenity and normality while also offering up tidbits that fed into various epithets like "Dave Deprave," "The Baron of Blood," "Canada's King of Horror," and "The King of Venereal Horror." He had a shirt made that said "More blood! More blood!" and wore it to interviews; in 1981, he told the *Los Angeles Times* that he'd created a special fake blood blend with cherry flavoring.

It's worth noting that sometimes he couldn't keep the story straight. In a 1988 interview with *Maclean's* for *Dead Ringers*, Cronenberg recounted a motorcycle accident in 1970 that required his shoulder to be reattached with a metal pin. He claimed that he asked the

---

1. A cloaked telepath (the incomparable Ronald Mlodzik) and an orderly proceed down one of *Stereo*'s many endless concrete corridors.

2. Little boy blue: Mlodzik holds his temple. His pouty, dandyish aura (and medieval clothes) defined Cronenberg's early films.

3. *Shivers*'s philandering husband Nick Tudor (Allan Kolman) kneels above his fresh kill: Dr. Rollo Linsky (Joe Silver). Silver, who also appears in *Rabid*, holds the distinction of playing most of the overtly, ethnically Jewish characters in Cronenberg's filmography. (In this, Silver enjoys a corned beef sandwich with a pickle while reading over Dr. Hobbes's research.)

4. After murdering her teacher with toy hammers, Candy Carveth (Cindy Hinds) is escorted to the Somafree Institute by two broodlets.

5. Nola Carveth (Samantha Eggar) holds her latest "baby" before licking it clean. Censors in Ontario imposed a cut that made it seem like she was eating the baby.

6. Cameron Vale (Stephen Lack) seems to lose the "scan off" with his brother Darryl Revok (Michael Ironside).

7. Scanner, artist, and family annihilator Benjamin Pierce (played by Cronenberg mainstay Robert Silverman) is fatally shot by Revok's goons. Pierce's sculptures were created by Montreal artist Tom Coulter, who'd go on to serve in the art departments of *Videodrome* (Cronenberg, 1983), *Billy Madison* (Tamra Davis, 1995), *Bride of Chucky* (Ronny Yu, 1998), and *Cold Creek Manor* (Mike Figgis, 2003).

8. Max Renn believes that *Videodrome* is a pirate TV broadcast that he's been able to tap into, but soon discovers that it's a projection of his most transgressive desires.

27

PART I. INDIVIDUATION

doctor not to use anesthetic. When the doctor protested, Cronenberg said, "Do you know what kind of movies I make?" But this was after he'd only completed two feature films and a handful of shorts; of course the doctor didn't know what kind of movies he made. (None of them could really be called horror films, either.) Still, it's a good story—one that fits his persona, and certainly the film about deviant twin gynecologists he was trying to promote. But this anecdote comes back, and changes slightly. In a 1992 article about *Naked Lunch* in *The Guardian*, Cronenberg is accompanied by one of his heroes, William S. Burroughs. While exchanging drug stories, Burroughs says that anesthetic is the one thing that freaks him out, and Cronenberg retells the motorcycle accident story—except he says he got a shot of Demerol.

Noting this difference isn't to nitpick or call Cronenberg a liar, but rather acknowledge the necessity for someone, particularly an artist, to manufacture their persona. Certainly, as you read through this production history, you will find things that perhaps don't line up with whichever Cronenberg interviews you've read. But trust me, they appeared somewhere. The man said it, possibly under intense scrutiny. Whether or not he knew what was said to be untrue isn't for me to know. However, I do suspect that the public image has grown closer to the real man with time. As he said in a 2022 interview, "Cinema is not my life. I have three kids, four grandchildren. That's life." I would agree.

THE CRONENBERG PERSONA

At the 1969 Canadian Film Awards, one of its jurors, the young British director Peter Watkins, declared that there was no Canadian film industry. There wasn't a more damning or humiliating occasion than the CFA, a government-funded institution created with the express intent of legitimizing (and, by extension, catalyzing) a Canadian film industry, to levy such a charge. In retrospect, Watkins, then known for 1965's *The War Game* (a wrenching documentary-style depiction of nuclear apocalypse) and 1967's *Privilege* (a portrait of a tormented pop star in a Christian-fascist state), was primed to call bullshit. His complaint was legitimate: for the first time in the CFA's twenty-year history, there were no feature films for Watkins or his fellow jurors, *Thoroughly Modern Millie* composer Elmer Bernstein and *3:10 to Yuma* director Delmer Daves, to view. Watkins also levied aesthetic criticisms at what he had seen, calling for Canadian filmmakers to shake off the yoke of British and American movies. "What we need today are filmmakers with guts, toughness. Because it's that flame that's so easily squashed out," he told a *Toronto Daily Star* reporter while softly punching one fist into another. "Once a filmmaker gets sucked into the commercial machine, chances are you never hear of that toughness again."

The day before the awards, a twenty-six-year-old Cronenberg held a "grudge" screening of *Stereo*, his sixty-five-minute fiction film about eight sequestered co-ed telepaths' carnal encounters. The CFA's selection committee had rejected *Stereo* on the basis it was actually an experimental film. (*Stereo* purports to be a "mosaic" of educational material, courtesy of the "Canadian Academy of Erotic Enquiry," an imaginary governmental body invested in a different type of social engineering; perhaps the parallel stung.) "If the film awards are ever going to mean anything, they've got to be more than just commercials," Cronenberg was quoted as saying in a brief article about the event. It appeared on the same page as Watkins's inflammatory remarks, mixed amongst notices and reviews of far less memorable entertainments.

Watkins was almost certainly too busy with his official jury duties and arguing about the finer points of socialism with Daves and Bernstein to know that the screening was taking place, let alone have time to attend. Still, it's unlikely it would be obvious that Cronenberg would assume the mantle of tough Canadian. Toronto's underground film scene was

9. The destroyed telepod. Carol Spier based the design on a component of a Ducati motorcycle (one of several Cronenberg owned).

10. Chris Walas and other crewmembers termed this stage of Brundle's transformation "the Space Bug." The final five minutes of the film took several weeks to shoot and required Geena Davis—whose scene partners were a series of animatronic and regular puppets—to constantly be in tears.

booming. An even larger group of cinéastes were making waves in Montreal—which was, before the separatist Parti Québécois took power in the mid-seventies and made French mandatory at businesses and schools (frightening away tons of corporations in the process)—Canada's most prosperous and international city.

The center of power in Eastern Canada has nothing and everything to do with exploding heads, tummy vaginas, and perverted identical twins, whether you like it or not. The Toronto that Cronenberg was born in on March 15, 1943, was a very different place to what it is today—even though Canada's a place that is most often thought of as no place at all. The alternative—that it's a sweet liberal wonderland, a smarter, nicer version of the United States where immigrants are welcomed and encouraged to retain their cultures—hides the virulent racism, xenophobia, anti-environmentalism, and spread of conspiracy theories that have taken hold of sizable segments of the population. Canadianness exists, at once hideous and just-sort-of-all-right to behold, and runs throughout Cronenberg's body of work, not simply in shooting locations but sensibility.

A particularly relevant part of that sensibility has to do with space: there's a lack of both people and industry. One in every three Canadians who served in WWI died, a demo-

Fig A. Filming *The Fly*, 1986.

graphic loss that some regions still haven't recovered from; the country is far less densely populated than its fellow continent-spanning neighbor to the south.

Save for wheat, a sizable number of products are still imported to Canada, be they cars or consumer goods. In the first half of the twentieth century, this reliance on sourcing things from abroad extended to culture: it was the Scot John Grierson who drafted the bill that created the National Film Commission (later the National Film Board of Canada) in 1939, and he, with the help of fellow Scotsman Norman McLaren, who focused its resources primarily on the production of nonfiction and experimental films. (Prior to Grierson's intervention, which garnered the NFB multiple Oscar nominations, the majority of Canadian films were either aimed at attracting immigrants and tourists or sloppily made B-movies made to meet a government-mandated quota.) It was only after the international success of Don Owen's 1964 film *Nobody Waved Good-bye* (it initially bombed in its native land) that the Canadian Broadcasting Company's television arm chose to partner with the NFB. Still, there wasn't a clear path for someone who sought to make narrative features in the country—again giving credence to Watkins's complaint. Although the young Cronenberg was a fan of westerns, comics, and horror movies, just like Steven Spielberg, Martin Scorsese, Tobe Hooper, or any other number of male American directors of his generation, his perceived access to narrative film and filmmaking was distant. This sets him

apart from the aforementioned movie-mad youngsters who shot 8mm before studying film at college and/or at Roger Corman's American International Pictures.

    Forms of expression far closer to home for little David—as in, actually, in his home—were writing and music. Cronenberg's father, Milton, originally from Baltimore, authored crime stories and a newspaper column about stamps (the adorably named "Stamp Chat") for the *Toronto Telegram* and had a lifelong devotion to the literary: during the Depression, Milton owned a bookstore in Toronto and was one of the first people to have copies of *Ulysses* in the city. An aspiring writer from very early on, David wrote his first "novel," all of three pages, when he was ten. Cronenberg devoured the works of William S. Burroughs, Henry Miller, and Vladimir Nabokov, along with then-disreputable science fiction (whose ranks included Isaac Asimov, J.G. Ballard, Philip K. Dick, Kurt Vonnegut, and Ray Bradbury). The louche, unrepentantly erotic, provocative, ideas-driven, experimental yet narrative nature of these works would go on to dominate his films. The director's mother, Esther, was a concert pianist who performed with the Boris Volkoff Ballet Company and the National Ballet of Canada, accompanying Rudolf Nureyev when he came to town.

    She taught her son how to play piano and guitar (as well as some Yiddish), and he seriously considered pursuing a career as a classical guitarist. Cronenberg's older sister Denise, born October 1, 1938, acted in his childhood plays and went on to dance in the National Ballet, appearing on stage (as part of the Candettes troupe) and television (her appearances included a 1961 Nat King Cole special). In addition to being in a creative household in the midst of the stifling, conservative postwar era, Cronenberg describes his parents as being supportive without being overbearing: "What I got at home was an unshakeable, totally realistic faith in my own abilities, and a confidence in being able to do what I wanted to do. We communicated a lot, and very well." Cronenberg's insistence on his normality while creating such viscerally disturbing narratives, imbued with such indelible horror images, can be understood in part as a well-balanced person's reaction to the unyielding, senseless cruelty of existence. After my mother died, a coworker told me that grief is a great teacher; he was a creep in the vein of *David Copperfield* villain Uriah Heep, but what he said is absolutely true (and another way to understand Cronenberg's work).

    Cronenberg attended Dewson Street Public School, Kent Senior School, Harbord Collegiate high school, and North Toronto Collegiate before heading to the University of Toronto. He described his upbringing as middle class and progressive: although both of his parents were Jews, they were neither religious nor adamantly anti-religious. Harbord Collegiate, which was predominantly Jewish and closed for Jewish holidays, was where Cronenberg says he learned about Jewishness, both as culture and religion. That he felt like an outsider in this regard, and wasn't tormented by the yoke of tradition or consumed by fear of Old Testament vengeance, makes his upbringing even more enviable. (His short *At the Suicide of the Last Jew in the World in the Last Cinema in the World*, 2007, a dark comedy about the realization of the persistent wish for the extermination of Jews, is his lone artistic engagement with Jewish identity: a pair of obnoxious TV anchors narrate a live feed of Cronenberg, alone inside a movie theater toilet, loading a gun with a single bullet and pointing it at different parts of his head. Recalling the sensibility of his early films, it's an impressive feat that is better seen than summarized.)

One could argue that this lack of faith opened up space for science and philosophy, but that would be a crass oversimplification best left to the religious right. His fascination with science, like the young Mantle twins in *Dead Ringers* (1988), came from an interest in the act of discovery and discerning function; making sense of life. (The costumes for the child actors in those scenes, created by his sister Denise, were based on an old photograph of Cronenberg as a kid.) This split between his artistic and technical ambitions was eventually resolved, as many things are, by the presence of women on the humanities side of campus and their scarcity on the other. (Cronenberg also won an Epstein Award for a short story he had written, but the point stands.) He switched to the English program.

2.

Sex and changing mores around it in the sixties formed the core of David Secter's *Winter Kept Us Warm* (1965), the film that permanently altered Cronenberg's relationship to the medium. Written, directed, and produced while Secter was still a student at the University of Toronto, the drama follows a male U of T student who has a girlfriend as he catches ambiguous feelings for another male U of T student, who also has a girlfriend. (*Winter Kept Us Warm* was shot on equipment Secter borrowed from Ryerson University, because, unlike the University of Toronto, it had a film program.) Many people Cronenberg knew acted in the film, which went on to screen at Cannes and other festivals internationally. Film was no longer merely something to be experienced, but something achievable. This sentiment was reinforced by people like gallery owner Avrom Issacs, who had connections to New York City's underground film scene and hosted screenings alongside other, more traditionally accessible art forms, such as poetry and jazz.

In an age where we suffer from a surfeit of images, it's difficult to express how earth-shattering and liberating that feeling was and not fall into the hellish pit of sixties hagiography. (As the COVID-19 pandemic showed, there is no uniformity of experience of any time, and really nothing more to add to the opening line of *A Tale of Two Cities*.) I wasn't there; Cronenberg was. He threw himself into learning the technical side of filmmaking.

This education simply involved reading books and magazines about photography and hanging out with cameramen who frequented the Canadian Motion Picture Equipment Company. After gaining a working knowledge of the medium, Cronenberg wrote, photographed, and directed his first short, *Transfer* (1966), a disjointed, Dadaistic tale of a neurotic (classmate Rafe Macpherson) who's in love with and relentlessly pursues his male analyst (classmate Morton Ritts). The premise is a play on the psychoanalytic notion of transference, a therapeutic phenomenon Sigmund Freud began to explore during the early days of analysis when there was an epidemic of female patients falling in love with their male doctors. (As Cronenberg would explain years later, his interest in Freud during this time was partly contrarian: Jung's writings were extremely popular in mainstream and counter-cultural circles.) *Transfer*'s bare-bones setting (a snowy field) and limited mise-en-scène (a dresser, a kitchen table, a chair) seem like a wise choice for an inexperienced filmmaker: lots of natural lighting, no limits on where to set up the camera, limited variables to preserve continuity. Still, it wasn't effortless: Cronenberg and his crew had to move three hundred pounds of equipment three miles through knee-high snowdrifts in order to shoot the climax, and, after successfully setting up for one key scene, the sun went down.

Other twentysomethings in Toronto who had been galvanized by Secter's achievement, such as John Hofsess, Iain Ewing, and Clarke Mackey, were also learning the hard way. In 1966, Hofsess founded the McMaster Film Board, an organization dedicated to screening experimental and independent films, modeled after Jonas Mekas's film co-op in New York; it shut down following a series of financial and obscenity-related scandals, but was soon revived by Ivan Reitman (yes, the *Ghostbusters* guy), who took it in a more wholesome direction. In 1967, Cronenberg, Robert Fothergill (a pre-Secter director), Jim Paxton, and Lorne Michaels (yes, the kinda evil *Saturday Night Live* guy) began the Canadian Filmmakers Distribution Centre, which rented its prints to film societies—organizations dedicated to screening foreign and arthouse films, typically located on college campuses—at the rate of $1/minute and split the profits with filmmakers. The MFB and

Fig B. Making *Scanners*, 1981.

CFDC were not simply places where filmmakers could vaingloriously screen their own films, but provided community, distribution networks, and a crucial form of aid to young directors. "Unlike the poet or novelist, the filmmaker must try to solicit public support for all his efforts," Hofsess explained in 1968. "What to a poet may be embarrassing juvenilia, best suppressed, is to a filmmaker something that must be displayed until its costs are met, enabling him to continue." It's worth dwelling on this point. The material side of filmmaking is often overlooked in favor of auteurism or stars, even though it's what makes or breaks one's ability to participate in the medium. The gender and racial imbalances in film directing remain staggering to this day, completely unlike those in writing, the plastic arts, or music. While it's certainly not the only factor at play, the fact that people in power like to give power to people like them is inextricable from film history. Toronto's scene was vibrant, but it was almost exclusively the domain of white, college-educated men. (This is an acknowledgment, not an all-consuming condemnation.)

Amidst screenings at the Isaacs Gallery, the CFDC's Cinethon (a marathon film festival), the MFB, and on the city's sidewalks, Cronenberg, Ewing, Fothergill, and Reitman founded the Toronto Film Co-op based at Cinecity, a post office that had been converted into a foreign and art house theater by gay Dutch lawyer Willem Poolman. It was 1967, the year he began an English master's program, started Emergent Films with Ritts (whom Cronenberg described as initially "jealous of me because I used to do push-ups on my knuckles in class"), and completed his second film, *From the Drain*. Two veterans—one childlike (Stefan Nosko), the other lisping and loquacious (Ritts)—share a bathtub. Although both men are dressed in winter coats and hats, the physical closeness of the actors, Ritts's stereotypically haughty nance, and the bathroom setting (a classic cruising spot, gleaned from Burroughs's writing or the numerous gay men Cronenberg knew) imbue the short with tremendous sexual tension. (There's also something to be said about "straight" servicemen's "solution" to the absence of women during deployments.) However, Ritts's character fucks Nosko's in another way, tricking him into sitting next to the drain, from where a vine emerges and strangles Nosko to death. The film's visual aesthetic, though still raggedy, was a large step forward from *Transfer*. This is most evident during the strangulation scene, which introduces new angles, framing (such as Nosko's POV), and close-ups, as when Ritts's character lasciviously strokes one of the faucet handles. More than merely being showy, it's here where the film breaks away from the feeling of being a filmed short story and approaches the cinematic.

PRELIMINARY EXPERIMENTS

Cronenberg had intended *From the Drain* to be first in a trilogy, each film starring Ritts and running for fifteen minutes. The second, *Sinus*, would be about a pregnant man, and the third, *Menopause*, would be about a man and a two-year-old girl.

These shorts were never realized, but elements of them would appear in his next two features, *Stereo* (1969) and *Crimes of the Future* (1970). (Another feature Cronenberg planned around this time, *Organic Toys*, about a courageous jet-propelled sperm, remained just a twinkle in the director's eye.) This is where a more familiar Cronenbergianism takes shape, even though neither film would be particularly satisfying to someone who's only seen *Videodrome*, *The Fly*, or *Eastern Promises*. As each film runs a little over sixty minutes and they are extremely connected in terms of theme, production, strengths, and weaknesses, it's possible to understand them as a single feature that's been split into two parts.

Stereo, shot on black-and-white 35mm at the University of Toronto's Scarborough College, marks Cronenberg's first foray into science fiction and movie blood. He again served as the film's cinematographer, cameraman, writer, director, producer, and con artist—while in production, he lived off of a $3,500 government grant obtained by claiming he would write a novel. To avoid the problem of camera noise (and serving as sound recordist while juggling those other tasks), all of the sound—which is only dry, overwritten psychological notes about the "experiment" and some instrumental music—was recorded in postproduction. *Stereo* was also his first collaboration with Ronald Mlodzik, a sylphlike youth whom Cronenberg once described as "a very elegant gay scholar" with "a medieval gay sensibility." (This also serves as an apt description of the character Mlodzik plays, albeit with the addition of "evil.") His presence defines *Stereo* as much as the Brutalist architecture of the campus buildings where the film takes place. Mlodzik's distinctive face, as well as the masterful swooping of his cloak, is as powerful as any of the great stars of the silent era. His seductiveness is key, as it's his method of monitoring and progressing an experiment involving eight men and women who can only communicate telepathically.

The unrepentant queerness of Mlodzik's physicality and the film's subject matter led to Cronenberg being propositioned following a screening in Montreal; he politely declined the man. In addition to self-financed screenings in Edinburgh, Scotland, and Adelaide, Australia, *Stereo* was accepted by the Museum of Modern Art's science fiction film festival and was shown alongside Stanley Kubrick's *2001*. The New York-based International Film Archives purchased the film's distribution rights for $15,000, as well as a $5,000 option on his next feature, *Crimes of the Future*. "*Crimes of the Future* will be more commercially viable than was *Stereo*, especially in large cities similar to the one which forms the backdrop to *Crimes*," Cronenberg told the *Globe and Mail* in 1969 following the sale.

I would take issue with that assessment. However, in the same interview, Cronenberg went on to describe *Crimes of the Future* as a detective story of sorts: a man goes on a search for a missing girl, and encounters various subcultures in the city, including an organization of street sweepers. The completed film also involves journeys through subcultures and a five-year-old girl, but in a far more menacing, sexually charged fashion: a man (Mlodzik) searches for his mentor who vanished after accidentally causing a plague that killed all sexually mature women and girls. (The only connections to the 2022 film of the same name are that the remaining men start growing new organs as means of survival and white goo dripping from children's mouths; the title is taken from a 1966 adaptation of Knut Hamsun's novel *Hunger*.) Though it's far less avant-garde than *Stereo*, the narrative is extremely difficult to follow, due to a lack, not an abundance, of formal complexity. Along with the continued theme of forced human evolution and pansexuality, Mlodzik's radiant presence dominates against a field of otherwise emotionally blank actors, all of the sound was added in post, and only the most soul-crushing parts of the University of Toronto were used as shooting locations. (Scenes set at the House of Skin, the institution that Mlodzik's character oversees, were filmed at Massey College, which Mlodzik attended.) Cronenberg used his grandmother's wheelchair to achieve the gliding dolly shots that are nearly as smooth as Mlodzik.

Crimes of the Future received a warm reception. Cronenberg did a stint as a clerk at Toronto's Sam the Record Man music emporium for a bit, then departed for France in 1971. There, with a 16mm camera purchased with a Canada Council grant, he shot several short, impressionistic documentaries for the CBC. (John Grierson would've been proud.) Two of these were about sculpture, which raised his interest in the medium. With assistance from an aluminum foundry in Nice, he made *Surgical Instrument for Operating on Mutants*, a piece that foreshadowed Beverly Mantle's tools for mutant women in *Dead Ringers*. (Unfortunately, it is long gone, as are the pages of a novel Cronenberg began to write during this period.)

In what can be understood as the dark twin of seeing Secter's *Winter Kept Us Warm*, Cronenberg went to Cannes, where he was exposed to the revolting extravagance of the big-time moviemaking machinery. (He was allowed to sleep on a couch at the Ritz-Carlton.) While there, a very different epiphany came to him: if he were to continue being a filmmaker—a professional one and not a hobbyist—he couldn't make movies like *Stereo* and *Crimes of the Future*. More specifically, he realized that he could no longer make films where he served as cameraman, editor, producer, sound recordist, and director. A real crew, and a real producer who could properly distribute the finished product, were required. He returned to Canada.

HIGH CULTURE FOR LOWBROWS

Like several of his contemporaries in the filmmaking underground, Cronenberg went to work with the CBC. The glow of the sixties was fading; he also had a daughter, Cassandra, to support. He continued to generate short documentaries for television, but also directed *Secret Weapons* (1972), a thirty-five-minute fiction film written by Norman Snider. The last movie produced by his college-era Emergent Films, it depicts a chemical weapons creator's return to a pharmaceutical company during the fifth year of the North American civil war, and his subsequent defection to the rebel side. Mlodzik, again wearing his own clothes, plays Mr. Lee, the queen bitch of the Holy Police, who attempts to make the scientist swear religious allegiance to the cause. It's the kind of film that abounded on state-funded

TV in the seventies, complete with a soundtrack of half-hippie fluting and menacing synths, provided by prog gods Syrinx. More importantly *Secret Weapons* moved Cronenberg a step closer to "real" moviemaking.

But there still wasn't an industry with which to align himself. The National Film Board held fast to its nonfiction mandate, and the underground's reach was, by definition, limited. But a little farther north lay the softcore wonders of Cinépix. Based in Montreal, André Link and John Dunning's company produced films that not only went to mainstream theaters with large audiences, but had soundtracks that got airtime on Quebec radio. Following the Quiet Revolution in Quebec—whereby the English language–dominant and Catholic church–controlled province became extremely secular, French language–dominant, and separatist-leaning—a newly liberated populace enjoyed their freedoms and stuck it to those who'd held them back for so long. (For context, one of the filthiest French Québécois swear words is "tabernacle.")

Cronenberg was nervous when approaching Cinépix because he knew his experience wasn't particularly strong—he'd made a bunch of gay arthouse movies and a handful

Fig C. Filming *Shivers*, 1975.

of documentaries for TV, neither of which were remotely similar to their output. Yet, upon seeing *Stereo* and *Crimes of the Future*, Dunning exclaimed, "We know you've got a sexual sensibility there, we're just not sure what kind it is!" Cronenberg secured their support for his next project, *The Parasite Murders*, aka *They Came from Within*, aka *Frissons*, aka *Shivers* (1975). Its simple premise—a half-bug, half-penis, half-turdlike parasite renders its host dead-eyed, extremely horny, and compelled to spread the contagion—took years to realize. Dunning sought funding from the Canadian Film Development Corporation, a governmental body that was created by a Liberal government in 1967 to encourage domestic commercial film production. They balked at its content and proposed a $400,000 budget, and also demanded an American distribution deal up front. No American company would agree to buy the rights to an unproduced, special-effects-heavy feature based on the strength of *Stereo* or *Crimes of the Future*. Closer to home, Reitman thought the script was too icky to fund. (He later served as its line producer.) There were years of rewrites that significantly shrank the budget, but the CFDC still refused. At one point Dunning approached Jonathan Demme to direct, a betrayal that Cronenberg only learned of during his first visit to Los Angeles. (This encounter took place at Barbara Steele's house: the horror icon had just finished her star turn as the prison domme in Demme's *Caged Heat*, and would soon play Betts, the sexiest neighbor, in *Shivers*.) Upon returning to Toronto, Cronenberg learned that the CFDC had finally ponied up.

This feeling of ownership over *Shivers* had nothing to do with a feeling of entitlement or careerism, but rather something deeply personal. Although Starliner Towers,

DAVID CRONENBERG: CLINICAL TRIALS

the soulless, self-sustaining luxury condo block in the film, drew heavily from the ideas and sensibility of J.G. Ballard (*Shivers* would be released the same year as Ballard's *High-Rise*), the core inspiration came from Cronenberg witnessing his father's prolonged, painful death at sixty-one: after colitis, Milton's body failed to absorb calcium properly, which led to him constantly breaking bones, even while doing something as simple as turning over in bed. "I think that might have influenced the 'extremeness' of the movie, if not the subject matter," he told the *Montreal Gazette* in 1975. "There was nothing in his death I found uplifting or redeeming. His mind was okay but his body was crumbling . . . It was horror without redemption." This experience is not simply painful but lifts up the curtain on humanity's pervasive desire to escape and control our bodies. We can lose ourselves in thought, we can go to the gym, we can get a BBL, we can follow multi-step Korean skin care routines; Silicon Valley psychos can even get infusions of blood from younger people and god knows what other treatments because they've amassed a wildly unethical amount of personal wealth. This doesn't change the fact that we are mortal beings. Still, there will be no brains kept alive in jars babbling devious commands through electrodes. This reality, and the attempt to process or exorcize those fears, became the guiding principle for Cronenberg's films going forward.

3.

Shivers also marked the start of another central feature of Cronenberg's career: unbridled outrage. In a three-page article that appeared beneath the withering headline "You should know how bad this film is. After all, you paid for it," Marshall Delaney (the name Robert Fulford, the editor of *Saturday Night* magazine, used to review films) excoriated the film's "perverted sex and violence" and its cynical use of "certain themes borrowed from avant-garde literature." However, Delaney devoted the majority of the space to questioning the concept of public funding for film, and, along with hurling abuse at the CFDC's output and its "discredited practices," concluded by calling for the secretary of state to investigate the organization. In 1975, a film reviewer at a respected publication frothing at the mouth was a scandal that had the potential to become a fertilizing event. Canada's parliament held hearings about the CFDC, and a chorus of criticism rose from all quarters, attacking the institution and the sicko who'd misappropriated public monies.

However, *Shivers* was the first CFDC-funded film to be profitable, and therefore cost the poor, abused taxpayer nothing. Only $70,000 of its $165,000 budget came from the CFDC, and American International Pictures purchased its rights for $150,000 (but shortened certain scenes to avoid an X rating from the MPAA). It was distributed in forty countries—again, a feat for any Canadian film, let alone one shot in fifteen days on Montreal's Nuns' Island. (The island used to house a convent and had been sold to developers—another sign of the province's rejection of its religious past.) The crew lived in the island's high-rises and put up fliers in the hallways, asking residents for use of their apartments for scenes. (Cronenberg's room also served as the special effects team's workshop, and he would often find his bed soaked with fake blood.) The production also fulfilled the CFDC's mission of building a commercial Canadian film industry, and not simply because it included a scene where Barbara Steele kissed Canadian softcore goddess Sue Helen Petrie: Joe Blasco, a special effects artist under contract for Universal (who also did makeup for *The Lawrence Welk Show*) came from Los Angeles to manage the gore and was shadowed by Montreal-based Suzanne Riou-Garand. The crew lived on the island for the entirety of the shoot, and it's where the director learned how to work and collaborate within a more organized, more mainstream film production system. The writer–director also learned a bit about press: he wrote open letters to Delaney and a critic at the *Globe and Mail* (who thought it was a failed attempt at camp) and did the interview circuit to defend himself and his intentions. Part of his response circled back to the question of Canadianness and English Canadian culture. "Surely it's obvious that there should be room for every kind of film from every possible country—I mean anything that disturbs you is not Canadian. It should be nice and somewhat serious if it's Canadian; that's the same old bullshit which has produced so many deadly films," Cronenberg told *Cinema Canada*. "Where else but in Canada do you get a critic not attached to a daily newspaper who is more conservative, more reactionary than a government body like the CFDC? Where else do you get a critic who quotes [Secretary of State] Judy LaMarsh for his definition of art?"

None of this abated the outrage cycle. *Shivers* wasn't allowed to compete in the Canadian Film Awards. The CFDC refused Cronenberg's subsequent requests for funding, which included *Pierce*, a proto–*Dead Ringers*, and *Mosquito*, a film that would soon become *Rabid* (1977). (Thankfully, he had secured work at the CBC before the release of *Shivers*, directing two episodes of an omnibus horror/ironic punishment series in the vein of *Tales of the Unexpected*.) In 1975, Dunning told the *Montreal Star*, "The Saturday Night piece is going to haunt Cronenberg in this country. He's got lots of talent but he may not be able to use it in Canada. AIP is interested in Cronenberg. So the Marshall Delaney article may be just the thing to push him across the border."

MORE BLOOD! MORE BLOOD!

That didn't happen. But Delaney's words did push Cronenberg out of his home. Cronenberg and his family were evicted after his elderly landlady read a *Globe and Mail* article about the forthcoming *Rabid*, which included the news that porn star Marilyn Chambers (of *Behind the Green Door* infamy) would be the lead and extensively quoted from the *Saturday Night* piece. She said there was a morality clause on his lease, and that she wouldn't house any pornographers. Cronenberg objected to the label, and clarified that the author, Robert Fulford (publishing as Marshall Delaney) simply deemed *Shivers* obscene. The landlady informed Cronenberg that she was a friend of Fulford's and trusted the writer completely.

Cronenberg was ordered out. As he wrote of the experience later (also published in the *Globe and Mail*), "The nightmare paranoia of my own films was coming home to haunt me. I was too rattled to see the wonderful symmetry of it all." Cronenberg purchased a house across the street from her and soon after a city zoning inspector demanded to search the premises. There had been an anonymous complaint that the building, in a residential-only area, held equipment used in the "photographing and developing of pornographic motion pictures for public sale."

4.

The inspector found nothing; it's unlikely he even knew what to look for. And after all, it was Reitman's suggestion to cast Chambers as Rose, the "Typhoid Mary" of a vampiric plague brought on by experimental skin graft surgery at mad Dr. Dan Keloid's plastic surgery clinic. (Cronenberg had wanted Sissy Spacek, who impressed him in Terrence Malick's *Badlands*, to star.) Cronenberg was beset by uncertainty throughout the entire process of creating *Rabid*. While writing the script, Cronenberg lamented to producer Dunning, "This woman grows a cock thing in her armpit and sucks people's blood through it. It's ridiculous! I can't do this!" Though Dunning talked him down, shortly after shooting began on November 1, 1976, Cronenberg urged his producers to switch over to his next script, *The Brood*. However, film production doesn't work that way. Cronenberg was obligated to follow through on his original vision, and Chambers's star power allowed for everything to operate on a much larger scale.

The director was nearly ten years into filmmaking when the cameras began rolling, and he had a better feel for how to work as a director within a conventional, Fordian movie production system rather than just doing everything himself. (A prime example of understanding how to break down filmic elements: Los Angeles–based Blasco created the "cock thing" and other latex special effects elements at home and shipped them to Montreal, where they were then attached to actors by Byrd Holland, a Canadian makeup artist.) Embracing this mode of filmmaking led to more expansive thinking: *Rabid* culminates

with the entire city of Montreal falling to its knees, its streets crawling with heavily armed soldiers and the infected. Caelum Vatnsdal, a great chronicler of disreputable Canadian genre pictures, likens the climax to the October Crisis of 1970, when militant Quebecois separatists kidnapped a British diplomat and provincial Labour minister, and Prime Minister Pierre Trudeau invoked the War Measures Act, which suspended civil liberties and granted wide-sweeping powers to the police. This would've immediately resonated with audiences watching at its initial release; for those of us who lived through COVID, the city-wide lockdown, fear of infection, and long vaccination lines conjure a different terror.

Chambers's innate toughness made her well-suited to play a biker. Using a crash as the inciting incident draws directly from personal experience: in the spring of 1970, Cronenberg got into a similar accident and flew over the handlebars of his motorbike; his shoulder was reattached with a metal pin. This leads into the aspect of Cronenberg's filmography that bedevils pure auteurists: Cronenberg's love of racing. There are certain parallels between the thrill of going fast (raising adrenaline and courting death in horror) or the intricacies slobbered over by fanatics (the science of motors). But his affection for racing is something that deserves to stand on its own. *The Italian Machine* (1976), a thirty-minute piece of episodic television Cronenberg made for the CBC series *Teleplay* while on movie probation for *Shivers,* fully indulges in the repressed contents of his other work: humor, unbridled bike love, and a happy ending. A trio of motorcycle enthusiasts attempt to wrench a mint Ducati 900 Desmo Super Sport from a decadent art collector (whose collection also includes a handsome young man, a living statue with a coke habit), and tool down the same lonely stretches of road Hart and Rose do at the beginning of *Shivers*.

5.

The Italian Machine's cast includes great Canadian actors who would help to define his next handful of films, such as Gary McKeehan, who would soon play Mike, the daddy-obsessed, bottomless pit in *The Brood*. By the time he made *The Brood*, Cronenberg would own not one but two Ducati Super Sports.

GET IN LOSER, WE'RE GOING FILMMAKING

The wryness and personality of *The Italian Machine* stands in stark contrast to *Fast Company* (1979), his feature-length "car guy" movie and follow-up to *Shivers*. Co-written by Phil Savath, Courtney Smith, and Cronenberg, its charm comes from being a rather straightforward genre picture, complete with a country rock theme song that repeats the name of the film in every other verse. Lonnie "Lucky Man" Johnson (William Smith, aka Arnold Schwarzenegger's dad in *Conan the Barbarian*) is an aging drag car racing star who takes Billy "The Kid" Brocker (Nicholas Campbell) under his wing as he travels to different races, beset by rival drivers and his sponsor's representative, Phil Adamson (played by the incredible John Saxon, who acted in films by Vincente Minnelli, Mario Bava, Curtis Harrington, and Wes Craven, among many others). Despite the

Fig D. On set, *The Brood*, 1979.

stars-and-stripes trailer that Lonnie drives and lives in, and its stated Montana setting, the film is purely Canadian: *Fast Company* was shot in Calgary, with local legends Gordie Bonin, Geoff Goodwin, and Edmonton International Speedway owner Graham Light providing the stunt driving. Boasting his first million-plus-dollar budget, Cronenberg created inventive ways to depict the various races and toiled to insert the vernacular of racing enthusiasts into the script, but otherwise the film remains unrecognizable as a product of his imagination, largely because he entered into the process so late. Well, almost: in a hot groupie sex scene that was removed to secure a PG rating (but was later restored for DVD release), the oil that sponsors Lonnie's races is poured over a woman's breasts—the faintest whiff of what was to come in *Crash*.

Though it's an outlier in his filmography, *Fast Company* marked his first collaboration with several key below-the-line creatives who would shape his work for years to come: cinematographer Mark Irwin (who'd written his film-school thesis on Cronenberg's previous work), editor Ronald Sanders, sound recordist Bryan Day, and art director Carol Spier. It was also notable for being his first tax shelter film.

Though the government had created the incentive in 1975, wherein 100 percent of an investment in a film could be written off, the heyday of this inglorious period of Canadian filmmaking began toward the end of the decade, as word of this insane loophole spread, and continued through the early eighties. Those looking to avoid paying their fair share could either invest in Multiple Urban Residential Buildings (deliciously abbreviated to the oppressive-sounding MURBs), factories, or invest in a film and, in Cronenberg's words, "visit the set, bring your kids, see Donald Sutherland in action."

This turn toward privatization led to a sharp increase in the amount of unbearable crap unleashed upon cinemagoers, but also placed Cronenberg, Canada's first commercially viable filmmaker, in a fortuitous position. When approached by Vision 4, one of many companies founded under the tax-shelter system, he offered them *The Sensitives*, another tale of troubled telepaths, and got the go-ahead. But when he began writing, what came out was the gorily personal story of a man going through a divorce: *The Brood*. When he showed them this entirely different script, they greenlit. All that mattered was that there was a movie to make. The investments had to be made before the end of the year, which meant that aspiring tax-dodgers wouldn't know they'd need a write-off until October. Production of Cronenberg's next three tax shelter films—*The Brood*, *Scanners*, and *Videodrome*—all began in the brutalizing cold of Canadian winter.

By the time he had finished the first draft of *The Brood* in late 1978, Cronenberg had divorced his first wife, Margaret Hindson, and married Carolyn Zeifman, a film editor he'd met while working on *Rabid*. He'd also flown to California, where Hindson was living in what producer Pierre David, in an interview on the Criterion disc of *The Brood*, has called a cult, retrieved their daughter, Cassandra, and taken her back to Canada. (Hindson had simply taken Cassandra there and informed Cronenberg that he'd only be able to see her for Christmases.) Given *The Brood*'s plot, which includes a husband strangling his estranged wife, it seems important to remember the difference between the autobiographical and the personal. Though Cronenberg has described that scene as "very satisfying," it's also important to note that to depict is not necessarily to endorse or confess a real-life transgression. "In *The Brood*, I'm all the characters," Cronenberg said in a 1981 interview with *Film Comment*—an admission that he's also the reckless psychiatrist-cum-guru whose treatment requires him to see all sides of interpersonal conflict and antagonize patients accordingly. While the filmmaker stated that certain arguments are near-verbatim, much of the overtly autobiographical material was shorn away to create the film's cyclical structure: trauma is passed through the generations, and nobody will be spared. (This calls to mind Philip Larkin's "This Be the Verse": "They fuck you up, your mum and dad. / They may not mean to, but they do. / They fill you with the faults they had / And add some extra, just for you.")

In the film, Nola Carveth (Samantha Eggar) is undergoing treatment at the rural Somafree Institute of Psychoplasmics under the care of Dr. Hal Raglan (Oliver Reed), the author of the self-help book *The Shape of Rage* and pioneer of psychoplasmics, which induces physical manifestations of mental pain. Nola's rage takes the shape of small humanoids—who, in their snowsuits, could pass for her daughter, Candy (Cindy Hinds)—that murder her drunken, abusive mother and her passive father. Frank Carveth (the affectless Art Hindle, brother of superbike racer Lang Hindle), begins investigating Dr. Raglan's methods in order to secure custody, finding a few Cronenberg regulars along the way (Robert A. Silverman, with his trademark combover, plays a former patient with massive, dangling neck lymph nodes caused by psychoplasmics). After Nola's "children" bludgeon Candy's teacher before the entire class and lead her to Nola, Frank confronts Nola and Raglan at the Somafree retreat. During this climax, Nola lifts up her flowing white tunic and reveals several gestational sacs (which were made out of condoms and glued to Eggar's abdomen). She bites the largest, bloodiest one open, pries the "baby" out, and licks it clean.

This final move was Eggar's idea, a decision made all the more impressive by virtue of the fact she was only on set for four days of the six-week shoot. The Ontario Censor Board, however, insisted on cutting the licking, which led many audience members to believe that Nola was actually eating the fetus—which is by far worse. "It's a very bizarre situation, because if they decide not to cut something that they were considering cutting, you are supposed to be grateful. It's like taking your child away, and instead of cutting off ten fingers, cutting off eight and asking you to be grateful that they've left two on," Cronenberg bitterly told *Screen International* in 1979. In the *Globe and Mail*, he lamented the inability to show an unadulterated version of his work in his home province. Each province had its own censor board, but Ontario's was the most stringent. They kept the excised pieces of prints, and often prints with those cuts were circulated in other provinces. If the uncensored version was screened in Ontario, the filmmaker went to jail. When Cronenberg was given a retrospective at Toronto's Festival of Festivals (later the Toronto International Film Festival) in 1983, the censor board refused requests to screen the uncut film.

6.

Nola showing Frank her new body is by no means the most disturbing scene in *The Brood*, but in this otherwise spare, restrained film, it is its bloodiest, making it even more unnerving. (On the other hand, this is the film where Cronenberg became famous for shouting "More blood! More blood!," which would become his catchphrase of sorts; he even wore a T-shirt that said "More blood! More blood!" while doing press.) During production, visits to the set were highly controlled, and the name of the most seasoned SFX artist in the crew, Jack Young, who'd worked on *The Wizard of Oz* and *Apocalypse Now*, was withheld. Young designed the wax masks of the broodlets and the corpse of the broodlet Frank kills. For the scene where Raglan goes into the broodlets' nest to retrieve Candy, the ghoulish babies were played by a children's gymnastic group. Though Reed said it was the best script he'd been offered since Ken Russell's *The Devils*, and was largely professional while cameras were rolling (off-set was another matter), the shooting of that scene went long and Reed had "rather a French lunch." The kids were then afraid to approach the loud, brown liquor-reeking thespian, so they were pushed off the bunk beds at Reed by their parents.

In a practice that would become common in his eighties work, Cronenberg excised much of what he'd originally written in the edit, including scenes with Candy that were parallel to the activities of the broodlings. It marked his first collaboration with fellow Torontonian Howard Shore, who would score the majority of Cronenberg's subsequent films. It also marked a turning point in his career, as the film received some critical accolades and a larger audience. Though the frenzy of *Shivers* and *Rabid* was there, the loneliness and despair of deterioration and transformation was clearer. Or, at least, it was apparent to those who saw the film rather than those trying to sell it. Roger Corman's New World Pictures picked up U.S. distribution, and the trailer—which makes the film out to be a bonanza of gore rather than the chamber drama it actually is—was cut by a young Joe Dante.

MIND CONTROL

After completing *The Brood*, Cronenberg started work on an adaptation of *Frankenstein*. "Thematically, the idea of a parent creating a child, and then rejecting the child and having the child reject the creator, that is the story," Cronenberg told *Fangoria* in 1981. "In Mary Shelley's terms, it was also the story of man and God—her opening quote from *Paradise Lost* sets that up . . . [my producer suggested that] in a sense, it was the idea that I'd been working with from the beginning." Though there was a full-page ad in *Variety* advertising the project, Cronenberg ultimately abandoned it. When asked why, he informed another *Fangoria* interviewer in 1983: "I'm fighting Frankenberry cereal. The legend has just been done so many times and debased in so many ways I would be fighting all of that instead of just trying to deal with the material itself."

The tax-shelter gold rush didn't always allow for such contemplation. When approached by Pierre David, a French Canadian who'd previously owned radio stations and flirted with joining the church before getting into the movie business, Cronenberg offered up *The Sensitives*, or as we now know it, *Scanners*. David loved the idea and informed Cronenberg that he'd start shooting in two weeks. David and his fellow Filmplan partner,

PART I. INDIVIDUATION

43

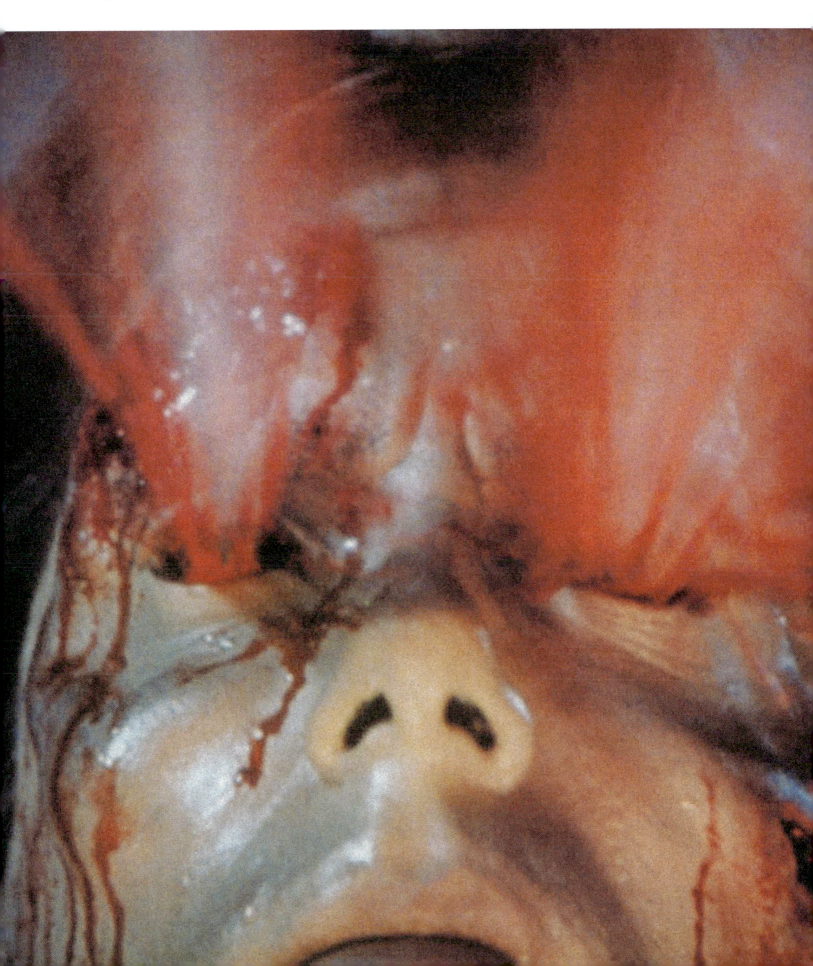

DAVID CRONENBERG: CLINICAL TRIALS

Victor Solnicki, were undeterred by the fact there was no script. If principal photography hadn't been completed before December 31, the investors wouldn't get their write-offs.

Two weeks of preproduction would be challenging for anyone aiming to make a feature film, even if they'd meticulously planned everything out and had a group of familiar collaborators (as Cronenberg did with Spier, Irwin, and Sanders) to work on it. The special-effects-heavy premise—Cameron Vale (Stephen Lack) battles against other man-made telepaths and ConSec, an evil, quasi-governmental corporation—exponentially compounded that difficulty. On the first day of shooting, the crew didn't have the 18-wheeler required for the first scheduled scene, signage for ConSec headquarters, or a costume for Lack. After these details were sorted out, the crew began filming on a highway. According to a story in *Cronenberg on Cronenberg*, two women who had stopped their car to observe the production were killed by a truck driver. The crew helped pull them from the wreckage.

Though there were no other tragedies during the rest of the nine-week production (to that point Cronenberg's longest), the process of realizing this paranoid spin on the thalidomide scandal of the late 1950s/early 1960s remained fraught. In what might be a case of cryptomnesia, William S. Burroughs's *Naked Lunch* describes "Senders" as those who can "control physical movements, mental processes, emotional responses, and apparent sensory impressions" of others, and who could potentially gain control of the entire planet; Cronenberg, however, has never cited this as inspiration for the film. Cronenberg wrote in the mornings before shooting began, during lunch breaks, in the evenings, and on weekends. The shooting schedule had to be constantly adjusted to compensate for absent or unfinished material. Lack, whom Cronenberg cast for his piercing eyes, struggled to deliver Cronenberg's verbose dialogue—he'd only acted in low-budget, largely improvisational films in Montreal, and had no formal training. (In fairness to Lack, there were no rehearsals and a stream of newly written or rewritten scenes that were often delivered immediately before the cameras started rolling.) When shown the dailies, Lack moaned about the sparse sets; "It looks like a fuckin' dentist's office!" is a quote he recalled to *Film Comment* in a 2014 interview. Actor Patrick McGoohan, who plays the creator and propagator of Ephemerol, the drug that causes the scanners' telepathic abilities, was, per recollections in *Cronenberg on Cronenberg*, far more combative toward the crew. Jennifer O'Neill, who gets the second-most screen time as scanner Kim Obrist, cried when she read a more complete version of the script. (For some reason, the version she'd been sent when asked to do the movie had no violence in it.)

Scanners was a constant act of invention to which everyone had to adapt: one of the guys in the scanners circle, where Cameron first learns of the incredible connection his powers hold, was the film's gaffer. The time allotted for reshoots the following June was instead used to shoot entirely new material, including a new ending. This latter half of production primarily involved the special effects, including the iconic exploding head scene. Dick Smith, the makeup and SFX mastermind behind *The Exorcist*, was exhausted after working for eleven months on Ken Russell's evolutionary fantasia *Altered States* and was unable to commit to being in Montreal for the first part of shooting. Spier, Cronenberg, and special makeup artists Chris Walas, Stephan Dupuis, Tom Schwarz, and Gary Zeller flew to Smith's home in Upstate New York, then traveled to New York City to purchase materials. Smith was present for the crucial reshoots and rigged the final fight between Cameron and his evil brother, Darryl Revok (the wonderful Michael Ironside), in which their veins burst open. He had devised a new bladder technique for transformations for *Altered States*, which would become a mainstay of eighties practical effects. (Coupled with advances in new types of latex, such ingenuity allowed for films like *The Howling, An American Werewolf in London,* and *The Thing* to make monsters the lead characters, rather than relegate them to merely hovering in the shadows.) Zeller invented Zel-gel, a substance that allowed the actors to cradle flame in their palms unharmed.

7.

DAVID CRONENBERG: CLINICAL TRIALS

The crew also used Dustin Hoffman's contacts from *Little Big Man*, which Smith had worked on, to signify that Cameron had defeated Darryl in the scan-off.

Louis Del Grande's infamous head, however, was manufactured and destroyed by the Canadian team: Walas created it from gelatin and stuffed it with half-eaten food and scraps from the FX lab; Zeller, who had done the explosive effects for George A. Romero's *Dawn of the Dead* (1978), was the one who blew it up from behind with a shotgun. (The team had originally asked Ironside to sit next to the head as it was shot, but Ironside wisely declined.) Anticipating censorship of the scene, Cronenberg shot an alternate scene where Del Grande suffers a scan-induced heart attack instead. "It's an incredible shot and very gruesome. But it's so surreal that it's also quite lovely in its own way. Dalí, I think, would agree," Cronenberg told *The Guardian* in 1981.

Released through Avco-Embassy, the company that distributed John Carpenter's films, *Scanners* appeared in more theaters but was far from a box office hit. But like *The Brood*, it began to grow a following on a new format: home video. A cult was forming, and despite its torturous filming, *Scanners* gained Cronenberg worldwide notoriety. "I knew if I survived *Scanners* I could survive anything," the writer/director later told Christopher Rodley.

In 1981, producer Pierre David told Cronenberg that November was fast approaching and his new company, Filmplan II Inc. (with Victor Solnicki and Claude Héroux), was looking to make a film. There were still Canadian doctors, lawyers, and dentists looking to dodge taxes. Cronenberg proposed *Network of Blood*, a treatment that he'd written eight years earlier. Inspired by Cronenberg's childhood experience of seeing channels from Buffalo and other parts of New York after Canadian television had gone off the air—signals that were weak, fuzzy, and/or lacking sound, which prompted the boy to project his own meanings on them—the original idea was, in Cronenberg's words, more of a melodrama. 8.

The finished product, *Videodrome*, was instead a surreal exploration of his harshest critics' accusations about his work. Max Renn (James Woods), a chauvinistic, unrepentant smut-peddler (whose station Civic TV is based on Toronto's real-life softcore broadcaster, CITY-TV), becomes obsessed with *Videodrome*, a torture and snuff film program emanating from Pittsburgh. He begins dabbling in BDSM with Nicki Brand (Blondie singer Deborah Harry), a therapist with a radio talk show and penchant for pain. Soon Max loses control, his sadistic hallucinations blurring with reality, and he discovers that *Videodrome* is actually a means of mind control devised by Spectacular Optical, a CIA cutout-style corporation. His salvation—if you choose to believe that Max is saved—comes from Brian O'Blivion (Jack Creley), a Marshall McLuhan–esque media prophet, and his daughter Bianca (Sonja Smits), who dutifully carries on her father's work à la Anna Freud.

Although Cronenberg was more prepared than he was for *Scanners* when production on *Videodrome* began, and had less of an insane timeframe in which to achieve it, the film we now know as *Videodrome* was primarily discovered during filming and in the editing room. The uncertainty and demanding nature of these long shooting days bothered many crew members, and an unflattering and embellished account of this tension (along with some intentionally secret elements of the story) was published before the film's release in *Mediascene Prevue* by Stephen Zoller. (It's worth noting that the journalist was never actually on set, according to an interview with Tim Lucas in the July/August 1982 issue of *Cinefantastique*.) It was reported that Harry only took requests through Libby Bowden, an assistant director who'd managed to strike up a rapport with the popstar, and, because the production was centered in an old three-storey frame house in Toronto that lacked soundproofing, the effects team couldn't work while scenes were being shot in other rooms. The eminently calm Cronenberg, who had to give several pep talks to his crew, was joined by regulars such as art director Spier, cinematographer Irwin, editor Sanders, and makeup artist Shonagh Jabour, as well as famed special effects guru Rick Baker, who would become the first person to receive an Oscar for Best Makeup for his work on *An American Werewolf in London*. A great deal of material in the screenplay—which was merely a second draft without an ending—was never filmed, such as a scene where Max and Nicki's faces melt off during a kiss, crawl across the floor, and then melt an onlooker. Though the decision to remove most of these special-effects-heavy scenes was made by the producers, Cronenberg himself nixed many scenes even though the special effects appliances and sets were ready. Woods, who was game enough to stand for eight hours straight (assisted by people massaging his legs) while shooting the scene where Max pushes a gun into his newly formed stomach slit, refused to stand in a pool of water while wearing a plugged-in television on his head. (Though the specialist who rigged the shot assured the actor that it was safe, Woods asked if the crew member would feel comfortable putting his young daughter in the same position; the crew member demurred.)

As with *Scanners*, Cronenberg continued writing through the final day of principal photography, which dutifully wrapped before the year's end; the crew were called back to shoot in March of 1982 and again in May. This led to a number of scenes that were shot and then discarded. Among them are a reveal that Bianca and Nicki are actually the same woman, Max having sex with Bianca and Nicki (both of whom have sprouted penises) on the *Videodrome* set, and Barry Convex explaining how *Videodrome*'s technology was developed.

Because *Videodrome* was being released by Universal Pictures—who were gracious enough to let him do whatever the hell he wanted—the film was subject to test-screenings. The studio chose Boston. The underpopulated audience who witnessed this seventy-five-minute, music-free cut of the film, in spite of the city's transit strike, included many women and their crying infants. Oscar Wilde once wrote that women aren't allowed to go to war because they're too cruel, and the feedback cards for *Videodrome* lend some credence to that assertion. (Some of these responses have surfaced online, including the masterful "SUCKED," and, "I fail to understand what would be accomplished by releasing such a movie on the public. What sort of person could enjoy it.") The overwhelmingly hostile reaction forced Cronenberg to recut and add scenes back into the film. It was subjected to additional cuts from the head of the studio (such as the dildo in the *Samurai Dreams* softcore video Max previews at the Japanese businessmen's hotel), which were reinstated for the unrated version of the film, which has an eighty-seven-minute runtime. A longer version made for broadcast television, which includes scenes that aren't in the unrated version, is, like the feedback cards, floating around online.

The studio's attempts to make *Videodrome* less objectionable proved fruitless. Universal did a wide release of 610 prints across North America, the largest Cronenberg had ever received; its run was cut short due to poor box office. (A slower rollout, typically employed for art house films, would've been more prudent.) However, the film found its audience on video.

ALMOST RESPECTABLE

In 1982, tax write-offs on investments in Canadian film were reduced to 50 percent, signaling the end of an era that yielded four of Cronenberg's films, *Meatballs* (Ivan Reitman, 1979), and a ton of terrible, mismanaged, and/or unreleased motion pictures that have long since been forgotten. It was also the year that Cronenberg got his first agent, who had Cronenberg regularly travel to Los Angeles to make connections. During one visit south, he met Carol Baum, a fan of *The Brood* and a producer who developed *The Stepford Wives* (1975) and was overseeing the adaptation of a number of Stephen King novels. It was Baum who suggested that Cronenberg direct *The Dead Zone*, and introduced him to the novel *Twins*, a pulpy, not-quite-true retelling of the misdeeds of twin superstar gynecologists who were found dead in their apartment. Cronenberg was familiar with the story of Stewart and Cyril Marcus, but the book—which was immune to legal action by the surviving Marcus family—pointed the way to telling their story.

The Dead Zone would be produced by De Laurentiis Entertainment Group, a company that straddled the commercial and the artistically ambitious. Founded by Dino De Laurentiis, a Calabrian-born superstar of Italian and American cinema, who'd at that point helped realize projects as diverse as *Nights of Cabiria* (Federico Fellini, 1957), *Serpico* (Sidney Lumet, 1973), and *Flash Gordon* (Mike Hodges, 1980), DEG offered Cronenberg his highest-profile, largest-budget production—$10 million. The project, which also involved John Carpenter's producer Debra Hill, already had a script written by King himself. Jeffrey Boam, screenwriter and film producer, and Andrzej Żuławski, the visionary behind another wrenching, goopy divorce drama, *Possession* (1981), had also generated versions. (Żuławski's was written in Polish, translated to English, and then translated to Italian so De Laurentiis could read it; unsurprisingly, the magnate disapproved of this mangled version.) Cronenberg, who had previously written all of the films he'd directed, was asked to shoot King's script. Cronenberg, however, despised King's version. "It was not only bad as a script, it was the kind of script that his fans would have torn me apart for doing; they would have seen me as the one who destroyed his work," he later said of the screenplay in *Cronenberg on Cronenberg*, which began with the wildly incompetent politician Greg Stillson torturing a child and was centered upon the Castle Rock Strangler. Following this refusal, DEG connected Cronenberg with Boam, and, after getting over the idea of not being a real auteur (because he hadn't written what he'd be shooting), Cronenberg agreed to direct.

This departure from his standard operating procedure extended beyond the script. Though it was shot in Niagara-on-the-Lake, Ontario, again in the bitter cold of Canadian winter, De Laurentiis insisted on using his preferred crew and actors rather than local talent; mainstays Spier, Irwin, Sanders, and Robert Silverman were given a pass.

Another notable exception was made for the seventeen-year-old special effects enthusiast Cathy Scorsese. Her father, Martin, had praised Cronenberg and *Rabid* during an appearance on *Late Night with David Letterman*. The elder Scorsese had attempted to connect with Cronenberg while in Toronto in 1978 for a screening of *The Last Waltz* (the Band's Robbie Robertson had somehow been recruited to be a juror at the Canadian Film Awards) but was informed by the abashed Canadians he was with that the Baron of Blood was unreachable. After this talk show confession, the king of New York met the king of Toronto; it was then that Scorsese remarked that Cronenberg looked like a Beverly Hills gynecologist. They became friends. Cathy was invited to work on *The Dead Zone* for a week, learning how to make blood bags and squibs with Jon Belyeu. (Belyeu, a special effects consultant on *The Dead Zone*, had most recently worked on the odd and beautiful *Halloween III: Season of the Witch*, Carpenter's first and last attempt to turn his franchise into a horror anthology rather than reheating Michael Myers.) On her last day, the crew threw Cathy a going away party that featured a cake that exploded when she cut into it.

Such warm feeling is absent from *The Dead Zone*, which is what makes it so powerful. The retelling of King's novel is filtered through the eyes of its wounded protagonist: mild-mannered, virginal schoolteacher Johnny Smith (Christopher Walken) who falls into a coma and awakens to discover he's lost his fiancée Sarah (Brooke Adams) and gained clairvoyant powers. Isolated and bereft, Johnny uses his powers to avert disaster, and ultimately decides to sacrifice himself in order to stop Stillson (Martin Sheen) from being elected president and starting a nuclear war. In addition to the sparse, puritanical misery of Castle Rock, Maine, the film also includes a foray into the Warsaw Ghetto, courtesy of the doctor (an unusually stoic Herbert Lom) who treats Johnny's body and mind.

Despite such flourishes, this story of unenviable psychic abilities retained a bitter sparseness, resulting in something closer to *The Brood* than *Scanners*, albeit far less rough around the edges. De Laurentiis initially attempted to reshape Cronenberg's vision during shooting but departed for warmer climes in order to meddle with another auteur, David Lynch, who was in the process of adapting Frank Herbert's *Dune*. In this far more orderly production environment, unburdened by the need to so heavily reinvent as he went along, Cronenberg did press for *Videodrome* while shooting *The Dead Zone*.

Paramount released *The Dead Zone* on Halloween of 1983, and it's considered to be one of the best King adaptations—perhaps, if I may insert my own snobbish opinion here, because there was limited involvement from studios and the author himself. *Cujo* and *Christine* debuted the same year but were nowhere near as critically successful. To honor his hometown, which only had one Dolby sound system, Cronenberg rented out the Crest Theater for a month to present *The Dead Zone* as it was meant to be seen and heard. Toronto reciprocated the honor by featuring a retrospective of his work at the Festival of Festivals. Piers Handling, chief programmer of the festival, told *Maclean's* that Cronenberg was the "only major filmmaker in English Canada to resist the realist impulse . . . David's fatalistic vision is very Canadian. He has an extraordinary sense of landscape and space—he is fascinated with the deadness of modern architecture and the schizophrenia of humans living in it." Though an accompanying book of essays about Cronenberg's work (titled *The Shape of Rage*) included a dissenting view from Robin Wood, a gay Marxist scholar who taught at Toronto's York University, Cronenberg was becoming respectable.

This clout by no means protected him from development hell. Cronenberg began work on another DEG project, an adaptation of Philip K. Dick's short story "We Can Remember It for You Wholesale," which would eventually become Paul Verhoeven's *Total Recall* (1990). Unsatisfied with Dan O'Bannon's script, Cronenberg wrote thirteen drafts over the course of fourteen months. He traveled to Dinocitta, De Laurentiis's studio in Rome, and scouted locations for Mars in Tunisia. William Hurt was cast as the lead; Ron and Judith Miller created concept art; production designer Pierluigi Basile created models for the film. However, Cronenberg's favorite version of the screenplay was vetoed by

DAVID CRONENBERG: CLINICAL TRIALS

PART I. INDIVIDUATION

10.

De Laurentiis and producer Ron Shusett, who said they wanted "*Raiders of the Lost Ark* goes to Mars," rather than a faithful retelling of Dick's original.

Cronenberg went in search of a new project, and was offered *Flashdance*, *Top Gun*, *Witness*, and *After Hours*. (Cronenberg had previously turned down 1982's *Return of the Jedi* and *Star Trek II: The Wrath of Khan*, which starred Samantha Eggar's fellow *Fantasy Island* cast member Ricardo Montalban wearing what may or may not be a fake chest.) Though it's tempting to fantasize about what these films would've been like had Cronenberg directed them, the alternate universes in which that happened are likely far duller than ours—well, maybe not the *After Hours* one.

HBO, which had only recently begun their foray into original programming, offered him the opportunity to write and direct a series and encouraged him to get weird with it. Cronenberg came back with an idea that he envisioned as "*Miami Vice* meets William S. Burroughs," and wrote treatments for episodes whose titles included "Inner Beauty" and "Sex With Monkeys." The series was not picked up. During this period in the wilderness, he also wrote *Six Legs*, a feature-length comedy about a group of entomologists who discover a new insect that proves addictive when eaten. Though there are shades of Burroughs and his own interest in bugs, elements of this script would ultimately make their way into his next project. In dire financial straits (old friend Ivan Reitman nearly talked him into doing an adaptation of *The Hitchhiker's Guide to the Galaxy*), Cronenberg received an offer from a team that was willing to honor his fatalistic Canadian vision. Mel Brooks, the boisterous comedic genius behind *Blazing Saddles* (and who had helped to bring Jewish humor to goyische audiences around the world), had garnered incredible critical acclaim for producing David Lynch's *The Elephant Man* (1980). (Nominated for eight Academy Awards, *The Elephant Man* lost them all to *Raging Bull*.) Brooks was remaking *The Fly*, a 1958 film that, save for star Vincent Price, was one of many in a long line of unremarkable "mad scientist and large bug" tales from the fifties. He wisely put faith in another sui generis writer/director who'd been fucked over by De Laurentiis.

Producer Mark Boyman had originally showed Cronenberg a script, which the director completely rewrote with some minor oversight by Brooksfilms. (Brooks was the one who came up with the iconic line "Be afraid. Be very afraid.") Cronenberg transformed the central relationship in the film from a long-married couple to a budding romance that's cut short by an agonizing death. Tech reporter Veronica Quaife (Geena Davis) meets Dr. Seth Brundle (Jeff Goldblum), a scientist who aspires to create a teleportation device. When trying out his teleportation pods on himself, a fly is trapped in the chamber with him, which leads to their genes being scrambled together. Though Seth first believes that the transportation has purified him, his body begins to take on more fly-like properties, physically and mentally shedding his humanity. At the end, after Seth's body is painfully fused with his own machine, Veronica puts him out of his misery with a shotgun. Though *The Brood* is thought to be Cronenberg's most personal film, the prolonged, visceral decay of a body—an irreversible process that a loved one is unable to stop and can only observe—harkens back to the writer/director's own experiences with his father's horrific bone-breaking deterioration and death.

The humor in the first half of the film makes its slide into grimness even more devastating. "People really have this idea that scientists are all sleek and everything they do is completely computerized, collaborative, and organized," Cronenberg told *Fangoria* in 1986. "It's absolutely not true. Many things are discovered in dreams, blunders, and sheer willfulness." To express that messiness, Cronenberg declined Brooksfilms' original lead, Pierce Brosnan, and proposed Goldblum for Seth, with whom he had acted alongside in John Landis's *Into the Night*. The pair had first met at Toronto's Festival of Festivals, during which Cronenberg defended *The Big Chill* against charges it was merely a rip-off of John Sayles's *The Return of the Secaucus 7*. (Other actors, such as Richard Dreyfuss, had objected to acting while covered in latex.) Davis was Cronenberg's first choice for Veronica, though producer Stuart Cornfeld was hesitant to cast her. This came in part from the fact that Davis and Goldblum were dating at the time. (Unless you're a fly, it's unwise to shit where you eat.) However, Cronenberg successfully fought for her, and cast John Getz (who'd recently starred in the Coen brothers' *Blood Simple*) as Veronica's editor and ex, Stathis Borans. The director's brief cameo in the film—as the doctor who delivers Veronica's larva baby—was not a Hitchcockian wink to the audience, but rather arose from Davis's unease with having Cornfeld between her legs.

Casting, which Cronenberg has frequently described as a "dark art," was overseen by Deirdre Bowen, with whom he had first worked on *The Dead Zone*. She would join the retinue of his regulars—Irwin, Sanders, Spier, Jabour, and Shore—as would Cronenberg's sister Denise, who was the costume designer. For special makeup effects, Chris Walas, a *Videodrome* alumni who'd gone on to make Joe Dante's madcap *Gremlins* (1984), oversaw an enormous team of makeup artists that included Stephan Dupuis (also from *Videodrome*) and puppeteers. Though Cronenberg approached most of the film as he always did by figuring out blocking and shots only once on the set and then shooting alternate takes (such as an ending where Veronica gives birth to a butterfly and a horrific scene where Seth, now

Fig E. Shooting *Dead Ringers*, 1988.

the crazed Brundlefly, fuses a cat and a baboon and then gnaws off a newly sprouted leg), he storyboarded the final scene, which took five weeks to shoot. It was a grueling experience, particularly for Davis, who had to cry nonstop for days at a time.

However, the infusion of American money allowed for a much grander scale of production inside Toronto's Kleinburg Studios, ensuring the flexibility of his earlier tax-shelter films. Spier modeled Seth's telepods on a motorcycle cylinder taken from one of Cronenberg's Ducatis. Shore, seeking to create a grand, Italian opera-influenced score, had parts of his music performed by the London Philharmonic. (Brooks was initially concerned by the baroque nature of the soundtrack, which led to Bryan Ferry recording a pop song titled "Help Me." It only briefly played in the background of Seth's arm wrestling competition and has been removed from most subsequent editions of the film.) Released wide by 20th Century Fox in 1986, *The Fly* became a critical and commercial hit. Walas and Dupuis won Best Makeup at the BAFTAs and the Academy Awards. Cronenberg had the world at his feet.

i.ii
THE PERSONA

PART B

For those who judge films strictly by awards and grosses, *The Fly* was the pinnacle of Cronenberg's career, generating over $100 million in revenue. This seemed like another opportunity to jump ship and go to Lipstick City. What led him to threaten to leave Canada in 1986/1987 wasn't marketability, but Bill C54, which sought to define and ban pornography—though the legislation didn't draw distinctions between pornography and eroticism and failed to offer new protections to those it sought to help (women and children). Libraries and art galleries opposed the bill, too; in a television interview, Cronenberg said it would "change what the country is." "Goodbye, David. Don't slam the door, just go. Our society can manage without your horror films," a letter to the *Toronto Star* read. Its author, Lois Elliott, didn't get her wish, as the bill stalled and died.

Offers poured in from Hollywood during this period, though they were decidedly the wrong ones: Cronenberg turned down *Beverly Hills Cop* and *Good Morning, Vietnam*. From the strength of *The Fly*, Warner Bros. funded the development of *Labyrinth Nine*, which Cronenberg described as "a sci-fi script, but it's more of a character study than a heavy-duty special FX film, though there would be some of that in it . . . based on two separate short stories, 'Rapuccini's Daughter' by Nathaniel Hawthorne and another by Paul Bowles. Neither one is sci-fi, but Hawthorne's has fantastic elements in it." It was abandoned.

But no matter . . . The idea of a deranged gynecologist—and the true story of the Marcus twins—had been floating around Cronenberg's head for more than a decade, and he was still under contract with De Laurentiis Entertainment Group. To avoid being sued by the Marcuses' relatives, they greenlit an adaptation of the novel *Twins*; Cronenberg had co-written the script with Norman Snider. (His old friend Ivan Reitman, who was working on an Arnold Schwarzenegger/Danny DeVito film of the same name, talked him into retitling it.) Cronenberg approached more than thirty actors for the lead role, including Al Pacino, William Hurt, and Robert De Niro. All of them balked at the idea of playing a gynecologist. Male studio executives would often ask: "Can't they be lawyers instead?" (Unsurprisingly, female executives never objected to the premise; after all, it was Carol Baum, who would eventually serve as the film's executive producer, who got the project going.) It was finally the classically trained British actor Jeremy Irons, then best known for the Granada-ITV adaptation of *Brideshead Revisited*, *The French Lieutenant's Woman*, and *Moonlighting*, who took up the Mantles. Cronenberg gave him three books "just to get him in the mood": the schlocky *Freaks* by Leslie Fiedler, *The Two* by Irving Wallace, and *Jeffcoate's Principles of Gynaecology* by Sir Norman Jeffcoate. The forty-six-year-old Geneviève Bujold, a French Canadian who came of age in the stifling era before the Quiet Revolution, was chosen for Claire Niveau, an aging actress with a trifurcated uterus who, at least momentarily, comes between the twins. Another storied Canadian actress, Shirley Douglas, the daughter of the first leader of Canada's leftist New Democratic Party and mother to Kiefer Sutherland, makes a cameo as a gossip columnist with a fantastic hat. (In real life, Douglas was known for telling all.)

However, as construction on the sets neared completion, De Laurentiis and his daughter Raffaella informed Cronenberg and his producers that, because DEG's 1986 releases—*Maximum Overdrive* (directed by a coked-out Stephen King) and *King Kong Lives* (John Guillermin)—had performed so poorly, *Dead Ringers* was canceled.

11. Prudish PR intern Ted Pikul (Jude Law) gets a taste of a bioport.
12. Allegra Geller (Jennifer Jason Leigh) prepares to jack video game virgin Ted into her pod, which contains the only, original copy of her masterpiece, eXistenZ.
13. Look who's cumming to dinner: Sigmund Freud (Viggo Mortensen) assures his very hungry protégé, Carl Jung (Michael Fassbender), that any topic is fair game.
14. Eric Packer (Robert Pattinson) looks at his wife, Elise (Sarah Gadon), with something resembling human tenderness.
15. Packer's pristine "Prousted" limo. It, like Eric, will lose its shiny veneer over the course of a single day.
16. "I think this bed needs new software. It's not anticipating my pain," Saul Tenser (Viggo Mortensen) tells his partner Caprice (Léa Seydoux). Saul's bed is one of several devices made by LifeFormWare that makes life bearable for him.

Tearing down the $300,000 worth of sets that had already been built would've cost another $30,000. This abrupt abandonment inaugurated a seven-month process of securing a $13 million budget by making presales for distribution. In the meantime, the warehouse with the unfinished sets was rented out for music videos and commercials. Telefilm Canada (formerly the CDFC), 20th Century Fox, Astral Films, Famous Players, and the newly formed Morgan Creek Entertainment stepped up. (It's worth noting that the fantastic restaurant and tearoom that Claire frequents were shot at an eccentric historical landmark in downtown Toronto: Casa Loma, a massive Gothic revival mansion built by the unfortunate Sir Henry Pellatt, a key investor in Canada's nascent hydroelectric industry who, because of financial difficulties, resided at his castle for less than ten years.)

Cronenberg was again joined by Bowen, Jabour, Sanders, Shore, Spier, and his sister Denise. His longtime cinematographer Mark Irwin, however, left for Los Angeles during preproduction, reportedly snarking, "How many ways can you shoot a clinic?" Instead, Peter Suschitzky, who had worked on silent film historian Kevin Brownlow's *It Happened Here* (1966), madman Ken Russell's *Listzomania* (1975) and *Valentino* (1977), and USC instructor Irvin Kershner's *The Empire Strikes Back* (1980), came on as director of photography and has fulfilled the role in every film Cronenberg has made since, except for *Crimes of the Future* (2022) and *The Shrouds* (2024). Cronenberg had refined his ability to innovate and retain a degree of flexibility with a large crew. Save for a dream sequence where Claire rips apart a growth between Beverly and Elliot, there were no special effects to navigate, though the crew utilized a computerized camera that could exactly replicate movements across takes for scenes where Irons shared the screen with his greatest acting partner: himself. (Irons had separate dressing rooms for each twin, and found a way to move his mouth slightly differently to distinguish Bev and Ellie.) The technology, devised by Balsmeyer and Everett, allowed the twins to appear in all parts of the frame together, not simply side by side, no mean feat in the days before digital VFX was de rigeur. Peter Grundy, the first assistant art director, designed the instruments for mutant women after looking through a surgical instruments catalog; the crew had nicknames for each torturous instrument, though they have remained secret. The shoot lasted eleven weeks and was subject to test screenings; the dream sequence survived.

Dead Ringers is typically considered a break from Cronenberg's previous films in terms of style, as it wasn't a creature feature and didn't offer lots of explosions. Not quite horror, though not quite art house, it received a mostly warm critical reception, and received awards from the New York, Chicago, and Los Angeles Film Critics' Circles. It also swept the Genies, the Canadian Oscars, but failed to make a dent with the Academy. However, Irons—an actor not known for his effusiveness when it comes to directorial collaborators—thanked Cronenberg when he accepted an Oscar for his performance in another superb film about a hermetic, rich psycho: Barbet Schroeder's *Reversal of Fortune*.

Cronenberg's plans to adapt *Naked Lunch* were made public during his press tour for *Dead Ringers*, but it would be another three years before it was released. Its producer, Jeremy Thomas, had broken from the broad film comedies his father Ralph (director of the *Doctor . . .* series) and uncle Gerald (director of the even more disreputable *Carry On . . .* series) had been famous for, first cutting his teeth in the editing rooms of *Family Life* (Ken Loach, 1971) and *The Harder They Come* (Perry Henzell, 1972). Later, Thomas formed the Recorded Picture Company, which became a powerhouse (or as much power that an independent-focused production company can achieve) after Bernardo Bertolucci's *The Last Emperor* won nine Academy Awards in 1988. Thomas first met Cronenberg at the Festival of Festivals in 1984, and the pair began discussing projects; accounts vary on how an adaptation of William S. Burroughs's *Naked Lunch* came up, but both men were enthusiastic. The strength of Burroughs's writing, along with Nabokov's, was one of the reasons why Cronenberg chose to abandon writing novels in favor of making films, and elements of el hombre invisible's work continue to pervade Cronenberg's output.

However, Cronenberg was not the first to attempt an adaptation of the infamous text: in 1963, Conrad Brooks had suggested creating a highly literal transposition (complete with camera effects to approximate being extremely high), and in 1970, Antony Balch and Burroughs's polymath collaborator Brion Gysin wrote and storyboarded a forties-style musical version (and wanted Mick Jagger to star). Frank Zappa had also wanted to turn it into a musical. Burroughs hated these projects, and had no interest in writing a script himself, as he abhorred the form. (He had previously written one closet screenplay, based on the life of mobster Dutch Schultz.) Cronenberg took a different tack, if not because a truly faithful transposition would've been infinitely more expensive and banned in every country. As he later explained to the *Los Angeles Times* in 1991, "One of the problems I thought that I would have, one of the things that kept me from wanting to do a literal translation of the book, was that it might seem like slightly pushed-to-the-edge *Saturday Night Live* routines... a lot of the dangerous aspects of that kind of humor comes from Burroughs and is now part of the American consciousness whether Americans are aware of it or not. Burroughs is alive whether they've read the bloody book or not." Instead, Cronenberg fused his own (heterosexual) sensibility with Burroughs's "Exterminator!," *Queer*, *Naked Lunch*, and personal history. The director wrote this paean to the typewriter on his first laptop while in London to act in Clive Barker's *Nightbreed*. (Yet again, Cronenberg played a doctor.)

Despite some reservations, Burroughs signed off on the fifth version of Cronenberg's script on January 20, 1991, via telephone. In it, exterminator and possible undercover agent William Lee (Peter Weller) shoots his wife, Joan (Judy Davis), during their "William Tell routine" in New York, then flees for Interzone, a cosmopolitan city in North Africa. There, amidst a sea of unsavory expats, his addiction to drugs worsens and he meets writer Joan Frost (also Davis). William's "controller" (a typewriter that is also a large bug) orders him to find out who's at the top of Interzone's drug trade and to have sex with men as part of his "cover." Geography, time, history, genre, and reality blur. The film ends when the seemingly victorious William shoots Joan Frost in the head as part of their "William Tell routine." "I was dismayed, naturally, to see the scenes that David wrote in which 'Bill Lee' shoots his wife, 'Joan'," Burroughs, who had actually shot his wife Joan Vollmer in the head, said later. "But on reflection, I feel that the scenes in his script are so different from the tragic and painful episodes in my own life from which he drew his inspiration that no intelligent person can mistake the movie for a factual account."

Instead, the centrality and repetition of Joan's murder provided more ammunition for those who believed Cronenberg to be a virulent misogynist, and the repressed, self-loathing nature of William Lee's homosexuality caused LGBTQ+ groups to decry the director as homophobic. Burroughs spent the rest of his life mourning and reliving Joan's death. But he also attributed his need to write, and by extension his career as a writer, as a means of keeping the "ugly spirit" that had possessed him that night at bay. It was also during this period of Burroughs's life, while he was writing *Queer* and *Naked Lunch*, that the famous gay author believed that his sexuality was not only disgusting but curable. These details, which Cronenberg drew from Burroughs's personal correspondence (and Ted Morgan's biography of Burroughs, *Literary Outlaw*), failed to mollify his critics. *The Advocate* pilloried Cronenberg and refused to print his statement on the matter. "I was sort of damned if I did and damned if I didn't. I myself am not homosexual and do not feel prepared to create a character as extreme in his homosexuality as in *Naked Lunch*," Cronenberg told *Film Quarterly* in 1992.

Nevertheless, this not-quite adaptation of an unadaptable book drew intense interest. Weller got wind of *Naked Lunch* while working on *RoboCop 2* with Suschitzky, and wrote to Cronenberg, begging to be a part of the project over the pleas of his agent. Judy Davis, who'd starred in Gillian Armstrong's *My Brilliant Career* and 1991's other surreal, tormented-author movie, *Barton Fink* (the Coen brothers), agreed to play the two Joans. The cast was rounded out by Ian Holm, Roy Scheider, Julian Sands, and a host of Canadian actors, which included the Palme d'Or–winning Monique Mercure as Fadela and Cronenberg regular Robert Silverman. Chris Walas, who had done the effects and puppetry for *The Fly*, along with a crew of nearly ninety others, began work on the bugs, typewriters, mugwumps (giant creatures modeled on the lanky Burroughs), and other drug-induced monstrosities that appear in the film, six months before shooting began.

Part of the reality in the film, historical and otherwise, was meant to come from the locations, making *Naked Lunch* Cronenberg's first film shot outside of Canada. In 1985, Cronenberg, Thomas, Burroughs, Burroughs's secretary James Grauerholz, and Recorded Picture Company's head of development had gone scouting in Tangier. For Burroughs, the trip was "a bit sad"; it was the first time he'd been back to Tangier since 1972, and only Paul Bowles (on whom the character of Tom Frost is based) still lived there. These fundamentally shaped Cronenberg's visions for the story. However, shortly before production in Morocco was set to start, Operation Desert Storm began, and neither the production nor the actors could secure insurance. Cronenberg rewrote the script over three days, restaging the film in more literal interiors.

Fig F. On the set of *Naked Lunch*, 1991.

This ultimately saved the production a great deal of money. Spier recreated the bazaars and streets of Morocco inside of a General Electric plant in Toronto, imbuing the film with a far dreamier feel—photographs and distorted paintings of Tangier and New York were placed in the windows of sets. Fittingly, the home of Olympic equestrian, artist, explorer, exotic pet owner, and actual predator of underage boys Norman Elder served as Cloquet's (Sands) home. Cronenberg was joined by his crew of regular collaborators— Suschitzky, Jabour, Bowen, Board, Sanders, and sister Denise—as well as his daughter Cassandra, who was one of the trainee assistant directors. Over the three-week shoot, the puppets were smeared with KY jelly in order to glisten and Weller, wearing suits made from fabric from the fifties, was only referred to as "Bill" or "Bill Lee" to remain in character. (Weller tried the same thing while making *RoboCop*, calling himself "Robo," but everyone just laughed at him.) It was Shore who suggested that the film use jazz as a reflection of its characters and hybrid form, and the final soundtrack uses music by Ornette Coleman (who had met Burroughs in Morocco while recording with the Master Musicians of Joujouka) as well as pieces written by Shore and performed by the London Philharmonic Orchestra and Coleman. Burroughs heartily approved of the finished product, and even kept a mugwump (sans robotic insides) at his home in Lawrence, Kansas.

The film bombed. Released wide, most unwitting cinemagoers likely had the same reaction as *The Simpsons*'s Nelson Muntz: "I can think of at least two things wrong with that title." It did however introduce a new generation of weirdos to Burroughs, and received awards from multiple critics' circles, most often for best screenplay. (*Naked Lunch* also swept the Genies, something that, since *The Fly*, nearly always happens when Cronenberg releases a new film.)

NEW SEX

Seeking a project that was less arduous, still true to his thematic concerns, and made "with serious people, so I don't have to worry about raising money," Cronenberg's agent offered him another adaptation, this time of a Tony Award–winning Broadway play: *M. Butterfly*. It was based on the true story of Bernard Boursicot, a French diplomat who was entrapped in a honeypot perpetrated by Pei Pu, a Peking opera star, who alleged during his espionage trial that he didn't realize Pu had a penis. The screenplay was penned by the play's author, David Henry Hwang, an unapologetically outspoken artist in the American theater. David Geffen, the openly gay head of the ambitious Warner Bros. subsidiary Geffen Pictures, had a long list of top-tier directors, including Peter Weir, whom he wanted to helm the project; Cronenberg wasn't among them. Cronenberg read the play, which he found difficult, but later saw a production of the play in Los Angeles and became interested. However, he balked at the film script, which he felt was far too didactic and political. Hwang's film version included a young Gallimard (the Boursicot character) sitting at his mother's knee while watching *Madama Butterfly* and weeping, as well as scenes of the Vietnam War. (Studio executives wanted bombs to make it more exciting.) Cronenberg worked with Hwang to excise material he felt made "assumptions about how the Occident sees the Orient and vice versa, about how males see women and vice versa."

It remains Cronenberg's most straightforwardly political film. The play presents Gallimard as a naïve idiot, which, according to most accounts of the case, was accurate, while the film departs from this. John Lithgow (who'd turned down *The Fly* because it was too gross) had originated the role on Broadway. Instead, Cronenberg brought back a leading man for the first time since *Stereo*'s Ronald Mlodzik returned for *Crimes of the Future*: Jeremy Irons. For Song Liling (the Pei Pu character), Cronenberg auditioned a number of trans women and drag queens for the role before settling on John Lone, who'd studied Peking opera as a child at Hong Kong's Chin Chiu Academy and starred in *The Last Emperor*. Lone only appeared in feminine clothes while on set up until the scene in the police van where Song appears fully naked before Gallimard. (An early scene in which Song reveals that they are "male" made test audiences uncomfortable during the proceeding sex scenes, so it was cut.)

In addition to Irons, Cronenberg was reunited with his regulars: Board, Bowen, Sanders, Shore, Spier, Suschitzky, and his sister Denise. After *Naked Lunch*'s false start, *M. Butterfly* became the first film he made outside of Canada, with exteriors shot around China, Budapest, and Paris, in addition to interiors shot on Toronto sets. The sense of scale achieved on the film's $17 million budget impressed executives. However, it was released around the same time as a seemingly similar tale of love or lust, Neil Jordan's *The Crying Game*, as well as another film set in the world of Peking opera, Chen Kaige's *Farewell My Concubine*. *M. Butterfly* failed to attract audiences or much critical attention, and is still largely (and unfairly) considered an outlier in his filmography. It also effectively ended Lone's career in English-speaking cinema.

Amidst this "failure," Cronenberg was honored with *The Strange Objects of Desire*, a retrospective of all of his films (including his CBC dramas and TV commercials) and gallery show that included over 300 objects from them (conceptual drawings, puppets, and video clips in the era before DVD extras). It was put together by Fern Bayer, chief curator of the Government of Ontario's Art Collection, and partially sponsored by Seibu, one of Japan's largest department store chains. Despite his protestations, Cronenberg was replacing Norman Jewison as Canada's grand old man of cinema.

BEYOND THE BOUNDS OF DEPRAVITY

His next project, an adaptation of J.G. Ballard's 1973 novel *Crash*, would undermine all conventional respectability. Jeremy Thomas, who once called Ballard "my Melville," had optioned the infamous book after its release, and approached Cronenberg with the opportunity to move another supposedly unfilmable work to the screen. Cronenberg's agent at CAA—who had proposed he do films more in line with the Demi Moore vehicle *The Juror* or *The Truman Show*—vigorously urged him not to do it, as it would end his career. "As a friend and a business associate, I felt I had to tell you," the agent continued. Cronenberg got a new agent.

Ballard's cold, clinical book was met with revulsion on its initial publication. In it, James Ballard, an author, gets into a head-on collision and, along with his wife, Catherine, is drawn into a subculture where people fetishize and derive pleasure from cars, car acci-

Fig G. On the set of *Crash* with James Spader, 1996.

dents, wounds, and scars. Their leader, Vaughan, dreams of crashing his 1962 Lincoln Continental convertible (the same one that Kennedy was shot in) into a limo carrying Elizabeth Taylor, killing them both. (The novel opens with Vaughan's happy accident.) Cronenberg, who, like Ballard, believed that the novel was "always spiritually set in North America," transposed its London setting to Toronto, the city that has so often played American cities in television and film, and made its protagonist, also named J.G. Ballard, a film producer. (As Ballard later noted, if Cronenberg wanted to go all the way he would've named the lead character "David Cronenberg.") The writer/director also ditched the Liz Taylor plot, as the actress had come to symbolize something very different than she had in the early seventies. Instead, this distance from midcentury Hollywood stardom was bathed in horny nostalgia, focusing on the parts of the book where James Dean's and Jayne Mansfield's respective fatal crashes are recreated.

The experience of the novel *Crash* is, much like *Naked Lunch*, one highly dependent on a very distinctive narration and prose style. However, Cronenberg opted not to use voiceover to reproduce the clinical descriptions of gearshifts and cocks. An approximation of this feeling, fused with Cronenberg's own sensibility, is achieved through Suschitzky's use of blues and a reliance on ambient light, even for scenes shot at night. (It should be noted that, as with his earlier films, this in part arose from budgetary constraints: the $15 million budget didn't permit them to light the standard five feet of road.)

Cameras were mounted slightly off the axes of the various cars, giving a slight yet pervasive feeling of unease. (Six Lincolns, one of which was cut in half to film the car wash sex scene over a period of three days, were used.) Spier created a replica of the Gardiner Expressway so that Cronenberg could visualize the driving beforehand, and spare, reflective set designs. His sister Denise provided bruise-colored costumes. The Miata convertible Catherine drives was reupholstered to emphasize this point. Shore, who composed for electric guitar and keyboards, recorded the soundtrack in Toronto, the first time he'd done so since *Videodrome*. The clean lines of the city itself also heighten this tone, just as the back alleys of Beijing provided *M. Butterfly* with a vibrant yet enclosed energy. Avoiding the clichés of nineties action films, such as slow motion, also gave it a distinctive, horrible feel. Cronenberg also told the thirty-five stuntmen working on the film to cool it—no triple flips and then a giant explosion.

The question of which stars would be willing to do so much fucking in the name of such a depraved philosophy seemed tricky. (*Crash* the film notoriously begins with three sex scenes in a row.) Holly Hunter, who'd gone from playing the chirpy wife in *Raising*

Fig H. On the set of *Crash*, 1996.

Arizona (Coens, 1987) to singing in *Broadcast News* (Albert Brooks, 1987) to the alternately dour and sexy protagonist of *The Piano* (Jane Campion, 1993), was the first to join the cast as Dr. Remington; her subsequent choice of roles, such as in Campion's *Top of the Lake*, show her continued investment in ambitious parts.

James Spader, who'd begun his career in John Hughes films, segued into indie fare with Steven Soderbergh's *Sex, Lies, and Videotape* (1989), and then went to blockbusters, was enthusiastic about the part. Other Hollywood notables in the cast include the enigmatic Elias Koteas (Vaughan) and Rosanna Arquette (Gabrielle, the sexy crutch-user). True to his homeland, Canadian actors, such as Deborah Kara Unger (who played Catherine), rounded out the cast. Cronenberg allowed all of the actors to watch themselves in a monitor after takes involving sex; the group of actors talked with the director beforehand, diving into the nuances and practicalities of what had been written for them. He also had the cast and crew watch Jean-Luc Godard's *Week-end* (1967).

Crash was Cronenberg's first film to premiere at Cannes and, like many great films that have debuted there before and since, it was booed. The press conference immediately after the screening was tense; Ballard, who was in attendance, rebuffed a Finnish journalist's assertion that the film was less extreme than the book. (Ballard and Cronenberg remained pals up until Ballard's death.) Gilles Jacob, the director of Cannes's selection committee, was pushed by crowds because of its inclusion. The following day, Cronenberg took a helicopter to Monaco to watch the Grand Prix. "It's my reward," he told a member of the press before stepping aboard. The Cannes's jury, headed by IMDb's favorite director, Francis Ford Coppola, awarded *Crash* a special prize for "audacity, originality and daring," but noted that "several members of the jury violently dissented in this choice." (According to producer Jeremy Thomas, it was most likely just Coppola, who had someone else hand Cronenberg the award during the ceremony.) Cronenberg had come a long way from the longhair who'd slept on the Canadian Film Development Corporation's couch, unsure of his involvement in film at all, while visiting the festival (and hating it) back in 1971.

The reaction to *Crash* was also a significant step up from Robert Fulford's salvo against *Rabid*: it became an international incident. The United Kingdom was about to hold elections, and *Crash* was the perfect target for politicians looking to, in the parlance of our times, establish their brand. It didn't matter that they hadn't actually seen the film; they were but humble public servants acting in the name of safety and morality. A mass-shooting at a school in Dunblane, Scotland—still the deadliest in U.K. history—in March of 1996, roughly two months before *Crash*'s Cannes premiere, was also looped into the outrage. Absurd hypotheticals flowed forth: What if teenagers saw this and were turned on? What if there were copycat crimes? This outrage was also a great business opportunity for Britain's eight major tabloids, which, in the nascent Internet era, published four editions every day. There were approximately four hundred stories about *Crash*, mostly penned by people who hadn't seen it. The effects of these attacks were quite tangible: while dining at a restaurant with Australian filmmaker Phillip Noyce on the Isle of Man, producer Jeremy Thomas overheard a group of people at a nearby table say that the people who made *Crash* "should be strung up." People also showed up outside of Thomas's home. The British Board of Film Classification had its entire staff evaluate the film: according to a piece on the BBFC's own website, when they passed it, *The Daily Mail* ran details about the staff's private lives. It was banned by Westminster City Council, but did, however, escape a ban that would've encompassed all of London. (The man who led the charge in these efforts also hadn't seen it.) "It's conceptually violent but not physically on the screen. *Braveheart* is a thousand times more violent and yet people think it's this great historical romp for children who walk in in the middle of it. It's not: *Braveheart* is quite excruciatingly horrifying. If I put everybody in *Crash* in a kilt would that be better, give you that distance?" Cronenberg said in an interview with Ballard that appeared in the May 1997 *Index on Censorship*.

Things weren't much better in the United States. Ted Turner, whose media empire owned *Crash*'s distributor, Fine Line Features, actually did watch it and was "appalled." He personally ensured that the film's October 1996 U.S. release date was pushed back several months. "Imagine the first teenagers that decide to have sex while driving 100 miles an hour, and probably the movie will get them to do that, I mean, mimic it," Turner said at New York's Museum of Television and Radio in 1996. As Cronenberg later quipped, this was pretty rich coming from a guy whose TV network showed reruns of *The Dukes of Hazzard*, a wholly unredeemable series about two good ol' boys careening around a southern small town in "The General Lee," a 1969 Dodge Charger, tricked out with a horn that would blast the first few bars of "Dixie" and had a Confederate flag on its roof. (Their cousin, the short-shorts-wearing Daisy Duke, solely existed to add an incestuous sex factor to proceedings.) Fine Line released two cuts—one rated NC-17 for limited theatrical, the other an R, which was eight minutes shorter, for home video. *Crash* was slapped with an R18+ rating and limited release in Australia. Meanwhile, in Canada, the film appeared in theaters on time and won five Genies.

In non-English-speaking countries, such as France, Italy, and Poland, the film was a huge hit. (Bernardo Bertolucci proclaimed *Crash* was a "religious masterpiece.") However, the controversy and its subsequent reduced availability hurt the film financially. "This whole idea that any publicity is good publicity is not true. Talk to Salman Rushdie," Cronenberg told *Filmmaker Magazine* in 1997. It had taken the writer/director, now in his late fifties, several years to complete *Crash*'s seventy-seven-page script. "[A]s I get older and things change, it becomes different because it's also three or four years between screenplays, and sometimes more. And so I sometimes can't even remember how to type," he said in another interview with Christopher Rodley. Around the same time of *Crash*'s development, Cronenberg began working on two scripts where a celebrated artist-protagonist was a stand-in for himself: *Painkillers*, what would later become *Crimes of the Future* (2022), and *eXistenZ*.

PLUG AND PLAY

eXistenZ, which was refined and released in 1999, can be viewed as a response to the hate engendered by *Crash*, but more directly invokes then supreme leader of Iran Ruhollah Khomeini's 1989 fatwa against Rushdie for his book *The Satanic Verses* (1988) and "all those involved in [its] publication." Scores of threats were made to publishers and bookstores, culminating in several bombings and the murder of its Japanese translator, Hitoshi Igarashi; the book was banned in multiple countries and many stores in the West refused to carry it. (Those that did tended to keep it under the counter.) Rushdie, fearing for his life, was forced into hiding and was under constant police supervision. His persecution was the cause célèbre of the literary world in the nineties. True to form, Burroughs once called him "Rush-die," a characteristically grim wordplay that implies a larger cosmic irony. In a 1999 interview with *Take 1*, Cronenberg more explicitly connected Rushdie's situation to Burroughs's work, citing a concept that Cronenberg foregrounded in his film version of *Naked Lunch*: "The terror of having to live with what you have created, because it goes away and develops a life of its own and comes back to haunt you."

In 1995, following a request from *Shift Magazine*, Cronenberg was escorted to London's Claridge's Hotel to interview Rushdie. During the interview, the two discussed the (then-newish) trappings of celebrity that artists were forced to assume, censorship, *International Guerillas* (a Pakistani film about two secret agents who hunt down the author at his palatial island compound), and, most germane to this part of the book, whether or not video games could be art and video game designers artists. Rushdie, like Roger Ebert after him, didn't believe that they could be; Cronenberg, perhaps playing devil's advocate, took a broader view.

Originally developed at MGM, and intended to be shot before *Crash* as Cronenberg's first big-budget action flick, the studio turned down *eXistenZ* because it wasn't "linear enough." *eXistenZ*—styled with random capital letters as a nod to intentional misspellings in the worlds of music and video games—follows Allegra Geller (Jennifer Jason Leigh), a world-renowned video game designer who is attacked by a Realist zealot at a preview of her latest game, eXistenZ. A hapless, virginal marketing intern, Ted Pikul (a baby-faced Jude Law), spirits her away from danger and across the countryside. Hoping to repair her semi-sentient masterpiece, which was wounded in the attack, they meet with her mentor, Kiri Vinokur (Ian Holm, who'd vowed to work with Cronenberg again after *Naked Lunch*). Allegra and Ted start to play eXistenZ in the hopes of accessing the damage and then . . . go into another game that's inside the game. Distinctions between these layers of virtual reality are fully scrambled at the film's climax where, after a wild shootout, it's revealed

11.

that Ted and Allegra have been playing another game entirely: transCendenZ, created by world-renowned game designer Yevgeny Nourish (Don McKellar). After other characters from eXistenZ (the game) provide some moronic feedback—and Yevgeny worriedly notes the anti-gaming themes of the test subjects' gameplay—Allegra and Ted reveal that they're the real Realists who oppose "the deformation of reality," and start shooting everyone in the room. The final line, "Is this still the game?," is not simply reflexive, but lends credence to the Realist's complaint.

The uncertainty of what is and is not real—as well as the parallels between video game companies and movie studios—recalls Cronenberg's foiled attempt at adapting Philip K. Dick's "We Can Remember It for You Wholesale." *eXistenZ* also includes a nod to the Dick novel *The Three Stigmata of Palmer Eldritch* with a fast-food bag emblazoned with "Perky Pats." (In the book, Perky Pats Layouts, Inc. is the name of the manufacturer of a simulated alternate reality, and Perky Pat, the main character in the simulation, has developed a real-world religion following rampant abuse of the drug Can-D.) This detail is one of the handful of words that appear on the screen: inspired by the then-limited pixel

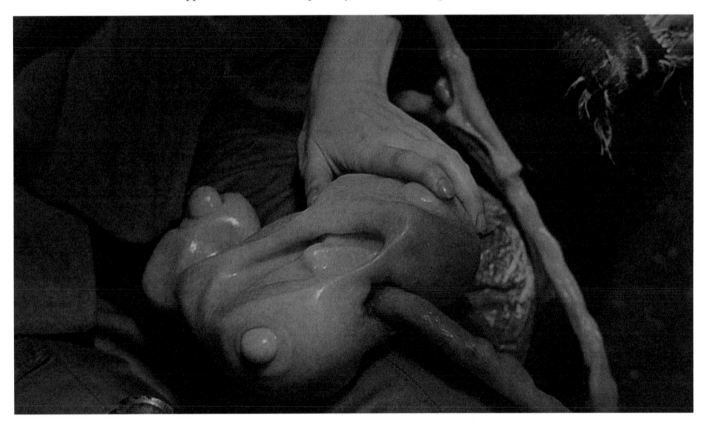

12.

counts of video games, all of the costumes are devoid of logos or any sense of time, and the sets are extremely simplistic in their design. This stripped-down world, built inside of a studio near Ontario's Credit River, feels strange, unclogged with the typical high-tech trappings of science fiction. There are no screens, radios, or wristwatches. Instead, both weapons (such as a bone gun that shoots teeth) and the bioluminescent game pods that are/contain games inside *eXistenZ*, are wholly carnal; Cronenberg originally intended to have microchips and circuit boards inside of the mutants (on whom ninety people, led by special effects supervisor Jim Isaac, worked on manufacturing), but scrapped it because it didn't work visually. "We wanted this very sweet little pet that goes through all kinds of things during this story," said Isaac in an interview. "You want to feel sympathy for it through Jennifer." Shore's score echoes the film's limited byte size and is melodic and trancelike; Suschitzky uses similarly soothing, naturalistic lighting. Despite the strangeness of its setting—or the two-headed VFX creature (created by Toybox) Allegra stops to marvel at—the film also has a gentleness that unobtrusive design often possesses.

A host of Canadian actors (Callum Keith Rennie, Silverman) and actor/directors like McKellar (he cast Cronenberg in his film *Last Night*) and Sarah Polley (who would go on to direct *Women Talking*) lend a similar familiarity. Law, who became involved after reading the script at Natural Nylon, a production company co-created with Ewan McGregor (among others), and Jason Leigh, who'd wanted to work with Cronenberg for years and turned down Stanley Kubrick's *Eyes Wide Shut* in favor of *eXistenZ*, were encouraged by Cronenberg to read canonical existential texts by Sartre, Kierkegaard, and Nietzsche. These labors proved futile, as Miramax marketed *eXistenZ* as a straight-up horror film. Despite the excitement around the project—Cronenberg turned down a spot at Cannes because of French and English interest, instead premiering it at the Berlin Film Festival, where it won the Silver Bear—the company chose to do a limited release in 1999. Critical and public interest shifted to a wide-release movie that also dealt with reality, will, games, and biological technology: *The Matrix*. It was yet another financial failure.

INDEPENDENT MUTATIONS

The Weinsteins' mishandling of *eXistenZ*, mostly motivated by the negative results from a few test screenings, was but one of many ill omens for American independent cinema. Miramax had come to dominate the market during the nineties, pushing out smaller development companies and leaving many up-and-coming filmmakers without financial, technical, and editorial support. *Shakespeare in Love* had beaten out the larger-budgeted, less-talky *Saving Private Ryan* for the Best Picture Oscar in February 1999 with a campaign that has now become de rigeur for all films (months of press, awards lunches, screeners for Academy members) with a little nastiness on the side (Miramax, named after the Weinstein brothers' parents, had also spread rumors about the other films in competition). Save for the open secret about his sex crimes, Harvey Weinstein's belligerent and bullying behavior toward everyone—be they creatives or executives—was heralded by press and industry insiders as a return to the moguls of old Hollywood such as Louis B. Mayer. (Mayer sexually and emotionally abused Judy Garland, made her wear painful discs to make her nose smaller, told her she was fat, and demanded that she go on diet pills, even after learning that she had an abuse problem—it was an apt comparison.) With more attention and money came more conventional, more star-studded "indies" that bore increasingly less resemblance to those made in the eighties.

In the face of this changing landscape of independent film, Cronenberg attempted one last dance with Hollywood: he signed on to direct *Basic Instinct 2*. Only Sharon Stone, who, as Catherine Tramell, iconically uncrossed her legs while wearing a white bodycon dress and no panties, returned for the sequel. (Michael Douglas maintained that he couldn't because his character dies at the end of the first film.) Securing a male lead proved difficult. The part was offered to Kurt Russell (who wanted a body double for the sex scenes), Robert Downey Jr. (axed because he was arrested), John McTiernan, Pierce Brosnan, Bruce Greenwood, and Benjamin Bratt. In an interview at TIFF Bell Lightbox in 2013, Cronenberg said that he'd suggested Rupert Everett, but was informed by studio execs that, because Everett was openly gay, there was no way he could play a straight man. Still, Cronenberg admired the script written by Leora Barish and Henry Bean (who worked on Chantal Akerman's *Golden Eighties*, among other projects), and did several months of intense preproduction.

Shooting was set to begin in March 2001, but the project was abruptly canceled. Page Six, the *New York Post*'s notorious (and frequently veracious) gossip column, reported that Stone and Cronenberg had gotten into vicious fights that led to its demise.

(Cronenberg later denied this.) "Hollywood is very strange," he told *The Ottawa Citizen* two years later. "They want your magic, but they want you to leave your magic wand at home. They wanted me not to use my cameraman, or my production designer, or composer. It's all about power: they want you, but they're afraid of you, and that's the problem." When reached for comment in the immediate aftermath of *Basic Instinct 2*'s demise, Cronenberg remained mum (that's what NDAs are for), save for the fact that he was hard at work on another script.

This might've been *Painkillers*, an early version of *Crimes of the Future*, or an adaptation of Patrick McGrath's 1990 novel *Spider*. In terms of subject matter and financing, both were about as far from Hollywood as a narrative filmmaker can get. McGrath, who had worked at a maximum security Canadian mental health facility and whose father had been a superintendent at Broadmoor, England's famous high-security psychiatric facility, used his experiences to fashion the tale of Dennis "Spider" Cleg, a schizophrenic who, due to budget cuts, is prematurely released from a similar hospital and sent to live in a dingy halfway house close to his childhood home. This move leads Spider to write down memories of his East End youth—his tender mother, his violent father—and, as the narrative progresses, events from the time that he couldn't have possibly witnessed—such as his father and a sex worker killing his mother and burying her in an allotment.

While the subject innately appealed to him, what caught his eye was a note attached to McGrath's script that said Ralph Fiennes was committed to playing the lead. Revealing such information is typically bad for business, but, as it turned out, Cronenberg received the screenplay from someone who only claimed to be the producer of the film. Drawing inspiration from Samuel Beckett (as Cronenberg noted in one interview, the story's structure echoes *Krapp's Last Tape*, in which the lone character, Krapp, listens to old recordings of himself from various points at his life) as well as his regular crew of existentialists, the director approached the project with the view that reality is what we make it. He removed any mention of schizophrenia along with all of the overtly hallucinatory incidents (glowing eyes, a bleeding potato, non-diegetic voices) to heighten the similarities between Spider's unreliable narration and our own—we constantly reshape and misremember our pasts, yet believe we have a constancy of self. Fiennes, who spent time with people with schizophrenia, excised much of the language from the novel—which he felt was too articulate for a case as severe as Spider's—in favor of muttering and understated body movements.

This English patient was joined by stalwarts Lynn Redgrave (the caretaker Mrs. Wilkinson), Gabriel Byrne (Spider's father, Bill), and Miranda Richardson (Spider's mother, the sex worker Yvonne, and, in a late scene, Mrs. Wilkinson). However, getting the money necessary for the eight-week shoot—three in Eton and London, five in Toronto (including a park where Cronenberg liked to race)—proved extremely difficult. Fiennes, Byrne, Richardson, and Cronenberg deferred their salaries, and the English crew went without pay (without agreeing to it beforehand) for three weeks. Cronenberg also served as producer for the first time, forgoing his usual lunch break naps for calls to investors and distributors. (He was also not paid for this role, which meant he forwent any remuneration for a full two years.) Though there were times he wasn't sure that the sets (or the crew) would be standing, and lacked many of his usual collaborators (only Suschitzky, Sanders, Shore, and his sister Denise joined him; Spier had a prior commitment to working on *Blade II*), *Spider* was still realized with great care: the wallpaper (vintage, imported from London), the nicotine stains on Spider's fingers, Spider's cuneiform (which Fiennes developed), the low-contrast film stock. Even 9/11 couldn't stop the production: after an hour, Cronenberg told the crew to "turn off the fucking TV" on the morning of the attacks. ("I know that might be considered heartless and ruthless . . . but I insisted we gotta continue making this movie. It's not going to change anything by watching TV. So we ended up working, which was probably actually a kind of relief," he later confessed to the *Toronto Star*.) Their collective effort was rewarded with a premiere at Cannes.

It also marked the start of another chapter of his career, what is often referred to as "Late Cronenberg." Though externalizing internal conflict was still at the heart of their stories, these films—*Spider*, *A History of Violence*, *Eastern Promises*, *Cosmopolis*, and *Maps to the Stars*—were met with befuddlement. Nearly every review and interview with Cronenberg for each film, regardless of medium, began with some variation on "Hey, there aren't any exploding heads in this one!" (Louis Del Grande's cranial burst was among the first wave of film scenes to be turned into an animated GIF.) This quintet of films were outside the realm of science fiction or horror (body or otherwise), and, like *M. Butterfly*, had a hard time finding audiences outside of true believers and fans of their hunky leading men. They were more often taken as curiosities rather than logical extensions of the themes that had preoccupied his entire filmography.

THE QUIET AMERICAN

After *Spider*'s release, Cronenberg mentioned directing adaptations of Iris Murdoch's 1978 novel *The Sea, the Sea* (about an aging, egotistical playwright's descent into delusion) as well as realizing *Painkillers*. Instead, he chose to "sell out." (His words, not mine.) Cronenberg was presented with Josh Olson's script for *A History of Violence*, which he had written for New Line Pictures—the new name of Fine Line Features, the Turner-owned studio that had held up the release of *Crash*. Olson had only loosely based the script off of John Wagner and Vince Locke's graphic novel of the same name and re-centered the narrative around questions of identity rather than the politics of la cosa nostra. (The film's development was so divorced from Wagner's original that Cronenberg did a rewrite of Olson's screenplay without realizing that the book existed; *A History of Violence* had a small print run that had been exhausted by that point.) "In the book, there's never a moment's doubt that the main character is the man the mob guys think he is," Olson later explained. It was exactly that element—the constant building and rebuilding of the self, the creativity involved in making and sustaining it—that attracted Cronenberg to the otherwise unremarkable project, and New Line agreed to let the director do whatever he wanted with it. Another factor, as is always the case with filmmaking at this scale, was money: Cronenberg also said that he didn't want to do another super-low-budget film like *Spider* where he didn't get paid for two years, which, depending on your view of art and capital, can lend some credence to the "sell out" admission. It was a deal that came with a $32 million budget and allowed him to bring all of his regular collaborators back for another film—one about America, his first since *The Dead Zone*, that was entirely shot in Ontario.

"Unassuming man hiding from a secret past called to deal with goons from the old days" is a story that Hollywood has told variations of for years, but has become more frequently repeated in recent years (consider 2021's *Nobody*, starring Bob Odenkirk, or 2023's *The Family Plan*, starring Mark Wahlberg): mild-mannered Tom Stall (Viggo Mortensen), the owner of a diner in Millbrook, Indiana, brutally overwhelms two would-be robbers and becomes a national celebrity. This draws the attention of his former Irish mafia associates, whom he'd left behind years ago. The gangsters start trickling into Millbrook with the intention of taking him back to Philadelphia. Tom's family, who were previously unaware of his past (and that his real name is Joey Cusack), struggle to come to terms with this revelation and the escalating threats against them. Tom/Joey finally agrees to go to Philly and meets with his brother Richie (William Hurt), which leads to a showdown between the brothers that recalls *Scanners*, sans telepathy.

A History of Violence required a leading man who, like Jeremy Irons in *Dead Ringers*, could inhabit two characters. Cronenberg met Mortensen at a Cannes party for *The Lord of the Rings* in 2001. (Maria Bello's uncle referred to him as "The Lord of the Kings [sic] king" in one of the tapes he made so Hurt could master the Philly accent.) Mortensen had only recently been catapulted to international stardom with the franchise, but, as Cronenberg noted in 2005, had "a kind of eccentricity that is more typical of a character actor than a leading man, and yet still has a leading man presence and charisma." Their partnership would prove fruitful: Mortensen remains the actor the director has most frequently cast in leading roles. Maria Bello (then of *ER* and *The Cooler* fame) came on as Tom's wife Edie Stall after meeting with Cronenberg about another (undisclosed) project, while Ed Harris (as the one-eyed heavy Carl Fogarty) and Hurt were actors Cronenberg had long wanted to work with. (Hurt, who'd turned down *The Fly*, also reads the audiobook of Cronenberg's first published novel, *Consumed*.)

The best account of the film's creation comes from *Acts of Violence*, a documentary shot by Cronenberg's wife Carolyn: Cronenberg, working out the opening scene with the actors and Suschitzky, walking around the hotel room set with a lens stuck in his eye; Spier and her team creating a bathroom for Tom and Edie's bedroom after Bello said she wanted to walk away and slam a door after the couple argue; Dupuis applying more fake blood to the top of the diner's bar with a paintbrush; the pieces of Americana that Mortensen brought back to set from his mother's house; the tapes of Bello's uncle and brother reading

Fig I. Cannes photocall for *A History of Violence*, 2005.

parts of the script, including the infamous "bro-heem," in their thick Norristown accents; the crew's mock election for American president (Kerry won); and "Fish Fridays," a custom started by Mortensen where the entire crew would wear fish T-shirts. In addition to "Scene 44"—a *Dead Ringers*–esque dream where Tom blows Fogarty away with a shotgun to the chest, gore and smoke spewing from a giant hole, and then awakes in fright—other cut scenes include an additional sensual scene where Tom and Edie have sex at the ol' swimming hole. (The latter was shot at night, in Toronto, in October, which meant that crew had to spray Mortensen and Bello down with hot water between takes.) The gore of Scene 44, though closer to his previous work, disrupted the feeling of violence in the film—Cronenberg had watched self-defense DVDs—which were essentially instructions on how to kill someone on the street—and, as the videos showed, kept the actors extremely close during attacks. (Most of the fight moves were also based off of these delightful educational items.) Like *Crash*, Cronenberg opted not to use fast cuts or slow motion for these moments of barbarity, instead focusing on their immediate aftermath, such as the blood spurting from one mafioso's destroyed nose after Tom had smashed it (as his family looks on, horrified). His stated goal was to make the audience complicit in this violence, just as he did with *Crash*'s eroticism.

Also like *Crash*, the film premiered at Cannes but was met with laughter rather than walkouts or boos. And because it was about violence rather than sex, there was no *Crash*-sized controversy in English-speaking territories. (Just two scenes were altered to sate the Motion Picture Association of America, who gave it an R: some of the blood spurts from the aforementioned schnozz-crushing scene were reduced; and there were softer crunching sounds when Tom stomps the neck of a henchman at Richie's mansion.) Released the year after George W. Bush's reelection—following "Operation Phantom Fury," the bloodiest offensive of the second Iraq War, and amidst the grotesquely mishandled response to Hurricane Katrina—*A History of Violence*'s commentary about America's relationship to force, and the country's ugly reality versus its mythology, eventually came to the fore. The film became part of the Oscar race, becoming the first Cronenberg film nominated for anything since *The Fly*. (It also won accolades from many critics' circles.) Even though it failed to win after ten months of promotion, its place in the cinema of the aughts was firmly cemented.

A History of Violence also achieved box office success, reestablishing Cronenberg as a commercially viable filmmaker. However, the scripts he was offered by Hollywood fell outside of his interests. Other times, they sat outside of his cosmology. "I don't do demons. I'm an atheist, and so I have a philosophical problem with demonology and supporting the mythology of Satan, which involves God and heaven and hell and all that stuff," Cronenberg explained to *The New York Times Magazine* when revealing why he'd turned down scripts like *Constantine*. "I'm not just a nonbeliever, I'm an antibeliever—I think it's a destructive philosophy." (He offered a similar rationale for turning down the ghost-powered *Dark Water*: "That suggests that there is some kind of afterlife. I'm philosophically opposed to that view.")

NOTES FROM UNDERGROUND

There was talk that Cronenberg would direct an adaptation of Martin Amis's 1989 novel *London Fields* (with a script co-written by the author) or *Maps to the Stars* (an original screenplay written by Bruce Wagner), or even design a video game created with his son Brandon. But what came next was another consideration of vicious desecrations of bodies in a godless world: *Eastern Promises*. "It's easier to forget that when we talk about violence,

69 | PART I. INDIVIDUATION

13.

we're talking about the destruction of a unique human being," he told *The Courant* in 2007. "To me it's an absolute irreversible destruction. Nobody goes to heaven or comes back in another form. It's a major act to commit. I take that seriously and in physical terms."

The only ghosts that haunt this story are the codes of the vory v zakone ("thieves in law," the Russian mob), the centuries-deep ethnic conflicts of Eastern Europe, and the Cro-Magnon capitalism that emerged after the collapse of the Soviet Union. Anna (Naomi Watts), the daughter of a Russian father and English mother (Sinéad Cusack from *V for Vendetta*, and wife of Jeremy Irons), is a doctor who delivers the baby of a teenage drug addict. She discovers the girl's diary and attempts to have it translated by Semyon (Armin Mueller-Stahl), a restaurateur and upstanding member of the Russian émigré community in London. There she runs into Semyon's idiot son Kirill (Vincent Cassel) and the icy-cool Nikolai (Mortensen), two thugs with a homoerotic charge running between them. Upon returning home, she finds that her casually racist uncle Stepan (director Jerzy Skolimowski) has also begun reading the diary, and he warns her not to involve anyone else: the girl was a victim of sex trafficking and shot up with heroin by the Russian mafia to keep her docile. However, Anna continues to visit Semyon, who is the head of the London vory v zakone. As she grows closer to the truth, she finds an ally in Nikolai, who turns out to be an undercover agent working with Scotland Yard who's penetrating Semyon's criminal empire. Though Anna and Nikolai have an unspoken romantic attraction to each other, Nikolai opts to continue to go even deeper into the underworld, eventually replacing Semyon as leader.

The script was written by Steven Knight, while his other film about London immigrants, 2002's *Dirty Pretty Things*, had been stuck in development hell at BBC Films for several years. Following an agent's offer, Cronenberg rescued it and worked with Knight to pare down and refine this first draft. After nearly forty years of making films, Cronenberg had honed his ability to recognize what would and would not be necessary for the final product: the days of shooting as much as possible just to have options (as he did in his tax-shelter era) were long gone. "We're at the point where we're all feeling we're not going to get too much better than what we are now," he said of his crew of regular collaborators.

Mortensen, with whom Cronenberg had formed an extremely close professional and personal relationship (they both read Dostoyevsky during filming), had also become one of those artistic partners. The actor, who spent six months preparing for the role, went to Moscow, St. Petersburg, Yekaterinburg, and other parts of the Ural Mountains region of Siberia without a translator to prepare (he only got recognized as Aragorn once), and even added more Russian dialogue to the script. (The Russian gangsters he encountered on his travels helped with the slang and gave a tattooed thumbs-up to the story.) In addition to devouring Russian television and film and adorning his trailer with Russian religious icons, he used plastic, prison-made worry beads that were fashioned from melted-down cigarette lighters.

Mortensen also gave Cronenberg a key text: the *Russian Criminal Tattoo Encyclopedia*, a now out-of-print book of Russian prison tattoos that was a staple of every hipster household in the aughts. Dupuis applied these every day, which were on full show during the infamous bathhouse knife fight. (Cronenberg claims it was Mortensen's idea to be naked; Mortensen reverses the claim.) The scene, which was shot in two of the fifty-three days of filming, was built in stages. First, Cronenberg and Spier located the perfect location—but had to build a set after the owners of the bathhouse decided to renovate. Then, working with models and stunt coordinators, Cronenberg built the action. Mortensen and two non-professional stuntmen—one Chechen was a Turkish Cypriot with a 47–0 amateur boxing record, the other a Georgian military veteran—rehearsed the fight a couple of hours for a few weeks. Then, the trio performed their movements (each fighting style unique to reflect their ethnic backgrounds) in slow motion so that Cronenberg could map out the camera movements. Finally, the scene was shot. (There were no pads, so in addition to touching up the tattoos, Dupuis was tasked with hiding Mortensen's bruises and swollen knees.) "These days with DVDs and screen grabs and so on, we know there will be naked shots of him on the Internet, so the natural vulnerability of the actors is increased," Cronenberg later told the *Globe and Mail*. "But we also know that's how the scene must be played."

Though Knight had based Semyon's character on a real person—a connected guy who also did public readings of the beloved Russian poet Pushkin—the film only used Russian émigrés as extras, as Russian actors, though good, often lacked strong-enough skills in English. However, external factors added another layer of verisimilitude to *Eastern Promises*: shot in the London districts of Harlesden and a pre-gentrified Hackney, the state-ordered poisoning of former FSB officer Alexander Litvinenko occurred a block away from the apartment where Croneberg, Cassel, and Mortensen were staying. (Litvinenko, an outspoken critic of Putin, had given various intelligence services crucial information about the real Russian mob and its connections to the Russian government and other mafias across Europe.) The trio would often pass people with Geiger counters on their way to the set.

As with *A History of Violence*, *Eastern Promises* was swept up into the Oscars race, with Mortensen nominated for Best Actor in a Leading Role. (Daniel Day-Lewis ended up taking the prize for his role in Paul Thomas Anderson's *There Will Be Blood*.) During the requisite press tour, Cronenberg remarked, "It would be fun, but it's not the validation that I need. I suppose the bad part of it is when you die they say 'Oscar-winning David Cronenberg found dead floating in a swimming pool,' as if that's the major thing that ever happened to you in your life. When in fact, it definitely wouldn't be." The film enjoyed commercial success.

He also admitted that he'd fallen out of love with *Painkillers*, and that *Maps to the Stars* and *London Fields* weren't happening. "It's sort of an IMDb problem, you know," he told the *Globe and Mail*. "Things have a reality on there and it's very difficult to get them off." This may seem like a slight quibble, but for the director (and eager audiences), this disinformation posed problems. It also pointed to larger changes in the way movies were being made. Three years would lapse before his next project was realized, entirely due to funding issues.

IN DREAMS

The 2008 financial crisis, so frequently diminished by ruling parties and finance bros, hit the arts particularly hard. Aside from the fact that countless nonprofit arts organizations were wiped out or permanently reduced to shadows of their former selves, film financing grew increasingly difficult. Distribution agreements became harder to secure, fundamentally changing what kinds of films made it to limited release. Everything got a lot safer. Even Cronenberg's most commercial proposed projects, such as *The Fly* 2 ("a meditation on fly-ness" without the original characters), *Eastern Promises* 2 (which would've continued Nikolai's story in Russia), and *The Matarese Circle* (an adaptation of Robert Ludlum's Cold War thriller, slated to star Denzel Washington and Tom Cruise) failed to get the green light because of a lack of funds. When asked about the status of *The Matarese Circle* in 2009, Cronenberg told MTV News, "Nobody has signed on. The Hollywood term is 'attached.' Nobody actually knows what that means. It's a very abstract, almost religious concept." The project's fate was sealed when MGM, the studio that had repeatedly enthused about the spy film, filed for bankruptcy on November 3, 2010.

This persistent cash flow problem almost derailed the film he was able to realize: *A Dangerous Method* (2011), which explores Carl Jung's affair with Sabina Spielrein, a patient who became a highly influential psychoanalyst (and was lost to history until John Kerr's book about her), and the breakup with his mentor, Sigmund Freud. Cronenberg became interested in adapting Christopher Hampton's stage play *The Talking Cure* when he heard that Ralph Fiennes was performing (as Jung) at London's National Theatre. (The play was only written after a script of John Kerr's book about Spielrein, Freud, and Jung was commissioned by Julia Roberts's production company and rejected—perhaps unsurprisingly, neither Roberts nor her handlers wanted to show Pretty Woman masturbating beneath her skirts.) Cronenberg read the play, collaborated with Hampton to rework it and remove anything from the unmade 20th Century Fox version, and secured funding that immediately fell through in the wake of the financial crisis. Christian Bale, who'd signed on to play Jung, dropped out, further complicating funding. New hope came when Christoph Waltz, then hot after his turn as a loquacious Nazi in *Inglourious Basterds*, begged Cronenberg to play Freud—his grandfather had been a student of the grand old shrink. However, in early 2010, as detailed in *The Hollywood Reporter*, Waltz informed Cronenberg via email that he'd be unable to participate; instead, he chose to do *Water for Elephants*, which had a much higher budget. His abrupt reversal wasn't just obnoxious: it meant that all of the German backers withdrew as well. Mortensen also declined the role of Freud because of his parents' ill health and because the blue-eyed Dane couldn't imagine himself doing it.

Actual help came in a familiar form: Jeremy Thomas. Casting still posed problems. Keira Knightley was initially hesitant ("In the age of Internet and all the rest of it, I didn't know that that is what I want particularly to be out there," she told Reuters in reference to the BDSM scene), but talked things through with Cronenberg. After Michael Fassbender (who rose to international acclaim with Steve McQueen's *Hunger*, and had also been in *Inglourious Basterds*) agreed to play Jung, Mortensen came on board. The first day of filming was precarious as agreements between the many production companies hadn't yet been signed. It impacted the film in other ways, too: because it was a German-Canadian production, only two days of the forty-two-day shoot were spent in Vienna (Freud's base of operations), and none were spent in Switzerland (Jung's homeland).

Nevertheless, the scenes shot in the grand seat of the Austro-Hungarian empire—such as the staircase of Freud's home, Café Sperl, and the Belvedere Gardens—added a layer of visual veracity to Hampton's dialogue, which was fashioned from letters between Freud, Jung, and Spielrein. (There were mail deliveries five to eight times a day back then, and the trio were not only trying to impress recipients with their letter-writing prowess, but were also incredibly forthright about their dreams and sexual habits.) Knightley spent four months in preparation to play Spielrein, reading her diaries, dissertations, and essays, in addition to essays about her. Her iconic movements are taken from Jung's notes from Spielrein's Burghölzli hospital file (which Hampton had accessed thanks to an elderly orderly who'd worked with Jung) as well as films of those diagnosed with hysteria and photographs taken by the French neuroscientist Jean-Martin Charcot of his patients. By contrast, Fassbender only had time to read a few biographies of Jung, peruse the gargantuan *Red Book*, watch some videos of Jung on YouTube, and have some chats with his sister, who is a neurologist. ("I had two and a half weeks before this started. Still, it's good to be under the cosh sometimes," he told *The Telegraph* in 2010.) Still, his work was enough to invent the "taking too much meat" moment at dinner with Freud and his family. Mortensen, who was given a prosthetic nose, thick eyebrows, and brown contacts in addition to a cigar, winkingly claimed that he'd based his interpretation of Freud on Cronenberg himself. This included imbuing a great deal of humor into the role, even between takes: while shooting a scene in Freud's office, Mortensen would move the various (and historically accurate) phallus figurines on Freud's desk closer to Fassbender while the camera wasn't rolling. The costumes, designed by Denise Cronenberg—as well as her commitment to telling the actors they couldn't take off their wool jackets, even when it was hot, because it would be historically inaccurate—imbued the film with a sense of another, more austere era that was being torn down by its three central characters.

Another force in the film is Sarah Gadon, a Canadian actress and University of Toronto cinema studies major whom Cronenberg has repeatedly brought back for his films. Her demure performance as Emma Rauschenbach, Jung's wealthy wife, deftly expresses the difficult reality of being a domestic goddess on a pedestal. Vincent Cassel portrays a different type of force in his brief appearance as the anarcho-psychoanalyst and patient-fucker Otto Gross.

A Dangerous Method premiered at the 2011 Venice Film Festival and was then sucked into the festival circuit (marking Cronenberg's first appearance at the New York Film Festival), and then awards season. The film was critically lauded (save for those who couldn't get over Knightley's chin-jutting) but was mostly nominated for and lost the top prestigious prizes. However, Cronenberg had already finished filming his next project, which starred a very different man who'd (begrudgingly) made his mark on sexuality and eroticism nearly a century after the fall of the Austro-Hungarian empire: Robert Pattinson.

CAR TROUBLE

It's a cliché for actors, whether they got their breaks on television or in big-budget blockbusters, to turn to independent film as a means of proving themselves a serious thespian. Pattinson, however, had the chops to back it up. As Cronenberg later noted in a making-of documentary included on the *Cosmopolis* DVD release, "[*Twilight*] was perhaps not the most demanding kind of movie... [But] those actors have to have a particular charisma for those movies to work and I didn't dismiss them as not indicating something about Rob."

However, his vampire star power wasn't what inaugurated the project. Portuguese producer Paulo Branco met Don DeLillo, the American author whose work frequently touches on the cinematic (either explicitly or through prose), at the Estoril Film Festival. It was Branco's son, Juan Paulo, who suggested that his father option DeLillo's 2001 novel *Cosmopolis*, and that Cronenberg should be the one to direct. (The elder Branco, a longtime fan of DeLillo's, felt that the book was somewhere between *Crash* and *eXistenZ*.) Though Cronenberg had read several of DeLillo's other works, he hadn't read *Cosmopolis*; after finishing it, he agreed to helm the project. In what was a new record, Cronenberg adapted the screenplay in six days: the first three were spent typing out all of the dialogue in the book, and the next three were used to add screen directions. The linearity of DeLil-

Fig J. Making *Cosmopolis* with Robert Pattinson, 2012.

lo's 223-page novel perhaps aided in this speedy turnaround: Eric Packer, a twenty-eight-year-old multibillionaire moneyman rides along the length of 47th Street in Manhattan inside his "Prousted" limo, seeking to get a haircut after he's destroyed his personal wealth (and possibly the world's economy) because he shorted the Japanese yen. Cronenberg's changes were minimal: he removed a scene where Eric walks onto a film set (too meta) and another where Eric and his virginal, old-money wife Elise (Sarah Gadon) join in a street orgy (clearly Eric's fantasy); Cronenberg also updated the currency in question to the Chinese yuan (the new economic threat from the East). Colin Farrell was originally selected to play Eric and Marion Cotillard to play Elise, but they both dropped out due to scheduling conflicts. Cronenberg then reached out to Pattinson, who nervously accepted the role. Pattinson was a fan of Cronenberg's and has a sizable knowledge of art house cinema—in one interview around the time of *Cosmopolis*'s release, he said his dream was to work with Jean-Luc Godard.

Because this was a Canadian and French coproduction, the number of American actors was capped at one: Paul Giamatti was chosen to play Benno Levin, Eric's disgruntled ex-employee. (This is yet another way in which film financing dictates what does and doesn't appear on the screen.) As such, Gadon returned to play Elise; Kevin Durand played Torval, Eric's head of security; Juliette Binoche played Didi, his art dealer and mistress; Samantha Morton played Vija Kinsky, Eric's chief of theory; Mathieu Amalric

DAVID CRONENBERG: CLINICAL TRIALS

74

75

PART I. INDIVIDUATION

15.

(Branco's former assistant director) played The Pastry Assassin, who pies Eric in the face; and K'naan, a Somali Canadian rapper, played the deceased Sufi rapper Brutha Fez. (K'naan performed DeLillo's lyrics to "Mecca," but wrote the song's haunting refrain.)

To prepare his crew for the extremely intimate shoot—the vast majority of *Cosmopolis* takes place in Eric's soundproofed stretch limo—he asked that they watch Samuel Maoz's *Lebanon* (a film set inside of a tank) and Wolfgang Petersen's *Das Boot* (a film set almost entirely inside of a submarine). A fake street was built, though much of the rear projection (and all of the exteriors) were shot on the streets of Toronto. Though the production used two limousines (a real one and one that came apart in twenty-one different pieces), the enclosed nature of the space meant that the camera was typically mere inches away from the actors; Pattinson, who typically looked at the cameraperson while delivering his lines, struggled to find a way to perform. "I just spent the whole movie in a perpetual terror. It wasn't like I could just spend the first few weeks getting used to the world. There were new people coming in every day," Pattinson told one interviewer. (It was, however, the first film he'd worked on where every decision wasn't run past a studio executive first, which allowed him to fully explore his own interpretation of the role. Freedom can be terrifying.) Morton described it as the most difficult filming environment she'd been in, due to the heat of the lights and tiny berth of the limo.

Things were also complicated by the international nature of the cast, who were flown in a day-and-a-half before their scenes were shot and left immediately after. There were no rehearsals, and costume fittings (again done by Denise) were tricky, save for Pattinson, who only wore Gucci suits. Cronenberg, however, was more confident than ever in what he wanted, which meant fewer setups, less coverage, fewer things to shoot only to discard later in the editing room. Every shot was completed in one or two takes. He would retreat to his trailer after blocking out a scene, watching the monitor feed as the electrical crew would set up lights, and communicate any changes via walkie-talkie—a benefit of digital filmmaking, which more accurately represents the light and color in a particular take. (Suschitzky disliked this method but went along for the ride.) The dislocated nature of this approach to production, and the eerie effect it created, was made stranger by real events in the outside world that unfolded as postproduction unfolded: the Occupy Wall Street protests, which mirrored the rat-throwing anticapitalists who shook Eric's limo; the London Whale, a (then-anonymous) trader whose hedging caused JPMorgan Chase to lose more than $6 billion; and Rupert Murdoch narrowly missing a fake pie (a paper plate covered in shaving cream) to his face by anarcho-comedian Jonnie Marbles during the media mogul's testimony at the Leveson Inquiry. (Piers Morgan, editor of one of several tabloid newspapers involved in a phone hacking scandal that led to the parliamentary investigation, was pied in the face in 2018 by another comedian, Harry Hill, for unrelated reasons.)

Despite being completely with the zeitgeist in a way few films ever are, *Cosmopolis* came and went quietly. It was released by Entertainment One in the United States to a few arthouse theaters on August 17, 2012—the month where wealthy New Yorkers decamp for their homes in the Hamptons—and in Canada on June 8, 2012. (The Upper West Side theater I saw *Cosmopolis* in on opening weekend had quite a few walkouts, but it would be unfair to say it was only the RPatz fans and their partners who left.) The film, which cost $20.5 million to fund, only made $7.1 million worldwide. In an increasingly narrow arthouse field, where the importance of box office began to matter more than ever, it was a failure. Still, it marked a crucial turning point in Pattinson's career. "Before I did this movie, I was really intending on hiding for the next couple of years. But this has really reinvigorated my ideas about acting. And I kind of like just—I like being slightly on the fringe, as well, rather than trying to get movies that are sort of vehicles. So, yeah. I'm kind of going more in that direction," the actor told the *Georgia Straight*.

It also marked a turning point in Cronenberg's career—a part where critics who'd been reared on his movies started reviewing them . . . negatively. (Amy Taubin, J. Hoberman, and Nathan Lee were among the handful of true believers who continued to champion Cronenberg during this fascinating period.) Though there was talk of a series for BBC America called *Knifeman*, about a visionary eighteenth-century surgeon (played by Tim Roth), the project was abandoned because of a post–*Downton Abbey* glut of period pieces; series based on *Scanners* and *Dead Ringers* also died on the vine. An adaptation of Jonathan Lethem's *As She Climbed Across the Table*, which had been announced in 2010, never moved forward either. Instead, Cronenberg completed *Consumed*, his first novel—finally, after fifty years—the result of a call from Nicole Winstanley, an editor at Penguin who was a fan. Published in 2013, the book follows Naomi and Nathan, a gadget-obsessed, unscrupulous photojournalist couple, who investigate the case of Célestine Arosteguy, a famous French philosopher who fucked her acolytes and was discovered partially eaten. (Her husband Aristide, another sexually adventurous celebrity intellectual, is the prime suspect.) Though both AMC (in 2017) and Netflix (in 2019) expressed interest in turning *Consumed* into a series, neither followed through. In the case of the streaming service, which also passed on *Crimes of the Future* (2022) and a series version of *The Shrouds* (2024), Cronenberg told the *Globe and Mail* in 2021, "My experience with [Netflix] was exactly my experience with studios. They're bright, literate, they know stuff. But underneath they're afraid. They say, 'We love your work.' Then you give them something, and they say, 'We want to work with you, but not on this'."

HOLLYWOOD OR BUST

His next project was another literary adaptation that, like *Naked Lunch* and *Crash*, was ten years in the making: Bruce Wagner's *Maps to the Stars*. Cronenberg had first met Wagner after the author sent the director his first novel, *Force Majeure*, in 1993. Wagner, like the protagonist, had been a writer who worked as a limousine driver in Los Angeles, and regularly ferried around Orson Welles, Larry Flynt, and Olivia de Havilland. (The author, a lifelong resident of Los Angeles, has likened the reality of limo driver to his previous job: ambulance driver.) Wagner had adapted *Maps to the Stars*, a novel he'd written after Paramount chose to permanently shelve a film he'd worked on, into a screenplay in 2005. Cronenberg was eager to direct it. The pair had worked on an unrealized television project called *Firewall* about the battle between Microsoft and Apple. Finding the $13 million budget for *Maps to the Stars* was difficult because of the material, which Cronenberg aptly described as "more like a docudrama than a satire" of Hollywood—and then there are the additional layers of incest, child murder, and gastrointestinal distress.

Agatha (Mia Wasikowska) arrives in Hollywood by cross-country bus and asks limo driver and aspiring actor Jerome (Pattinson) to take her to the childhood home of Benjie Weiss (Evan Bird), a thirteen-year-old star whose father, Stafford (John Cusack), is a celebrity self-help guru. The house is no longer there—it's been burned down. Through her Twitter friendship with Carrie Fisher (Wagner is Fisher's daughter's godfather), Agatha becomes a personal assistant to Havana Segrand (Julianne Moore), an actress who's the daughter of Clarice Taggart (Sarah Gadon), a big star who abused Havana and died in a fire. (In a pathetic coup de grace, Havana's latest movie is a remake of one of Clarice's biggest films.) When Agatha reunites with her brother, Benjie, she tells him that she was the one who started the fire. Stafford attempts to pay her off, but Agatha remains undeterred: she confronts their parents about their incestuous relationship, bludgeons Havana to death with an award, and eventually extinguishes her family's cursed bloodline.

When financing was secured—through Entertainment One, Prospero Pictures, SBS Productions, Integral Film—the production was limited to one American actor (Cusack; Moore is a dual American-British citizen), and all but five days of the twenty-nine-day shoot were spent in Toronto and its environs. (Coproductions also typically restrict the nationality of any co-writers, which further prolonged the funding process.) Those precious five days marked the first time Cronenberg had filmed a movie in the United States, in the city that, for the past fifty years of his life, he'd been asked if he'd leave Toronto for: Los Angeles. Union Station, Rodeo Drive, the Beverly Hills Hilton, the Hollywood Walk of Fame, Hollywood Boulevard, Runyon Canyon, Park Way Beverly Hills, and the iconic Hollywood sign—places that, if you don't know them by name, you'd recognize instantly if you saw them—were used.

Pattinson agreed to do the film before reading the script, which Cronenberg gave him while they were at Cannes for the premiere of *Cosmopolis*. Moore had been attached to the script for eight years by the time it was realized; prior to that, Rachel Weisz and Viggo Mortensen had been cast as the incestuous couple (but dropped out due to scheduling conflicts). Cronenberg cast Bird, a Canadian actor, after seeing him in the American version of Scandi-noir TV serial *The Killing*.

Cronenberg, confident in his abilities, did no rehearsals or storyboards, and, after blocking the action, went to his trailer to watch a monitor feed as the shot was set up. Again, most of these—composed in a way to heighten the characters' isolation—were completed in one or two takes. He completed his director's cut in two days, just as he'd done with *Cosmopolis*. Save for slight changes to the technology (the original screenplay was written before iPhones or texting were in regular use) and a scene where child ghosts pass Agatha on a street at night (the presence of which were objectionable to the devout anti-believer), Cronenberg made no substantial changes to Wagner's script. In one interview, Wagner said that Canadian sets are far quieter than American ones. Perhaps it was just the director's calming influence, and the rapport he'd established with his longtime

16.

collaborators. Sadly, this would be the final time that David Cronenberg worked with his sister Denise; she passed away in 2020 in the midst of her younger brother's lengthy period of cinematic dormancy.

THE LOST YEARS

This was not the only loss Cronenberg suffered during the eight years that passed between *Maps to the Stars* and *Crimes of the Future*—his wife Carolyn died in 2017 at the age of sixty-six. "I felt I didn't have the heart for [filmmaking] because she had been with me through all of my career. And that was part of it," he told *Vulture* in 2022. "It wasn't the only part. I felt that I could really live without making another movie. It wouldn't crush me." The other reasons are at once old and new. During this period, getting money for independent film grew even more difficult to pin down: Prime Minister Stephen Harper's government reduced Telefilm Canada's budget in 2012, and there were myriad changes made to how projects received funding.

Individual producers had a harder time securing investors—the increasing alternatives to cinema (video games, the Internet, television) sidelined its status as the mass medium, and the decline of theatrical exhibition made putting money into a film an even less appealing proposition. *Maps to the Stars* grossed a little over $4.5 million worldwide and was nearly universally panned, which was yet another reason to avoid gambling on a beloved old man of cult cinema. Cronenberg was honored with lifetime achievement

awards, retrospectives, exhibitions, remakes of *Rabid* and *Dead Ringers*, and a restoration of *Crash*, but couldn't be trusted to do a new film—a common fate befallen older directors. (He was offered the opportunity to direct season two of *True Detective* in 2015 but turned it down because he disliked the script. A wise choice.)

Then there was the streaming gold rush. Netflix began original programming in earnest in 2013 with *House of Cards*, and other Silicon Valley entertainment companies—eager to avoid being left in the dust as they had been with streaming music—began pumping money into new content. By greenlighting a successful series, a streamer would not only get more subscribers to their platform but deny a competitor of that chance. (People typically only subscribe to one or two streaming services, and the turnover is constant.) After *The Handmaid's Tale* became the first streaming show to win an Emmy in 2017, this competition intensified. In 2022, 599 scripted English-language shows were released, more than double the number in 2012; non-English-language programs (such as *Squid Game*) and "unscripted" reality shows (such as *Squid Game: The Challenge*) also proliferated. The recklessness of this era is best exemplified by Carl Erik Rinsch, who, with a single unprofitable, risible feature film credit to his name (*47 Ronin*), received $55 million from Netflix for a high-concept sci-fi/fantasy show that he never completed. The promise of nabbing the next *Game of Thrones* was more appealing than seeing through projects by Cronenberg or the thousands of other established or (reliable) up-and-coming directors.

As is often true when Silicon Valley "disrupts" an industry, this new model made things significantly worse for workers (as evidenced by the 2023 Writers and Actors Guild strikes) and wasn't actually viable. "It was our belief that cord-cutting losses would be offset by gains in streaming," AMC executive chairman and Knicks owner James Dolan wrote in 2022. "This has not been the case. We are primarily a content company and the mechanisms for the monetization of content are in disarray." While streaming had disproved many long-standing ideas about what audiences don't like (such as unconventional women and subtitles), its glut of choices is difficult to navigate. Still, like many people, Cronenberg has regularly voiced his preference for home-viewing. "I think *Lawrence of Arabia* looks great on an Apple Watch, and it probably sounds better because it would stream directly to my hearing aids by Bluetooth," Cronenberg told Spike Lee during a talk at the 2018 Venice Film Festival. "I don't think I've ever had that orgasmic, democratic experience in the cinema. Maybe that's my problem." True to his fervent nonbeliever, technology-as-extension-of-the-human-body stance, Cronenberg has repeatedly refused nostalgia for the art form he spent his life working in. "Cinema is not my life," he said in another interview. "I have three kids, four grandchildren. That's life."

Though there were intermittent murmurs of *Eastern Promises* 2 between 2015 and 2022, Cronenberg routinely found work as a performer in films like Albert Shin's 2019 film *Disappearance at Clifton Hill* (for which he reused scuba skills learned while shooting *The Dead Zone*) and Viggo Mortensen's 2020 directorial debut, *Falling*, or television shows like *Alias Grace* and *Star Trek: Discovery*. "As I say, my main attraction as an actor is that I'm cheap and available," he quipped to *The Guardian* in 2020. He also acted in his daughter Caitlin's NFT, *The Death of David Cronenberg*, in which he nuzzles his own dead body (a highly lifelike prop from the series *Slasher: Family Ties*, in which he plays the maniacal patriarch of a wealthy family), a role he'd spent his entire life rehearsing. In it, he lies in the bed he shared with Carolyn, on her side of the mattress, making the short film even more affecting.

LONG LIVE THE NEW FLESH

Sometime before the COVID pandemic, Cronenberg received a call from producer Robert Lantos, the founder of Canada's Alliance Communications, who'd worked with him on *Crash*, *eXistenZ*, *Eastern Promises*, and *Maps to the Stars*. Lantos asked Cronenberg if he had any interest in finally realizing *Painkillers*. Though Cronenberg initially demurred, thinking that the twenty-year-old first draft was out-of-date; some of it had grown out of conversations with the French performance artist Orlan (who unsuccessfully sued Lady Gaga for copying her.) He realized nothing had to be altered after rereading the script. (It was retitled *Crimes of the Future*, mostly because it's a great title and there have been dozens of very lousy films and series called *Painkillers*.) The production secured funding from Greece, which offered an extremely generous 40 percent rebate, and the thirty-day shoot began in Athens in the blistering heat of June 2021, amidst continent-wide wildfires and COVID. (Protocols for film crews during COVID required daily tests and masks for anyone who wasn't in front of the camera.) Unfortunately, because his longtime director of photography, Peter Suschitzky, was not a citizen of the European Union or Canada, he was unable to work with Cronenberg on the project—yet another casualty of Brexit. (As of this writing, Suschitzky is in the process of applying for E.U. citizenship.) Instead, cinematographer Douglas Koch, who'd known Cronenberg since the eighties and lensed stand-out Canadian independent films such as Patricia Rozema's *I've Heard the Mermaids Singing* and Don McKellar's *Last Night* and *Through Black Spruce*, joined the production. Ronald Sanders, who'd been Cronenberg's editor since *Fast Company*, didn't join either. Another *Last Night* alumni, Chris Donaldson, who served as an assistant editor on *eXistenZ*, also joined. Other old collaborators—Deirdre Bowen, Howard Shore, and Carol Spier—came aboard. The rest of the crew were Greek, such as costume designer Mayou Trikerioti, who worked on the Weird Wave classic *Homeland* (Syllas Tzoumerkas, 2010).

The ruins of Athens—dating back to antiquity or the 2008 financial crisis—litter the landscape of a film preoccupied with the physical and psychological debris people intentionally or unintentionally leave behind. (It is also littered with references to Cronenberg's previous films, showing an actual "inner beauty pageant," a concept proposed by Beverly Mantle in *Dead Ringers*—and one that the writer/director has repeatedly proffered in interviews throughout his career.) Set during an indeterminate future in a barren, multicultural city, humans no longer feel pain or get sick, and the government closely monitors any new evolution. In this environment, surgery and body modification has become a pastime, or, as the excitable bureaucrat Timlin (Kristen Stewart) suggests, "surgery is the new sex." Saul Tenser (Mortensen) is a world-renowned performance artist who has the new organs he spontaneously grows removed by his partner, Caprice (Léa Seydoux), before reverential audiences. Saul works with Detective Cope (Welket Bungué) to infiltrate a group of radicals who seek to evolve (or augment their bodies) so that they can digest plastics. The group is foiled by a live autopsy performed by Saul on a boy who had the ability to do so—Timlin removed the boy's new organs before the procedure began, maintaining the government line. In the end, Saul, who struggles to comfortably digest food or sleep, embraces his "accelerated evolution syndrome." Caprice records him consuming one of the group's plastic bars with a beatific smile on his face.

To express the themes—and to show Mortensen, who wears a black plague doctor cloak for most of the film—Koch revisited *Naked Lunch* and *Spider* and used wide lenses in close-ups. The images are crisp and detailed; the tiniest movements of the actors are never obscured, and there was no "atmosphere"—no fog machines, no radiance hazers. Caprice's grainy ring camera was a cheap endoscopic one, sent from Canada. (The iconic final shot was not captured with one of these, and the effect was achieved in post.) As with *Spider*, Cronenberg adopted a Beckettian approach, opting to take away things (such as extras) rather than add to the scenes. He also wanted to control the exact amount of white goo dripping from the boy's mouth and the blood in surgery scenes, and digital VFX were used to do so. As is common in contemporary filmmaking, many of the digital VFX were blended with practical effects. ("I don't fetishize any of it. I'm very pragmatic," Cronenberg said when asked whether he preferred practical or digital. "It's movie magic.")

By contrast, the actors were given a great degree of freedom in their performances, only given feedback when asked. (Saul's jerky movements and discomfort were mostly Mortensen's invention; one wonders what would've happened if Nicolas Cage, who was at one point attached to the project as Saul, would've made of them.) Though there were no rehearsals, the actors would discuss the scenes amongst themselves. Like *Cosmopolis* and *Maps to the Stars*, Cronenberg would block a scene with the actors, then watch a monitor in his trailer while the electrical department set it up. Continuing with the themes he'd been drawing from for decades, Spier's designs drew from our insides, with many objects, such as the treasured Sark autopsy unit, possessing sharp, boney elements. She used a photograph of the inside of a cello—an instrument that mirrors the curves of an idealized female body—as inspiration for Saul and Caprice's bedroom. Even the soundtrack has the feeling of coming from an internal source: Cronenberg told Shore that he wanted the audience to be uncertain if the music was music or a sound effect.

Though Cronenberg has assiduously avoided overt political commentary and never sought to be prescient in his science fiction, *Crimes of the Future* was both in the worst way possible. It premiered at Cannes a day before a study was released that revealed the presence of microplastics—from plastic bottles, food packaging, bags, among other sources—in human blood. About 80 percent of people in the study, who were all healthy, had microplastics rushing around their veins and possibly getting lodged inside their organs; more research is required to determine if or how these particles are impacting bodies and minds. Before the film's debut, the U.S. Supreme Court's decision about *Dobbs v. Jackson Women's Health Organization* was leaked to the public: *Roe v. Wade*, which granted the federal right to abortion, was going to be overturned. (Though obtaining an abortion in many states had been extremely difficult for years, the procedure was banned outright and criminalized.) In the intervening months and years, sweeping prohibitions on trans healthcare were implemented across the United States, further tightening the grip the government has on individuals' bodies. And even if you don't live in the United States, you aren't just eating plastic, you are plastic.

Cronenberg returned to Cannes again two years later for *The Shrouds*, which interweaves his career-long interests in conspiracy, technology as an extension of consciousness and physical desire, decay, memory, and mortality. Its laconic dialogue is suffused with details of the most painful losses in Cronenberg's life, a whisper-quiet gasp rather than a loud moan. For this delicate task, he assembled his longtime collaborators Howard Shore and Carol Spier, as well as editor Christopher Donaldson and cinematographer Douglas Koch, both veterans of *Crimes of the Future*.

Karsh Relikh (Vincent Cassel, done up to look like Cronenberg) is the head of GraveTech, a company that has created a stylish burial shroud (designed by Saint Laurent, a co-producer of the film) made up of thousands of tiny cameras, which record the decomposition of a loved one inside their casket. Karsh's wife, Becca (Diane Kruger), has recently succumbed to bone cancer, and Karsh's teeth mimic her decline, weakening from grief. Becca appears in alternately sexy and tragic flashbacks, losing body parts or crumbling from Karsh's touch (echoes of *The Fly* and Cronenberg's father's decline), but also as not-quite herself: Terry is Becca's recently-divorced twin sister, who's turned on by conspiracy theories, and an AI named Hunny, who looks and sounds like Becca/Terry and is often disobedient.

Amidst negotiations with a rich Hungarian, Karsh's graveyard is vandalized. Terry's ex Maury (Guy Pearce), who also programmed Hunny and GraveTech's software, suspects foreign interference—Chinese and Russian entities, naturally. Karsh goes on a subterranean search for the truth, not unlike Adrian Tripod in *Crimes of the Future* all those years ago, though some characters suggest it may be Maury and Hunny throwing interference. *The Shrouds* is a perfect comment on "now" (whatever that is) and, in its themes and subtle connections to his past films, an eloquent summation of a career that spans over fifty years. Still, like the surfeit of data that the dead exude and the implications of postmortem surveillance, there could (and should) always be more from David Cronenberg.

ii.
THE SHADOW

STEREO [1969]
CRIMES OF THE FUTURE [1970]
SCANNERS [1981]

WHAT IS THE SHADOW?

Shadow permeates Cronenberg's films. This is the part of the unconscious that serves as a repository for all that is "bad" about ourselves and humanity. It is shaped by cultural norms and personal insecurities—the ego sometimes fabricates a false idea of who we

17. Limited hangout: Mlodzik on top of a telepathic cuddle puddle in *Stereo*.

18. *Crimes of the Future*'s Adrian Tripod mourns the unexpected loss of one of his guinea pigs at the House of Skin.

19. The feeling is mutual: Cameron Vale overhears a woman complaining about his presence at the mall.

20. Cameron experiences the beauty of connection—and alternative ways of being—that his scanner abilities hold.

21. Demon-like Darryl attempts to consume Cameron during their scanning battle.

22. Victorious synthesis, represented by the same contacts Dustin Hoffman wore in *Little Big Man*: Cameron has fused himself with Darryl Revok.

are in order to protect itself and hides all that fails to conform inside the shadow. As with the persona, this Jungian concept asserts a simple truth: everyone is capable of misdeeds or outright evil. However, the shadow can also house positive traits and insights such as creativity—what someone considers positive or negative is shaped not just by society, but by our upbringing, partners, and personal biases. Trauma and unmet needs can also force otherwise positive traits or impulses into one's shadow. But even the most negative things can give rise to goodness: rage can be used to achieve justice. The act of confronting our shadow and integrating it into our psyche gives us access to a deeper knowledge of ourselves and the world. The struggle of shadow work—a methodology that has been gaining popularity in non-Jungian circles—offers an opportunity to confront and grow from what we have previously pushed away. You can spend a great deal of time and energy denying the things that you don't want to admit are a part of you and beating yourself up for possessing those traits. Even acknowledging those self-punishing efforts can be a step in the right direction.

Cronenberg's films probe the fact of body over mind: disease; aging; decay; sex; violence; and death. "To me, film is really a mirror of the unconscious, and I guess I am busy exorcizing my own demons," he told *Guardian* in 1981. In this light, all of Cronenberg's films are shadow work—but go beyond something as facile as art as therapy. The death of Cronenberg's father shook him greatly and set him on a course for confronting that fear through his art—in a way, rehearsing his greatest fears and coming to embrace them. Turning your shadow from adversary to companion is key to individuation or any kind of personal growth. In Jung's schema, your shadow becomes the guide to the rest of the unconscious, leading you deeper; in plainer terms, you learn how to live with all parts of yourself.

The mad scientists that recur throughout Cronenberg's oeuvre are mad because of their commitment to rationality and scientific methodology over emotion and morality. They seek immortality through fame—the classic workaround to death—by breaking new ground. But they fail, time and time again, as though they may be able to reason their way around adhering to basic precepts of decency, they cannot defeat death or disease. They cannot see themselves as anything other than heroic, which gives rise to their shadow consuming them. Ernest Becker, author of *The Denial of Death*, argued that all we do comes out of our reaction to death; in the final interview before his death, he explained the ideas of fellow psychoanalyst Otto Rank thusly: "The fundamental dynamic of evil is the attempt to make the world something other than it is... free from accident, from impurity."

What makes for the best way of living, and what is and is not acceptable behavior, also underpins politics. Another key element of Jung's concept of the shadow is the phenomenon of shadow projection: the tendency to view the evil inherent in ourselves as exclusively belonging to others and blame them for our own shortcomings. "It is in the nature of political bodies to always see the evil in the opposite group, just as the individual has an ineradicable tendency to get rid of everything he does not know and does not want to know about himself by foisting it off on someone else," Jung wrote. This approach necessarily slides into scapegoating entire groups and reducing them to subhuman or demonic. It also gives us a blank check to behave as badly as we'd like in order to defeat this evil Other. There are myriad instances of this happening throughout history, though those that took place during Cronenberg's lifetime—such as the Cold War and the War on Terror—most intimately shape Cronenberg's dissection of the Western world's shadow.

In his first two features, *Stereo* and *Crimes of the Future*, as well as *Scanners*, a secretive, hyper-rationalist approach to attacking the Other—and using unsuspecting people as guinea pigs for larger political and social aims—form the crux of the drama. They form an exquisite critique of science and its abuses, something that could only be created by someone with an intimate understanding of science and the darker side of the Free World's methods of preserving order.

17.

ON *STEREO*, *CRIMES OF THE FUTURE*, AND *SCANNERS*

Paranoia and occultation run throughout Cronenberg's filmography, whether it's Spectacular Optical in *Videodrome* or the government Saul Tenser reports to in *Crimes of the Future*. While some of this comes from the writer/director's approach to editing and narrative structure, it's also an important part of the stories the films tell. Whereas the previous chapter offered a production history with some digressions into other economic and social forces guiding how the films were made, there's another important element that has indelibly shaped Cronenberg's filmography and deserves a greater degree of scrutiny.

Over the decades, Cronenberg has repeatedly cited the conformity of the Eisenhower era as the inspiration for the confrontational, subversive nature of his work. Though Canada is a sovereign nation, its role in the Cold War was one dictated by geography (as it's wedged between Russia and the United States) as well as overt and covert interactions with its neighbor to the south. The latter took many forms, but to give a sense of its extent, JFK's final cabinet meeting before his assassination was about quashing Canadian nationalism in order to preserve the interests of American business. This control came with the advent of nuclear bombs. The role of the U.S. presidency fundamentally changed after 1945, and from that moment came the ability to exert horrible power over the rest of the world, or even eliminate all life on earth. It's this reality that motivates newly psychic Johnny Smith (Christopher Walken) to sacrifice himself and attempt to assassinate the unscrupulous, inept political candidate Greg Stillson (Martin Sheen) in 1983's *The Dead Zone*.

18.

In light of this new reality, between 1945 and 1948, the U.S. and Canadian governments began creating elaborate, secretive national security apparatuses. In 1947, with the passage of the National Security Act, formerly distinct branches of the U.S. armed services were consolidated into one, the Department of Defense, and the wartime Office of Strategic Services became the Central Intelligence Agency, which offered clandestine (and more often than not immoral) ways to influence and reshape other governments as they saw fit. Think tanks espousing highly rational, evidence-based, technological approaches to the fight against Communism, such as the RAND Corporation, proliferated. These changes moved power away from offices of democratic accountability—and therefore operated with little to no accountability at all. It was all in the name of national security or the preservation of the free world. The obvious contradictions of, say, agencies steaming open the letters of leftists and reading them, lying to the public about the survivability

19.

of a nuclear attack, forcibly relocating indigenous people to the High Arctic, purging LGBTQ+ individuals from government jobs, or planting false stories in the exalted free press were ignored. Such acts became the Western world's shadow. Seemingly morally upstanding characters beset by paranoia and the moral unscrupulousness of governments, corporations, and mysterious institutions in between the two abound throughout Cronenberg's filmography. Their acquiescence to these powers is the site of his horror.

Though the Cold War is considered bloodless, it is estimated that there were 1,200 deaths a day for forty-five years as a result of American "interventions" against Communism. However, this number doesn't include the toll taken at home in North America. Aside from the angst, depression, drug addiction, and malaise caused by the conservative conformity of the Cold War era, there were inhuman experiments—conducted entirely in secret, without the consent of the participants—that sought to break down and reform an individual's will. These would go on to inspire the narrative and tone of Cronenberg's *Scanners*, as well as other anti-governmental, anti-corporate, and anti-authoritarian elements in his oeuvre.

Though it sounds extreme to connect conformism, anti-Communism, and unethical psychological experiments, they are inextricably linked. As a member of the North Atlantic Treaty Organization (NATO), Canada provided troops and other forms of support to its southern neighbor's bloody excursions around the world in the name of freedom. More than 30,000 Canadians were involved in the Korean War, a conflict incited by the United States in order to provoke the Soviets and establish itself as a global hegemony. The invasion ended in a stalemate and devastated both halves of the divided Korean peninsula. Millions of civilians were killed. The unscrupulous approach to fighting Communism—with help from the CIA, whose unofficial motto was to do it first and ask questions later—involved secret operations across Asia and the use of chemical weapons, which had been strictly forbidden by the Geneva Convention. The public was horrified when American soldiers—who'd either deserted in disgust or been captured by the Chinese or Russians—issued statements admitting they'd committed war crimes or used biological weapons. They had. But the CIA convinced itself—and the rest of the free world—that these deeply unpatriotic individuals had been brainwashed by the Reds. Mind control was a new concept, but as Stephen Kinzer, a historian who has chronicled the activities of American intelligence services during this period noted, it was the ideal explanation for any deviation from the Eisenhower era's rigid consensus. If you didn't conform, you had been tampered with and were unstable, unworthy of listening to. Having convinced themselves that the Soviets possessed advanced psychological warfare techniques, the CIA embarked on a frantic race to perfect its own methods of brainwashing. This culminated in a project known as MK-ULTRA, overseen by Dr. Sidney Gottlieb, the man who'd spearheaded the development of the biological weapons for the agency. The most inhuman of these experiments took place in Montreal. They would go on to inspire the narrative and tone of Cronenberg's Montreal-shot *Scanners*.

20.

But MK-ULTRA wouldn't become public until the mid-seventies following a Senate hearing. What inspired this ghoulish testing was the then-dominant school of psychology: Behaviorism. It was premised on the notion that every good or bad or neutral part of ourselves comes from conditioning and environment. This approach also had the benefit of making psychology resemble other, older sciences. Behaviorism offered measurable, rational explanations—a chemical reaction isn't subjective, so why should human behavior be? Different forms of conditioning—a method exemplified by Pavlov's dog salivating at the sound of a bell—offered a way to shed negative traits and reinforce good ones. In the postwar glow, Behaviorism suggested there could soon be a future where everyone was not only mentally well but behaved in an ideal manner—if only you pushed the right buttons. The morally upstanding West saw no issue in mashing the controller.

While Behaviorist approaches can be extremely helpful, it's not the universal cure-all that it was believed to be in the first half of the twentieth century. Furthermore, what qualifies as good—save for universal taboos about murder, incest, and defiling the dead—is both highly subjective and dependent on culture and time period. This notion of an idealized, perfected form of humanity, and the rational yet morally dubious path to reaching it through scientific experimentation, is explored in Cronenberg's first feature, *Stereo* (1969).

Though most of the gore occurs off-screen, the sixty-five-minute film can be understood as a psychedelic gothic horror. *Stereo* presents itself as an "educational mosaic" created by the Canadian Academy of Erotic Inquiry and depicts an experiment where the test subjects are a group of beautiful co-eds with telepathic abilities. They are kept inside a Brutalist building and are occasionally fed pills or pursued by researchers in white lab coats; mostly, they lounge around and play with each other. Yet the relationship between any given shot or scene is left for the viewer to invent. Another layer of potential association or frisson is the soundtrack: in keeping with the tradition of an industrial film, their actions are accompanied by a calm, clinical voiceover—a parody of scientific language—recorded by various, unidentified parties. This droning sometimes, but not always, intersects with the actions depicted on-screen. Like stereo sound, two things play at once; more often than not, this verbose narration adds a dry, absurd sense of humor to the film. (The line between horror and comedy is very thin.) Mostly, it discusses the work of Luther Stringfellow, the godlike researcher whose work has led to this experiment in "omnisexuality." In the end, the empty, sterile building triumphs over the subjects: casual violence increases as the film progresses, and it concludes with a man slapping a woman who approaches him for an embrace. (One could argue that, given the blatant disregard for the participants, the CAEI is only searching for omnisexuality in order to destroy it.)

Stereo's exquisite shot compositions and radical approach to form critique the ultra-rationalist nature of science, in particular its strictly Behaviorist approaches to the psyche. The "observable reality" we are offered in the film is ambiguous at best and frequently confusing—just like life. It cannot be entirely contained or explained by its accompanying voiceover. Thus, the experiment, this quest for a higher sense of humanity (or, as the voiceover puts it, "a possible prototype of three-dimensional man"), is nothing more than Stringfellow's cult. Religious overtones abound, from Ronald Mlodzik's priestly cloaks to the stated goals of the experiment, the "need for love" in erotic research, and the reverential descriptions of Stringfellow's genius. Participants are ritually scarred (through brain surgery and the removal of their vocal cords), given man-made drugs to induce their adherence to his ideas (recalling entheogens), kept in check by researchers (who function like shamans), and wander around his sanatorium, often in a trancelike state.

The researchers and subjects are looking for unity (through telepathy) and the numinous—a container for the wild, broken-down state of modernity—and reach something that existed long ago in a time of myth. But this cannot be manufactured—even though the researchers supposedly adopt a non-scientific, subjective approach to Eros—and at the end the participants who have survived it are more alone than they were at the start, destroyed and lacking a sense of self. Through no fault of their own, they are as empty as the concrete Petri dish in which they are stored. Science, when directed by someone without any doubt in themselves, has a limit. Its shadow takes hold.

Crimes of the Future (1970) continues this exploration of scientist as a flawed god or father figure. But instead of *amor vincit omnia* (love conquers all), its motto and driving force is *timor mortis conturbat me* (fear of death disturbs me). Possessing a less experimental approach to narrative but an equally loquacious, scientific voiceover, *Crimes of the Future* explores a classic science fiction concept: a world where one gender has been eliminated. "The mad dermatologist Antoine Rouge," leader of the House of Skin, caused a plague—through cosmetics he created—that has killed all post-pubescent women. A close disciple of Rouge's, Adrian Tripod (Mlodzik), travels through a variety of hapless scientific organizations—the Oceanic Podiatry Group, the Institute for Neo-Venereal Disease, and the Gynecological Research Foundation—in a fumbling quest to find his father figure. Adrian and his fellow male scientists, many of whom have taken to wearing bright red nail polish, carry out therapies that are essentially new mating rituals, such as "the invocation of the genetic history of feet," which consists of patient and practitioner aggressively groping each others' feet and falling back in ecstasy. Rather than conducting these in a strictly clinical setting, Adrian wanders the grounds of brutalist buildings, cruising for subjects. (Similarly, at the Metaphysical Import/Export Corporation, where Adrian takes a job as a courier, he lustily observes candidates for CEO positions sorting bags of panties and socks in wooden structures that recall bathhouse architecture.)

Everyone is damaged, but still seeks gratification. Eventually, Adrian abandons these homoerotic tasks when he falls in with a group of underground pedophiles who seek to artificially induce puberty in a five-year-old girl and impregnate her. What moves the hesitant, effeminate Adrian to commit this heinous act is not the continuation of the species, but the feeling of Rouge's presence within (or that Rouge is possessing) the young girl. However, she succumbs to Rouge's Malady, white goo spilling from her mouth. Adrian also contracts the fatal illness, and a single tear rolls down his cheek. Though we do not see him die, it's clear he's become another victim of masculine, ultra-rational scientific curiosity. However, he's not an entirely innocent one: like Rouge, his predicament is the direct result of putting a girl, unable of giving consent, through a medical procedure that is untested and self-serving. This is the dark side of enlightenment, of a quest for knowledge that disregards humanity. The shadow of science has triumphed.

On March 11, 1980, the Canadian news magazine program *The Fifth Estate* broke an incredible story. It revealed that from 1957 to 1965, Montreal's Allan Memorial Hospital had been the site of a secret, CIA-funded mind control experiment known as MK-ULTRA Subproject 68. The patients—most of whom were admitted with mild mental health problems—had not been informed they would be undergoing this experimental treatment and several survivors were now suing the U.S. government. (This was before the advent of universal healthcare in Canada, which meant they also paid for the privilege.) The project was overseen by Dr. Ewen Cameron, who, because he lived in New York and commuted to Montreal for work, held the distinction of being the head of the American Psychiatric Association and the Canadian Psychiatric Association at the same time.

Aside from prestige, Dr. Cameron was recruited by the CIA because of a research paper on his new therapy called "re-patterning," which would wipe a subject's slate clean and pave the way for implanting them with new attitudes and beliefs. Though his initial methodology was excruciating—a patient would be isolated, stunned, put into an artificial coma, and then, while drugged, forced to listen to a simple, pre-recorded message on a loop for hours and days at a time—he intensified its variations for MK-ULTRA. In another approach called "psychic driving," unwitting patients were first blindfolded, had their arms sheathed and ears plugged; others were given electroconvulsive shocks that were thirty to forty times as strong as the standard. They were then put into artificial comas for weeks to months at a time. (Sometimes these were partial comas, so that they could feel the disorienting passage of time.) Upon waking, they were drugged (with LSD, paralytics, or experimental tranquilizers), given meager amounts of food and water, and then exposed to a single recorded message like "My mother hates me" for up to sixteen hours a day, for weeks at a time. Some patients were given special helmets with speakers inside them so that they couldn't break up the grueling monotony by smashing their heads against the wall.

The results of this part of the treatment were extreme: in one report, Dr. Cameron described a nineteen-year-old honors student who'd been reduced to sucking her thumb, wetting herself, talking like a baby, and only feeding from a bottle. Though Dr. Cameron repeated the "re-patterning" with positive messages, sometimes for longer periods than the negative ones, it didn't work. The patients were irreparably broken, and then simply discharged.

Little is known about what went on in these experiments—which, rather helpfully for the CIA, did not take place on American soil. The only information about them comes from Dr. Cameron's notes and from the diaries of subjects; the CIA destroyed the majority of its documentation on MK-ULTRA, and the agency's responses to the victims or their families have never been made public in the name of national security. (Even an official apology was suppressed by Pierre Trudeau's government; his son, Justin, placed confidentiality agreements on a recent out-of-court settlement.)

While Cronenberg has never explicitly cited MK-ULTRA (or *The Fifth Estate* episode, which features harrowing interviews with two survivors) as inspiration for *Scanners*, its parallels are striking. And, given the film's numerous rewrites, reshoots, and re-editing (over the course of its principal photography but especially during its protracted nine-month-long postproduction period), it seems like a likely potent source to draw from. The film follows Cameron Vale (Stephen Lack), a man who seemingly suffers from schizophrenia, but actually has telepathic powers—what is called a scanner. He's recruited by Dr.

DAVID CRONENBERG: CLINICAL TRIALS

Paul Ruth, played with seething, anxious aplomb by Patrick McGoohan, star and creator of *The Prisoner*. (The show's pervasive paranoia, byzantine narrative, and expressionist flourishes were also likely an inspiration for *Scanners*.) Dr. Ruth is a psychopharmacologist and board member at ConSec (an ambiguously private corporation that provides weaponry and private armies for international security), who trains Cameron and instructs him to track down other scanners who haven't allied themselves with the anarchic Darryl Revok (Michael Ironside). Cameron soon joins up with a group of non-aligned scanners that includes Kim Obrist (Jennifer O'Neill) and experiences the beauty of fusing his powers with others. Eventually, Cameron and Kim discover that Darryl is manufacturing mass quantities of Ephemerol, the drug that gave them their telepathic powers, in order to create an army of scanners. In the penultimate scene of the film, Darryl reveals to Cameron that Ephemerol was created by their father, Dr. Ruth, who gave it to his pregnant wife (and other expectant mothers) in order to study its effects on their offspring who would be used as weapons.

Darryl demands that his brother join his quest for world domination, and when Cameron refuses, they battle each other telepathically, blood and flames shooting from their bodies. In the end, Cameron is victorious—he has taken over Darryl's body. This fight, one of the most indelible images of Cronenberg's career, is also rich with significance, as it literalizes the act of confronting one's shadow and integrating it into one's psyche: the agonizing struggle; the cleansing, elemental nature of fire; and Cameron's penetrating blue eyes (the window to the soul) representing the brothers' successful synthesis. With Dr. Ruth and Darryl gone, Cameron now has a fighting chance for himself and humanity.

More poignantly, despite the elaborate special effects, Cameron's journey represents the painful alienation and stigma of neurodivergence. *Scanners* possesses a profound sadness, one that often gains expression through Howard Shore's half-orchestral, half-electronic baroque score. The film begins with Cameron, dirty and wearing shabby clothes, emerging from the darkness into the fluorescent, tacky hell of a shopping mall. He seems to be unhoused, an all-too-common experience for untreated mentally ill people. As such, Cameron's reduced to picking at food and smoking cigarettes that others have left behind. When he turns to look at an elderly woman and her friend, one says, "I've never seen anything more disgusting in my life . . . I don't know how they can let creatures like that in here." He returns the favor by giving the woman a seizure, letting her experience the pain and confusion he does. This gestures toward another sad history: long before the advent of modern medicine, seizures were lumped in with mental illness; a short film of Darryl at the Crane Psychiatric Institute in 1967, in which he discusses his decision to put a hole in his skull to stop the voices he's hearing, also harkens back to that time—trepanation was a means of letting the "demons" that were causing mental illness or epilepsy to escape.

The experience of being scanned is painful, and being a scanner totalizing. As Dr. Ruth posits, "With all those voices in your head, how can you hear your own? How can you develop a self? A personality?" (These are also questions that run throughout Cronenberg's filmography: What is self, and how is it constructed and reconstructed through our own choices?) Though Dr. Ruth is pretending he doesn't know how scanners came to be at this point, he spits out these philosophical questions without any shred of penitence or sympathy. His need to observe and see through his experiment, one callously conducted on his own sons and other unsuspecting victims, trumps his basic humanity.

By contrast, when Cameron connects with the group of scanners led by Kim and they scan each other while sitting in a circle, he experiences a moment of grace, one that is "beautiful and frightening." Their shared trance brings emotion and agency back to the victims, but it also leaves them vulnerable, and it is cut short when Darryl's gunmen break into their apartment and start blasting shotguns. Those scanners who survive feel the pain of others dying, of being ripped out of existence, and are returned to their victimhood. Nevertheless, this scene shows that it is emotional connection, not a cruel assertion of

PART I. INDIVIDUATION

21.

22.

power over others, which is what makes scanners truly unique. They aren't freaks or weapons as Dr. Ruth and Darryl envision, but rather they are capable of incredible empathy and attaining higher planes of consciousness, of the transcendent.

Deeper connections—to the Montreal experiments, to a hero's journey—can be found in the stylish, idiosyncratic name of its protagonist. (This is often the case in Cronenberg's work.) A vale is an antiquated word for valley, and thus "Cameron Vale" can be understood as a person caught inside of Dr. Cameron's world: a depression where the schizophrenic and the psychologically maimed reside. But it can also be understood as a homonym of "veil," as in lifting the veil of silence and secrecy of the true horrors unleashed by deep-state apparatuses hell-bent on controlling and defeating their enemies. Cameron is a hero because he defeats the evil in himself, rather than attempting to maintain or reshape the world to fit his values. His harmony at the end of the film offers hope not only in the sense that a "damaged" person can survive and achieve greatness, but that they can heal themselves. In short, it's a happy ending, one of the few in Cronenberg's fifty-year-plus filmography.

iii.
ANIMUS/ ANIMA/ANIMUM

DEAD RINGERS [1988]
NAKED LUNCH [1991]
M. BUTTERFLY [1993]
CRASH [1996]

WHAT IS ANIMUS/ANIMA/ANIMUM?

Despite his disdain for the dogmatic, and a profound openness that is evident in his visionary approach to psychology as well as his personal life (not just the open marriage stuff—he was doing yoga in the 1910s), Carl Jung was in many ways a product of the Victorian era. He rejected many of its social and intellectual trappings, but, as progressives often do, carried on some of its worst biases unexamined. (His writings about race, both during and after Hitler's regime, are appalling by modern standards.) This failure to shear away such tendencies, even while producing something wildly new, becomes apparent while discussing his concepts of the anima and animus. Jung states that each person has a contrasexual element in their psyche: that within every man there is a woman—the anima—and that within every woman there is a man—the animus. Glimpsed in dreams, the anima is beguiling whereas the animus is imperiously correct. It is a psychopomp, a guide to the personal and collective unconscious. Familiarizing ourselves with the anima/animus, and integrating it into our whole being, can allow us to access deeper knowledge that would otherwise be hidden, potentially alleviate previously intractable problems, and achieve individuation. Yet it's also something quotidian and concrete: the anima/animus

23. Beverly dreams that he and Elliot are actually conjoined, and that only his anima, Claire Niveau, can separate them.
24. The showboating Mantles flaunt their supremacy in the field of gynecology by donning blood-red surgical gowns.
25. Claire as a bringer of light (and self-awareness) to Beverly.
26. Beverly and Elliot return to their amniotic positions.
27. "William Lee, I have arranged all of this just to be alone with you." The unspeakable object of Bill's desire—and his greatest tormentor—appears in a pile of insecticide at the police station.
28. The throbbing, erogenous innards of Tom Frost's Mujahideen reveal themselves to Bill after he asks Joan Frost to type up a filthy tale in Arabic.
29. The Mujahideen's enormous proboscis/penis/appendage extends itself as Bill and Joan get into even heavier petting.
30. An actor never heals: Song during one of their many performances, this time on an actual stage.
31. Half-Peking opera, half-Italian opera, and entirely tasteless: René concludes his pathetic attempt to recreate Song's glory by slitting his throat in prison.

has a hand in forming all types of relationships, and the ability to unexpectedly intercede in any internal aspect of ourselves—our habits, our moods, our confidence.

The notion of the anima/animus was revolutionary because it asserted gender parity during a wildly sexist time. It hints that we are inherently fluid or nonbinary beings; Jung sometimes stated it directly. However, he also assigned qualities like tenderness, caring, and patience to the anima, and logic, complex thought, and assertiveness to the animus. If a woman is overwhelmed by her animus, it can manifest in controlling or power-seeking behavior, or being loud—so, not knowing her place. Like all aspects of the psyche, Jung argued that the qualities of the anima and animus are a priori, and are therefore unchanging, essential, and universal. "This image is fundamentally unconscious, an hereditary factor of primordial origin engraved in the living organic system of the man . . . of all the ancestral experiences of the female, a deposit, as it were, of all the impressions ever made by woman." Therefore, there are but two genders. Women are "naturally" passive caregivers and men are "naturally" rational leaders.

Not to put too fine a point on it, but I fucking hate that.

But I also recognize that this was written long ago. The cultures and visual records that Jung was looking at to form his theories were recorded and filtered through a Western European worldview. (There are also plenty of instances where Jung and Marie-Louise von Franz bent the mythological canon to fit their misogynistic, androcentric, heteronormative worldview.) The best records of the Incas were made by the agents of the inquisition who went to Peru to convert them to Christianity on pain of death; the ability to understand quipu, the colored threads that served as the Incan "writing" system, beyond an agricultural accounting tool has been lost forever. Humanity has self-extinguished an untold number of its greatest accomplishments—even through ostensible preservation acts like archeology. And though we are now aware of the multitudinous counterexamples to the gender binary, gender as a fixed, lifelong category, and heterosexual attraction around the world, there are still Jungians who cling to these outdated notions. Not only do they dismiss and devalue the changing role of women in society as some kind of wacky trend, but decry trans and gender nonconforming persons as sick. The existence of this anti-trans industry, of course, lies in the fact that there's good money to be made by playing the haughty, authoritative contrarian—whether you believe in it or not. Even when identified as stereotypical or normative, ideas about sexuality, gender, and bodies eschew their true nature, as well as their differences. It places those who argue against those ideas on the back foot, forcing them to rebut the irrelevant rather than elaborate on what's actually extant.

However, there have been plenty of post-Jungian practitioners and theorists who've questioned this. Is there really a need for gender specific traits or figures that function as our opposite? I've clearly posed this question to immediately offer the answer, "no." I find James Perrin's definition of the animum, which replaces the anima and animus, to be the best: that it is the "container and center of the unresolvable definitional and causal tensions between bodily facility (sex), sociality (gender), and identity (sexuality). It is archetypal sex, archetypal gender, and archetypal sexuality itself." (It's also worth noting that, in his initial writings about the anima, Jung himself did not gender it.) Other post-Jungians have argued that rather than being contrasexual, the anima/animus is in fact an Other that resides inside of us. Rather than a horned-up facsimile of the *Downton Abbey* actor you're thirstiest for, Jung himself observed that this figure can take the form of an animal, a person of the same gender, or any object, and progressive adherents of his philosophy use that definition. It can exist in opposition to you without being gendered. And this is what gets to the core of what was truly radical and important about Jung's concept of the anima/animus: we harbor an Other that's distinct from the shadow. What's more, we must come to terms with that Other, and learn to work with it. For Jung, in Switzerland, in the early twentieth century, the most radical Other he could envision was a woman; for us, with a greatly expanded worldview, that Other can be anything.

32. Catherine Ballard exposes her perfect ass, on her perfect balcony, as she wistfully gazes out over the expressway below.

33. A car wash experience like no other: Catherine's semen-soaked hand gropes the leather interior of Vaughan's Lincoln.

34. Gabrielle proudly shows off her scar, reminiscent of lips or labia, at the luxury car dealership. After teasing a salesman, James Ballard will savor Gabrielle's third labium with great gusto.

35. Coitus interruptus: James pins his wife to the grass after successfully running her Mazda MX-5 Miata off the road. The accident, sadly, isn't fatal.

ON *DEAD RINGERS, NAKED LUNCH, M. BUTTERFLY,* AND *CRASH*

David Cronenberg's 1988 film *Dead Ringers*, 1991's *Naked Lunch*, 1993's *M. Butterfly*, and 1996's *Crash* hinge upon their characters' engagement with the anima/animus/animum—and their failure to integrate it. Each film starts off with a fairly straightforward doppelganger. (Jung believed that all psychic life is opposites, and all psychic energy—which Freud frequently reduced to sex—proceeds from the tension between those binaries.) As these films progress, these doubles fracture and multiply into angrier, more self-destructive beings. These opposites inflame and torture each other, and conclude with brutal, frustrating murders—of themselves, of their animum.

In the case of *Dead Ringers*, it's Toronto's marvelous Mantle twins, Elliot and Beverly, star gynecologists who specialize in female fertility. (To keep things exactly identical, both are played by Jeremy Irons.) They cohabitate, work together, and swap places whenever expedient—an inside joke on the rest of the world. Things change as Beverly falls for one of the women they share, and, through fits and starts, begins the process of finding what's behind his shadow, pulling away from Elliot. However, Beverly's descent into drug abuse aborts this process, and instead generates another person, one who is paranoid and obsessed with perfection. In an attempt to cure his brother, who he believes to be weaker, Elliot begins ingesting the same pills as Beverly, and spirals into a similar yet entirely different kind of addict. Though their bodies are intertwined at the end of the film, shadows fully occluding who they once were, each twin dies alone.

ANDERS WOLLECK:
"Mutant women? That's a great idea for a show."

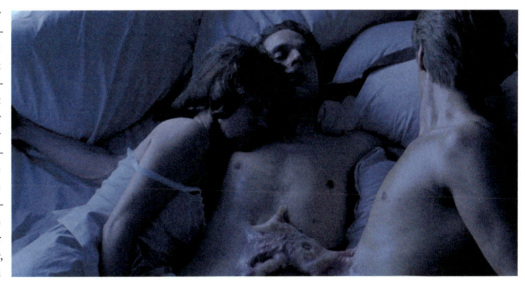

23.

You're lying in bed with your lover in the blue light of morning. You've finally patched things up after a horrible fight that seemingly ended your relationship. It's musty bliss. Except he's there—your double, your exact double, disapprovingly looking down at this most intimate of moments. And while the border between you two has never been that firm or important—it's a gift to have him as your backup, your helper, your confidant, your cheerleader, your reminder to do the things that you don't want to do—his presence here is terrifying. It's malicious, destabilizing, and sacrilegious. Then your lover coos in your ear, "I'll just separate you two." She sees the fibrous growth connecting you and him on your stomachs. She's probably always seen it, but you've never noticed it before. Your lover gently leans over and bites into it like a dog gnawing away an umbilical cord. (That's probably what it is; you're a doctor, you can look into it later.) There's blood, but not a lot of blood. She's got a giant piece of bloody tissue in her mouth, perhaps a tendon. It's painful to you, and you alone. Your double silently looks on. You thrash around and scream.

And then you fall out of bed. It's just a dream.

DAVID CRONENBERG: CLINICAL TRIALS

This scene from *Dead Ringers* is the lone "genre" element in an otherwise more "mature" arthouse style film. Just like the appendage connecting Elliot and Beverly Mantle, this film is typically identified as a turning point within Cronenberg's oeuvre. But it's much more than that. Based on the true, unsettling case of a real pair of gynecological wunderkind twins in Manhattan who had a penchant for fucking their patients, swapping places, and popping pills, Cronenberg hinges the drama on classic narrative themes and psychoanalytic ideas about doppelgangers, showing the best, the worst, and the most homoerotic prospects of having an exact double. Though the Mantles have some opposing qualities—Elliot is the shameless showman, obsessed with *Lifestyles of the Rich and Famous*, while Beverly is bookish, shy, and sensitive—they share all aspects of their lives. (You can't really say that Beverly is "the good one" if he's been pretending to be his brother in order to get laid for years.) Sometimes they appear complementary, but more often they're the same person on a different day or a slightly worse mood. They possess qualities that can be contained in a single person, which, as the film makes clear, they are.

In his adaptation of the material, Cronenberg wisely makes a mature, beautiful actress named Claire Niveau (Geneviève Bujold) serve as the film's love interest and antagonist. She is the Mantles' anima made flesh. Rather than their overly confident, ultra-rationalist, consumerist outlook, Claire operates on impulse, feeling, and intuition—a Cassandra of sorts. Although Beverly and Elliot have convinced themselves they're better than everyone else by virtue of their intelligence, Claire quickly detects the difference between the two of them while they're pretending to be one person. She sees through everything about them, and frequently tries to bring Beverly—literally and metaphorically—into the light. Aside from the bright, white bedroom of her Rosedale apartment, her most damning insight comes as she uses a long match to light multiple candles as she tells Beverly, "I don't think you two have come to terms with the way it really does work between you."

24.

Like Cassandra, Elliot dismisses Claire as "crazy," "a flake," "a showbiz lady," and merely using these assignations to procure prescription drugs—all before he identifies her as a possibly "destructive element" in the Mantle brothers' saga. (A true misogynist, this doesn't stop him from sexually desiring her, even after she has rejected him multiple times.) Overconfident Elliot, whose identity is a direct product of his birthing order, societal prestige, and bank account, doesn't believe anything needs to change. However, as little brother Beverly falls for Claire, he stops sharing everything with Elliot and identifies a potential for growth. He hesitantly begins to split away and individuate. Like a teenager eager to prove how mature they are, Beverly starts taking Claire's drugs—having spent his entire life with Elliot, he believes the only way to get close to someone is to imitate everything about them, including the bad. But the process is too much for him to bear, as Claire tells Elliot, "He's not alone, but he's lonely." Beverly's reliance on substances soon surpasses Claire's, and when she leaves Toronto for her next film role—in which she plays a character who may or may not be "an emotional hooker" who's involuntarily handcuffed to someone else—Beverly stands in the dark hallway of her apartment wearing a bathrobe, cowering next to her door and close to tears. Separation is painful, made even more so by Beverly's belief that Claire has been unfaithful; his addiction worsens. But he's at least attempted it—unlike Elliot. During one of Elliot's attempts to ease Beverly off pills without outside intervention, baby brother lies next to drawn venetian blinds and mumbles, "Don't you have a will of your own?" The answer, of course, is not quite. Elliot's belief that he's the stronger twin leads to their mutual destruction: Elliot's final attempt to help Beverly is to get on an identical pill regime in order to "synchronize" their systems. The single organism maintains homeostasis.

That a gynecologist would believe he could successfully treat such serious substance abuse, let alone in such an obviously dangerous fashion, speaks to the level of delusion only very smart people can achieve. It's a product of a society where intelligence, prestige, and financial success puts you at the top of the hierarchy. *Dead Ringers* exposes how such an overemphasis on rationality and achievement, unchecked—uncheckable!—breeds the fucked-up, unethical, dangerous mess that the Mantles unleash upon their patients and themselves. The twins have not just gone into any kind of gynecology; they specialize in fertility—something that was and still largely remains reserved for affluent white women. This affords them wealth, but also access to a certain type of person—such as a peripatetic film star like Claire. (To put a very fine point on this heady mix of misogyny and classism: the Marcus twins, the real life Mantles, were among the few doctors at the time to have perfected the "purse string," a procedure that aids women who have difficulty carrying a fetus to term.) It is not enough to be so uniquely gifted that they win awards, do guest lectures, and plan to take over the department, but they mark themselves by wearing movie blood-red scrubs. The Mantles and their assistants are not like any other type of medical staff; today, we'd call it branding. These uniforms, one of the film's most iconic images, invoke the theatricality of the operating theater and of Catholic mass. However, the Mantles' surgical wear also reads as an executioner's hood—a reminder that doctors have the ability to fatally harm, too.

25.

This unsettling costume is matched by Beverly's urge to devise new tools for "mutant women" whose "insides are all wrong." He never elaborates on what exactly is wrong with their anatomy, nor what their anatomy "should" be like. Though this mysteriousness suggests the degree to which Beverly has lost it, turning even further inward (after his aborted attempt to individuate), it's very much in line with the history of medicine, which is still largely geared toward the treatment of male bodies. (My current insurance carrier considers gynecologists "specialists," and therefore I pay more for those visits.) Prior to the nineteenth century, births, birth control, and abortions were managed by midwives. As the medical field professionalized, these procedures were wrested away from female caregivers, or were made illegal. "Professionalized," like many verbs, is culturally relative.

DAVID CRONENBERG: CLINICAL TRIALS

Consider Robert Liston, the English surgeon who rose to fame for his ability to amputate limbs quickly; he would ask to be timed by onlookers and used his mouth to hold instruments. (Only one in ten of his patients died on the table, a record for the era.) Then there's J. Marion Sims, often called the father of modern gynecology, who developed his techniques by experimenting on unanesthetized slaves and Irish immigrants. Though his defenders are quick to point out that the use of anesthesia was uncommon at the time, it's undeniable that his subjects—such as Anarcha, a Black woman he operated on thirty times—could not give consent, and that he absolutely benefitted from (and personally endorsed) the institution of slavery. Sims's influence is everywhere in the field: for example, he invented the speculum, a tool that is used in every modern gynecological examination. (For the uninitiated: it always feels fucking awful.) Although *Dead Ringers* doesn't explicitly mention this history, Beverly's interest in doing research (even before slipping into addiction and deeming every woman he examines abnormal) and fashioning "radical techniques" parallels Sims's work: just as Beverly seeks out the artist Anders Wolleck (Stephen Lack) to build the tools he designed for treating mutant women, Sims had a jeweler create a special silver hook for his fistula surgery.

How Beverly's personal problems manifest in his work—and that they manifest in his work at all—are a very clear critique of the midcentury Western medical mindset. In this ultra-rationalist, androcentric model, the doctor is the unquestionable, unimpeachable expert. The patient is there to be "corrected" by this authority, regardless of how harmful (physically, emotionally) that experience may be. Only the disease—which is very often a patient's failure to fit into the larger patriarchal, capitalist, white-supremacist society that evinces its superiority through its technological advancements—is present in the examination room; palliative care is nonexistent or relegated to less scholarly staff (like nurses).

Though the Mantles' specialization in fertility evinces a certain interest in maintaining that status quo by enabling (wealthy, white) women to achieve their biological destiny of making babies, this deeper need to reshape and rectify bodies becomes Beverly's primary preoccupation—a change propelled by the belief that Claire betrayed him and his worsening substance abuse. He is overtaken by his shadow, the worst aspects of either brother. Formerly the twin who was "good with the serious ones," Beverly examines a fully awake, middle-aged patient with a retractor meant for surgical procedures, and grows indignant when she yelps in pain. (He also asks the poor woman if she's engaged in bestiality—a vulgar, childish question that speaks to the level of his regression.) Beverly not only remains unrepentant after his mistake has been pointed out but seeks to validate his medical opinion by getting new surgical tools made. If the tools exist, so must the mutant women they're intended to treat, and vice versa.

26.

Though history repeats itself, it sometimes bends towards progress: unlike Sims, Beverly's attempt to test out his newly minted instruments on a patient is foiled. Similarly, Elliot's attempt to be Beverly before the medical review board—and pass off such a wildly dangerous gambit as merely the result of overwork—fails. "We could've killed her," Elliot informs Beverly, in one of the twins' many slipups between "you" and "we." Beverly, who is high as a kite, recites the story of the deaths of Chang and Eng, the conjoined brothers who toured the country and begat the term "Siamese twins," in a childish, singsong voice. This simultaneously harkens back to Beverly's nightmare of the hideous appendage that connects them and foreshadows the film's cataclysmic ending.

What makes the culmination of the Mantles' folie à deux so tragic and so relatable, despite its strangeness, is that Beverly is given a way out but chooses not to go. Though Beverly remains constantly, dangerously high, Claire returns, unaware of Beverly's mania. After Beverly accuses her of infidelity, Claire explains that it was her "defiantly gay" male secretary (the superb Damir Andrei) who'd answered the telephone in her hotel room when he'd called. That Beverly couldn't detect this isn't dwelled upon, not unlike the many other indications that neither he nor Elliot know much about sexuality, save for their private understanding of it. The twins' habit of abbreviating each other's names to the feminine-sounding "Ellie" and "Bev" is at once a signifier of their insufferable upper-class Britishness—which they have retained despite living in Toronto for at least two decades—and their alternately infantile and sexually charged relationship. The Mantles view themselves as a complete being, alternately feminine and masculine. Even the flashback to their childhood, in which their crude sexual proposition to a neighborhood girl is rebuffed and they retreat to their bedroom in order to "operate" on a visible woman model, doesn't show their parents. (The visible woman's limbs are tied and pinned down with the same medical supplies and in the same fashion as Claire's are in a later scene, foreshadowing the creepy rituals they reserve for women.) The absence of parents reinforces the eeriness of their existence, that they are no men of woman born. It's undeniable that their single cell became two, but it seems as if there was no gestation or birth, and that they merely came into existence through sheer force of will. Aside from providing them a framework by which to interact with and use women, their interest in gynecology no doubt arises from their interest in their own rarified creation—yet another form of self-love, just more Mantleology.

Though "narcissism" has been overapplied so many times that it's beyond parody, the Mantles experience Narcissus's fate, drowning in their own reflection. This parallel isn't simply sadism on Cronenberg's part: the myth was a touchstone for psychoanalysts like Otto Rank and Sigmund Freud, who argued that narcissism is a crucial component of development, part of what allows a baby to understand what is and is not them, and part of our obsession with doppelgangers. With twins, this process is muddled: rather than being individuals, they simply exist in the twinship, permanently primordial. This becomes increasingly explicit as the film's conclusion approaches: drugged-out Beverly leaves the garbage-strewn Mantle Clinic to go see Claire; when he doesn't hear from Elliot, Beverly returns to the clinic to discover Elliot has taken his place. Reunited, they regress to babyhood, going on a bender of pills and cake; Elliot starts bawling when he learns there's no ice cream. Without any sort of obligation other than eating, shitting, and getting high, the passage of time ceases to exist. It's unclear whether or not it really is their birthday—the cake was just lying around anyway.

It's also unclear what leads up to Beverly operating on Elliot. Before returning to the clinic, he'd told Claire that the tools he'd designed to treat mutant women were actually for separating Siamese twins. The procedure is a barbaric parody of a gynecological surgery; Elliot refers to the clawlike device Beverly uses for his first incision as the "morticulator," a Latin-derived word that means something like "death wrestler." Elliot bleeds to death on the table, and Beverly passes out. Upon waking, Beverly can't process what he's done, and starts calling for "Ellie" in a high-pitched, childlike voice. But he gets dressed. He packs a bag. He goes downstairs in the blinding, sharp sunlight and calls Claire on a pay phone. When she picks up, he says nothing, and she asks who's there. His back to the camera, his face impossible to read, Beverly hangs up the phone and returns upstairs. Beverly lies in the fetal position on Elliot's body, which he's propped up. It's like a pietà amongst the filth.

Doppelgangers are terrifying because they are uncanny, the familiar turned strange, calling into question what is and what is not us. These doubles pose a threat to at least one aspect of our lives, be it social (through the double's evil deeds) or biological (being killed and replaced by a double). Like twins, doppelgangers were, across cultures and times, almost universally reviled and feared. But, as Rank noted, the notion of a soul that persists after death is a double, and an idealized one at that. Without his brother, without his soul, he had no identity, affirmed by Claire's confusion. There was nothing left for Beverly to do but go back.

KIKI: *"I'd like you to meet a friend of mine.*
He specializes in sexual ambivalence."
WILLIAM LEE: *"Sexual ambulance, you say?"*

It's fitting that the only bare female breasts glimpsed in *Naked Lunch* are actually made of rubber—and are aggressively torn apart inside what is an actual dick-sucking factory. Although it doesn't appear in the book *Naked Lunch*, this act is a perceptive extension of William S. Burroughs's work: something that's queer, slapstick, profane, larger-than-life, and legitimately surprising. This rug-pull moment reveals that Fadela (Monique Mercure), a witchy, butch lesbian with a harem and a massive drug operation who's been abusing Joan Frost (Judy Davis), is actually Dr. Benway (Roy Scheider), the man who put Agent William Lee (Peter Weller) onto the addictive black meat of the aquatic Brazilian centipede—which means that, with his various investigations, Lee has been chasing his own tail the entire time. It renders everything that has come before—the question of whether he's actually a globe-trotting flatfoot or just a junkie slumped over in a smoky room—completely moot.

But Fadela is and isn't more than a full-body lady suit. She also exemplifies the negative anima, the enchantress or witch that lures the huntsman away from the trail in many a fairy tale. Dr. Benway's feminine side—which he crassly accuses of being "subversive" and "on the rag"—isn't the main force that's been leading Lee deeper down the rabbit hole. She's just like any other inhabitant of the liminal fantasy metropolis Interzone, a disposable curiosity that can trick or treat Lee. As much as he'd like to believe otherwise, he's not really into women. Over the course of the film, there are not one but two identical Joans, and while he relentlessly pursues the second one, she is not a manifestation of his animum. Instead, Lee's animum appears as an assortment of talking male bugs with pulsating anus-like mouths, a hideous manifestation of his true desire filtered through his internalized homophobia.

Naked Lunch fragments and mangles characters, places, and reality itself. William Lee is clearly based on the author of the novel *Naked Lunch*, William S. Burroughs, and works as an exterminator in New York City. Lee also commits the original sin of Burroughs's writing career: killing his wife Joan (Davis) while attempting to shoot a glass off of her head. On the orders of a mugwump, a giant reptile-like creature (whose hunched back mimics Burroughs's/Lee's posture) who serves at an undisclosed intelligence agency, he heads for Interzone, a place that sometimes looks like Morocco and other times New York. Along with some rent boys, Lee meets the Frosts, a marriage between a homosexual man, Tom (Ian Holm), and a heterosexual woman, Joan (also played by Davis). The Frosts, who are based on the real Paul and Jane Bowles, mirror Lee's arrangement with his own deceased wife; Lee becomes obsessed with her, sublimating his sexuality through drugs that, in his words, may or may not exist. Additional agents, who are monstrous bug-typewriters, give Lee instructions to follow. When it seems as though he's escaped, Lee kills Joan Frost in an identical manner as his wife Joan Lee.

Control is a major theme in Burroughs's work, and these bugs are literal controllers in the film's shifting universe, doling out investigative leads and bits of tradecraft that mitigate Lee's self-hatred—such as telling him he was programmed to kill Joan, or instructing him to forcefully type "homosexuality is the best all-around cover an agent ever had." Most importantly, they connect him to his unconscious and to the mystical flow-state of writing, which in turn allows him to produce the text that will become *Naked Lunch*.

It seems heretical that Cronenberg's adaptation of this famously "unadaptable" book, considered obscene because of its casually graphic descriptions of gay sex, is premised on the author-surrogate's inability to accept his sexuality. But then, to faithfully represent a vision as unique as Burroughs's would've been far more gauche (as well as expensive and impossible to distribute). Instead, Cronenberg extends that vision, fusing his own sensibility with elements of Burroughs's life (mainly sourced from Ted Morgan's 1988 biography

Literary Outlaw), the novels *Junky* (1953), *Queer* (1985), and *Naked Lunch* (1959), as well as the short story "Exterminator!" (1973).

True to Burroughs's most famous device, the cut-up method, in which writing, audio tape, or film is cut up with scissors and randomly reassembled, the combination of these sources forge new insights into Burroughs's identity and his work.

Beyond transgressive pulp, what emerges in the film *Naked Lunch* is a pervasive sense of loneliness. Along with Burroughs's substance abuse, this arises from Cronenberg's choice to anchor its plot in two key biographical details from Burroughs's life around the time he wrote *Naked Lunch*: the hatred of his homosexuality and the infamous "William Tell routine," during which he fatally shot his wife, Joan Vollmer, in Mexico City. The former exemplifies the knotty contradictions of selfhood, an antiestablishment that doesn't believe in itself: after completing *Naked Lunch*, Burroughs wrote to his former lover, Allen Ginsberg, and claimed that writing the book had "cured" his gayness. (Ginsberg, meanwhile, was seeing a shrink to excise his own.) However, Vollmer's death, whether or not you believe it was an accident, remains an unredeemable tragedy that further set Burroughs apart from the rest of society. In addition to believing he'd ruined his son's life, he'd also lost Vollmer—a brilliant, integral part of the early Beat scene, and, by nearly all accounts, someone whom Burroughs adored. *Queer* was largely written while he was awaiting trial for Joan's murder and was only published in 1985. In its foreword, Burroughs wrote of the shooting: "I live with the constant threat of possession, and a constant need to escape from possession, from Control. So the death of Joan brought me in contact with the invader, the Ugly Spirit, and maneuvered me into a lifelong struggle, in which I have had no choice except to write my way out."

It sounds like a neat self-hagiography, but like Jung, Burroughs did not believe in coincidence. He too was interested in, studied, and took seriously customs and belief systems of non-Western and premodern societies. These viewpoints became inextricable from Burroughs's own, evident from both his personal life and writing. Also like Jung, Burroughs's first contact with these systems came through the women in his life: Burroughs's mother loved crystal balls and was supposedly clairvoyant, while his Welsh housekeeper, "Nursey," regaled the boy with stories of magic and superstitions from her homeland. (The curse in 1983's *The Place of Dead Roads*, in which a thinly veiled Burroughs surrogate exacts revenge upon a tormentor from his teenage years, originates from an identical source.)

From an early age, Burroughs knew (and disliked) the fact that he was gay and felt that he was an outsider. Sometimes he felt his homosexual desires were the influence of an external spirit. However, Burroughs also acknowledged that invisible, non-rational forces of the universe were not necessarily evil. "To me 'genius' is the nagual: the uncontrollable—unknown and so unpredictable—spontaneous and alive," he explained in a 1988 interview with writer and researcher Matthew Levi Stevens. "You could say the magical." Although the term "nagual" became slightly less obscure during the 1960s because of Carlos Castaneda's *The Teachings of Don Juan*, a book about shamanism that was either mostly or entirely fabricated, naguals are indeed part of pre-Columbian, Mesoamerican shamanistic practices; they are born transforming trickster-figures who can use their powers for evil or ill. Cronenberg's *Naked Lunch* operates on an identical principle of the g-word. Lee is an archetypal trickster—cunning, foolish, rule-breaking, wise-cracking, treacherous—and the magic that he performs—in trancelike states, in orgasmic reveries, or sometimes without even pressing his typewriter's keys—is akin to writing a masterpiece that he's unaware exists. It's a fitting way to represent a man who created a work of transgressive fiction that reverberated across the twentieth century's pop mainstream and multiple eras of the avant-garde. As Jung wrote, "[the trickster] is a bridge, or even a waterfall, between the subconscious urges of the animalistic, primitive, and the divine aspects of the individual. For this reason, he neither fits into the animal life, nor the godly life, but he does point out the humor and inconsistencies of a life in ignorance of either of the two."

The trickster's contradictory, hybrid nature also points to why Lee's animum appears 27.
as a series of enormous bugs that speak through gigantic, clenching assholes. They are
inhuman, but also his most constant companion: Clark Nova (Peter Boretski) is a typewriter in front and pink bunghole in back, at once functional and erotic. Yet it is also too
impractical and revolting to use for either writing or sex. Jung notes that trickster narratives allow modern people to look back on the mores of the past with condescension—
which rings particularly true with Cronenberg's decision to focus the narrative around
Burroughs's inability to accept his sexuality.

This alignment with tricksters is established even before the film's images begin,
with the quotes "Nothing is true; everything is permitted" (Hassan I Sabbah) and "Hus-
tlers of the world, there is one Mark you cannot beat: The Mark Inside" (from *Naked Lunch*).
On the most basic level, this sets up the wild unreality of the narrative and identifies its
protagonist as a rent boy. (Unlike the book's text, "The Mark Inside" is capitalized, as you
would a name—perhaps honoring the existence of the Lee who is freely queer, and the fact
that Lee cannot hide from this version of himself.) Still, the lengths Lee goes to in order to
avoid reality—by pursuing Joan Frost (whose marriage to Tom is, like his own, a cordial
agreement between a gay man and a straight woman), by believing that homosexual acts
are part of his spycraft—only go so far. Lee runs away from all types of sexual situations
which are simultaneously real, metaphorical, and fictionalized versions of something that
really did happen—save for when he "penetrates" by typing with a typewriter.

Fig K. David Cronenberg with *Naked Lunch* author
William S. Burroughs and Peter Weller, 1991.

When Kiki, a sweet-hearted Interzone rent boy with whom Lee shacks up with for a
bit, has intercourse with the effeminate dandy Cloquet (Julian Sands), Lee perceives it as a
grotesque consumption of flesh rather than what he's been up to. Though this scene in particular has drawn ire from gay critics, it's worth noting that this—a well-heeled European
literally sucking the life out of a poor North African—is an apt metaphor for the power
dynamics of late nineteenth-/twentieth-century sex tourism in Morocco. (Is this secretly
what Cronenberg wanted to convey with this gore? Probably not, but the film exists outside of his intent.) Similarly, when Lee visits Joan alone at the home she shares with Tom,
the pair get high, and Lee starts kissing and nuzzling Joan as she types an erotic story in
Arabic on Tom's imperious Mujahideen typewriter. The machine opens to reveal pulsating
organs and sinew as Joan's writing grows dirtier, and then grows a penis-like organ from
out of its anus. As Lee and Joan writhe on the floor, a half-bug, half-human torso (only the
backside, of course) flops on top of the writhing couple and starts furiously humping both
of them; Joan's fingers flit around its asscrack. Fadela interrupts this ménage à trois by
crying out, "Mrs. Frost! This is an evil and insane thing you're doing!"—objecting to the
violation of her sexual ownership of Joan, as well as Joan indulging Lee's fantasy of hetero-
sexuality. A similar stretching of the reality principle is evident when Martin (Michael

Zelniker), a Ginsberg surrogate, and Hank (Nicholas Campbell), a Jack Kerouac surrogate, find Lee sleeping on a beach that's at a combination of Morocco and New York City's Chelsea Piers (a famous cruising spot). When the pair look inside the pillowcase he claims holds his writing instrument, it's full of pill bottles and needles.

28.

Another common feature of tales about tricksters involves the trickster being tricked, which forms a crucial component of *Naked Lunch*'s ending. A scene of Dr. Benway revealing himself as Fadela by ripping off his costume is a grand fuck you to Lee, underscored by the muzzled mugwumps' joyous exclamations of "Benway!" (The mugwumps, mammoth, skeletal creatures that have penises growing out of their skulls, are rather po-faced while they're being suckled by the unfortunate souls who are tasked with extracting their jism.) When Benway asks Lee what he wants, he asks for Joan Frost. Benway is incredulous. "I can't write without her," Lee tells him in a soft and sad tone, a sharp break from his typical drollness. When Lee is stopped by border guards while attempting to enter Annexia, a fabulated Soviet satellite, they demand that he prove he is a writer by writing something. They hand him a pen. He wakes up Joan, who is sleeping in the back of the van, snuggled up in Moroccan textiles. Unprompted, he tells her the same thing he said before he shot Joan Lee: "It's about time for our William Tell routine." He fails to hit the glass on the second Joan's head, then rushes to her side, horrified. The guards welcome him to Annexia. Lee stares off-camera in disbelief. Did Lee trick himself into believing he could make the shot this time? Was it motivated by a need to make a macho show of force and prove that he's a real man, not a queer, to the guards? Or did they trick him into becoming a writer again, which necessitated him killing Joan once more? Or was there no trickery at all, and that on some level, Lee knew killing her was what allowed him to write, and he simply has to live with the guilt? Is he damned to repeat this cycle forever? It's a chilling ending, one that rips us out of the magical realism of all that has come before it and underscores the senseless horror of what actually happened, Orpheus losing Eurydice. Tricksters, after all, can be cunning or stupid, or both. As Jung wrote in his essay outlining the trickster archetype, "repressed contents are the very ones that have the best chance of survival."

29.

> RENÉ GALLIMARD: *"Sir, with all due respect: you don't really think those little men could've beaten us without our unconscious consent, do you?"*

It's tempting to understand 1993's *M. Butterfly* as another film about a man who can't accept that he's gay: set in the mid-sixties before, during, and after the Cultural Revolution, it was inspired by the true story of Bernard Boursicot, an accountant at the French embassy in China who began passing state secrets to the Communists during his nineteen-year-long affair with Shi Pei Pu, a Beijing Opera star whom he believed to be female. However, this frequently-overlooked entry in Cronenberg's filmography exposes a different set of raw truths about identity and sexual desire. It also stands out as the director's most overtly political work, not simply because of its setting and the fact it deals with espionage. This impetus comes from David Henry Hwang, who authored the original play and also adapted it to the screen. Hwang was not simply part of the vanguard of Asian American theater in the eighties and nineties, he was very often its face: among other achievements, he became the first Asian American playwright to win a Tony Award and led the charge against Jonathan Pryce playing a Eurasian character in a 1993 West End production of *Miss Saigon*. His frequently autobiographical work explores the lives of immigrants, the stereotype of the perpetual foreigner, the burdens of representation, and the projections the West flings eastward and the East throws westward. (This, specifically, probes the notion that the East is weak and inherently feminine, which extends from the relationship at its center to the ideological dictates of American and Chinese foreign policy.) The edge and directness Hwang brings to the film—through pointed dialogue, intimated critiques, and the radical act of interweaving a very real story with the grandiosity of Puccini's opera

30.

31.

Madama Butterfly—sit uneasily next to Cronenberg's more overtly romantic directorial approach. Yet this tension is perfectly suited to the inexplicable nature of love and sex, the messiness that exists behind the spark of desire and its carnal expressions. It shatters the illusion that we really do know a partner, or even ourselves—a difficult lesson learned every day, quietly and loudly, by all sorts of people under far more quotidian circumstances.

Casting choices also heighten *M. Butterfly*'s ambient tension and confusion. Instead of choosing an unknown, androgynous actor to play Song, the fictionalized version of Pei Pu, they are portrayed by John Lone. There are clear limits to Song's ability to physically present as female—to the audience, at least. (This is a significant departure from the Broadway original, where BD Wong, who was then an unknown actor and could pass more easily as female, played the role.) This reality, combined with a viewer's potential familiarity with the true story, means that Song's "big reveal" carries no shock; surprise is one of the most basic forms of narrative enjoyment. By denying this pleasure and avoiding this cheap twist, it elucidates the fact that gender is not simply a social construct, but also a collaborative fantasy.

The typically intimidating and authoritative Jeremy Irons as René Gallimard, the fictionalized Boursicot, cuts a similarly complicated and contradictory figure. Whereas Boursicot was a twenty-year-old, pimple-faced high school dropout who'd never been with a woman before he became involved with Pei Pu, Gallimard is in his mid-forties and married to an equally arrogant Frenchwoman (tellingly played by one of Rainer Werner Fassbinder's frequent collaborators, Barbara Sukowa). Aside from the obnoxiousness of his Eurocentrism and wild overconfidence in everything he does, he's a tattletale who rises through the ranks of the embassy by badgering his colleagues about their suspicious spending. (The open disgust for accountants in art and life is only outstripped by that for lawyers.) Though Gallimard's first interactions with Song only underscore his fundamental loathsomeness (he reduces Song's thoughtful criticisms of why the Chinese disdain *Madama Butterfly* to "because the white man gets the girl"), his passion for them renders him extremely weak and reactive. He enjoys being the cruel and dominating white man, educating them in the art of Western lovemaking and demanding their total submission in one moment, to falling to his knees the next and crying out for "my butterfly." Gallimard's blind affection is like a teenager's, but for that reason is also infinitely relatable. It's a potent reminder that even the most unlikable people are capable of falling hard and losing themselves in another person.

The depths and pureness of Gallimard's love come from the fact that Song is not just a woman, but the perfect woman. When the couple visit the Great Wall, the scene is shot almost entirely in close-up: despite being in such a grand location, all Gallimard can see is Song. He believes Song's construction because it so perfectly embodies what he believes an oriental woman to be: slender, modest, long-haired, innocent, suffering, selfless, and pliable—far superior to the Western variety. (When Song shows Gallimard "their" baby, they complete his ideal of "womanliness.") As Song tells their controller, Comrade Chin (Shizuko Hoshi), "Only a man knows how a woman is supposed to act." However, Song's true feelings (and gender identity) aren't as transparent as Gallimard's. Earlier, when Chin catches Song wearing women's clothes, splayed out on their bed reading old movie magazines, her disgust is mortifying. "Don't you understand how degrading those images are to women? And why do you have to behave this way when he's not even here?" Chin spits. "Comrade," Song gently lilts, shyly casting their gaze downward every so often, "in order to better serve the great proletarian state, I practice my deception as often as possible. I despise this costume, yet for the sake of our great helmsman, I will endure it along with all of the other bourgeois Western perversions." It's unclear if their use of such clunky Communist rhetoric is ironic or not; there's a genuine sadness in Song's voice. Is it the weight of being who the party wants them to be, who they want to be, or who Gallimard wants them to be weighing them down in this moment? The knowledge that this self-objectification is the only way Gallimard can love them? Guilt? That they can no longer see themselves without this "costume" anymore?

More than the simplistic notion of being "a woman trapped in a man's body," the burden pre-transition persons who do not identify with the sex they were assigned at birth more directly suffer is the inability to see themselves as they want to be; mirrors are painful reminders of this disconnect, while imagining who they may become only goes so far. Or is it the weight of all of these burdens at once? "I try my best to become somebody else," Song murmurs. But who is that somebody? Song looks down at a magazine with a portrait of Anna May Wong, the alternately trailblazing and crudely typecast Chinese American film star, on its cover. Wong is a remnant of a past that is temporally close and culturally distant: Song can never be an actress outside of the role they play for Gallimard and the Party in this new China and is consigned to being a functionary. The freedom from Confucian patriarchy Chin enjoys, along with the sadistic pleasure she derives from the job, is unavailable to Song—unless, of course, their desire is to have sex with a man, even if it's one who may not be the one they really want, and take out their frustrations by (or get off on) tricking that man through invented, expedient customs of Chinese lovemaking. The refusal to state Song's wishes outright again points to the irrational, mystifying essence of human desire.

Things aren't made any clearer once the couple are arrested in France. As they are being driven back to prison from court—where the question of "how didn't he know?" provokes laughter from the lawyers and the gallery—Song taunts Gallimard. "You still want me, don't you? Even in a suit and a tie," they say. "Come here, my little one. Oh, my mistake. I am *your* little one." Gallimard, incredulous and quietly enraged, is now the one with the shameful downward glances. The gaze has been switched, and Gallimard is no longer in control. Song strips naked, finally giving Gallimard what he wants, and Gallimard cowers in a corner. But suddenly they begin to use their feminine voice again, adopting the softness of their former role. Kneeling before him, rubbing his hands on their face, Song informs Gallimard, "I am your butterfly. And underneath the robes, it was always me. Tell me you adore me." The power of seduction, of the traditionally feminine, begins again. When Gallimard rejects Song, Song begins to cry. The last time we see Song, they are sitting in an airplane bound for China, wearing a suit and an ambivalent expression. They remain a cipher.

But it's not the last time we see "Butterfly." Jung wrote of the necessity for an unfeeling man, one convinced of his pure masculinity, to fall in love with a woman onto whom he projects all things feminine, and then have his heart broken upon realizing that she is a real, entirely different human being. The resultant pain and confusion is what forces him to practice the functions once assigned to the anima, and once they've been practiced enough, they become a part of him and cease being a gendered thing. In the film's final scene, Gallimard does exactly this—but can't handle it. He stands before an audience in prison as "Un bel di, vedremo" (the aria from *Madama Butterfly* he saw Song perform) plays and begins to slather on red and white makeup, a poorly done reproduction of that worn by female characters in traditional Chinese opera. "I'm a celebrity. I make people laugh. I made all of France laugh. But really, if you'd understood, you wouldn't laugh at all. Quite the contrary. Men like you should be beating down my door, begging to know my secrets. For I, René Gallimard, have been known and loved by the perfect woman," he begins. He summarizes the Orientalist fantasy that he fell so hard for: "Women in cheongsams and kimonos who die for the love of unworthy foreign devils. Who are born and raised to be perfect women, to take whatever punishment we give them. Strengthened by love, unconditionally."

As his transformation nears its completion, he abruptly switches his identity: "My mistake was simple but absolute: the man I loved was not worthy. He didn't deserve even a second glance. Instead, I gave him my love, all of my love." Gallimard begins to cry, puts his hand into a prayer position, and delicately bows. "My name is René Gallimard. Also known as Madame Butterfly," he says before stabbing a shattered pocket mirror into his neck. Even in death, Gallimard confuses Japanese and Chinese culture. (It's also worth noting that the aria is about Cio-Cio-San, Puccini's protagonist, saying that she will wait for her American lover, fantasizing about the day he arrives on a ship, rather than her big suicide scene.) He's clueless to the end.

Before the credits roll, there's a shot of a stewardess sealing the door of an Air China airplane. She too is the perfect woman, pretty and attentive and deferential—albeit one that gets to take off her uniform at the end of the day. Though the drama of Gallimard's death and the closing door suggest a tragic resolution, it also makes clear that many different women carry Song's burden.

> VAUGHAN: *"Was I glib? 'James Dean died of a broken neck and became immortal.' I couldn't resist!"*

Cars speed across steel and concrete over a bridge in the distance, their drivers undeterred by the oppressively gray, almost foggy weather outside. But there's no time to contemplate the inherent dangers of tooling around in Toronto, the city that so often plays New York City, Los Angeles, and everywhere but itself. The foreground is deathly still. It takes you a moment to figure out why there's a black Mercedes-Benz convertible parked on a tile floor in the foreground: it's a showroom. The blue-tinted outdoor lighting and the indoor, orange-tinted fluorescents, separated by a large glass window, heighten the unsettling, unnatural juxtaposition of the two planes, of machines in motion and machines at rest.

Shiny surfaces reflect off of one another. Then a black cane enters the frame from the left, cautiously probing the slicked wax floor. Gabrielle (Rosanna Arquette) is grasping it, slowly loping her way toward the convertible. Her legs are covered by metal braces and fishnet stockings; they are on display, just like the luxury automobiles around her. Although she is petite, each footstep lands heavily with a crunch. James Ballard (James Spader) trails behind her, face blank, inconspicuously conspicuous. He's there as a voyeur, to generate contrast between Gabrielle's physicality and his own, and to beg the question: What would a man like this be doing with a woman like that, all sex and leather and steel?

A bespectacled man who works at the dealership—whose desk is surrounded by cars, part of some frozen, nonsense traffic jam—notices them. He approaches Gabrielle and James while she lovingly caresses the convertible's body. We see a close-up of the long, labia-like wound on her leg as she faces the car and splays against it. "Is there something here that interests you?" he asks, looking at her head and not where the scopophilic camera is. The camera doesn't represent the point of view of any person, but rather the philosophy-cum-psychopathology that has overtaken the protagonists' minds.

"This interests me," Gabrielle coos. "I'd like to see if I can fit into a car made for a normal body. Could you help me into it please?" The salesman obliges, and Gabrielle cutely struggles to get into the convertible. (James quietly slips into the passenger seat, eyes fixed on the salesman and Gabrielle.) She struggles to get in. "I'm caught," she says bashfully, playing the victim, playing into the notion that the disabled are to be pitied and doted on, playing the damsel in distress. The salesman smiles and then looks behind him, as if he can't really believe this is happening, and then kneels to help her. It's somewhere between chivalry and the start of a letter to *Penthouse*. Gabrielle paws at James's crotch as the salesman tries to separate her leg brace from the leather passenger seat. The salesman touches her brace gingerly at first, trying to avoid her skin. But he tugs too hard, and the fine German craftsmanship rips—a kind of premature ejaculation that breaks the fantasy. "Oh shit. Fuck! This is bad, this is really bad," he hisses to himself. Gabrielle grabs James's sex harder.

And then James and Gabrielle are in the dark of a parking garage. Gabrielle splayed out in the back seat of a car. Some car, it doesn't matter. There's no sense of how much time has passed, how much distance has been traveled to get here. The garage is a non-place: anonymous, concrete, and empty. James roughly positions Gabrielle's leg vertically before him, tears open her fishnets, and fucks her scar.

The incautious viewer will say that the sex in 1996's *Crash*, based on J.G. Ballard's 1973 novel of the same name, isn't romantic, playful, or procreative. What is present, and what confuses our sense of familiarity with this basic act, is not only that it is used as a mode of character development, but that it's treated as the paradox it truly is. As author Garth Greenwell said while discussing desire in his own (extremely different) writing, "Sex is inextricable from philosophy. It is a source of all of our metaphysics. It's the experience that puts us most in our animal bodies, and yet also gives us our most intense intimations of something beyond those bodies." Vaughan (Elias Koteas), a barking-mad wiseman who's the president of a car crash club, and his disciples (particularly those who have given up their lives and reside with him) are becoming part of the future; he is the negative animum that guides all. Rather than "the transformation of the human body through technology"—a "crude sci-fi concept" that Vaughan uses to separate out the fakers from the real heads—car accidents are "a fertilizing rather than a destructive event. A liberation of sexual energy, mediating the sexuality of those who have died with an intensity that is impossible in any other form."

In practice, Vaughan's philosophy means that gender, sexuality, and anatomy are irrelevant. What matters are scars, bruises, and other traces of past crashes and violence: connections to that force, to all those who have died before, a path forward in a world of endless consumer choices and potential futures. This is exemplified by the scene in which James lies alongside his wife Catherine (Deborah Kara Unger) in bed, tracing the large bruises that Vaughan left on her body; James watched Vaughan aggressively fuck Catherine from the front seat of Vaughan's 1961 Lincoln Continental while driving through a soapy, yonic car wash. Although the novel *Crash* is replete with car and bodily fluids freely mixing, the lone cum shot in Cronenberg's adaptation comes when, after Vaughan finishes, Catherine puts her hand up on the driver's seat. The placement of the semen, like wounds themselves, is suggestive of stigmata: Catherine and James are forgiven, healed, and reborn through this brutalizing act of cuckoldry. Scarification, branding, and other types of intentionally inflicted harm are often part of religious or coming-of-age rites.

Whether they should be saved requires a level of faith in humanity few possess. The Ballards in the film are devoid of affect—a charge unjustly leveled at other Cronenberg protagonists—exactly because they are both young, conventionally attractive, white, heterosexual, cisgender, healthy, and extremely rich; their every need has been met, and they are safely sealed away inside their luxury high-rise—which doesn't seem much different from the hospital James recovers in. Nothing can reach them, including pleasure. They've learned the hard way that the most valued tenets of late capitalism are in fact hollow and joyless. Catherine, first glimpsed getting fucked against the wing of an airplane in a hangar, takes flying lessons, a classic pastime for the ultra-wealthy who've run out of other ideas. Similarly, though the term "ethically non-monogamous" wasn't common parlance in 1971 or 1996, open relationships often (though not necessarily) signal a couple's misplaced imagination. Catherine and James live on the surface and understand their fundamental uselessness. While the misery caused by their material conditions are unsympathetic and unrelatable, their dissatisfaction with the world and their place in it is, increasingly, universal. They embrace the mutation promised by Vaughan's psychopathology because it offers a way out.

But why the car crash and archetype of the car, and not electrocution or some other interaction with twentieth-century technology? As the story goes, Ballard began   32.

writing *Crash* in 1969 after staging an exhibition of three wrecked cars, presented without explanatory labels, at the New Arts Laboratory in order to test the "hypothesis that a repressed fascination lies behind our conventional attitudes to technological death and violence, a fascination so obsessive that it must contain a powerful sexual charge." On opening night, a topless woman (who had agreed to be naked before seeing the cars) interviewed visitors on closed-circuit television, and the show quickly descended into drunken chaos. (Just like Stravinsky, Tzara, Buñuel, and many other twentieth-century avant-gardists, Ballard took the riot as a good sign.) In a 1971 essay titled "The Car, the Future" for the appropriately titled *Drive* magazine, Ballard wrote: "We spend a large part of our lives in the car, and the experience of driving involves many of the experiences of being a human being in the 1970s, a focal point for an immense range of social, economic, and psychological pressures. I think that the 20th century reaches almost its purest expression on the highway. Here we see, all too clearly, the speed and violence of our age, its strange love affair with the machine and, conceivably, with its own death and destruction." As Ballard ponders later in the same article, "Are we merely victims in a meaningless tragedy, or do these appalling accidents take place with some kind of unconscious collaboration on our part?...If we really feared the crash, most of us would be unable to look at a car, let alone drive one."

    The self-destructive impulse that Ballard identifies here, as well as its repetition, lead back to psychoanalysis. Although Freud popularized the concept/term of "death drive" in his book *Beyond the Pleasure Principle*, its first incarnation was in Sabina Spielrein's 1912 paper, "Destruction as the Cause of Coming Into Being." She builds off of Jung's assertion that the libido (or "passionate yearning") contains "the power that beautifies everything and under certain circumstances destroys everything," and goes on to detail the biological and historical sources of this paradox, exploring the potential pathologies of this "drive toward death and destruction." Vaughan's coterie of banged-up travelers are indeed cruising through their own psychopathologies, as well as the concept itself. Again, in the midst of this absolutely bizarre scenario, we find ourselves. Intercourse has never only been about reproduction, but that fact has only come into wider public consciousness in the West relatively recently. *Crash*'s frankness about the panoply of sexual options available to human beings is only shocking within the confines of a wide-release Hollywood film, a visual ecosystem that has almost exclusively presented extremely chopped-up versions of the missionary position as the peak of eroticism. This is parodied in the scene where Dr. Helen Remington (Holly Hunter) sits stick-upright while watching a VHS of automobile test crashes. Though the rest of the degenerates are casually paying attention, Helen loses her mind when the tape freezes. She can't get off unless she sees something very specific, and angrily declines the offer of another tape. We, like Helen, won't see the big crash or big orgasm we want to see.

33.

    Cronenberg makes other visual choices that deny pleasure when dealing with violence. Although the car archetype is derived in large part from our own experiences—sublimating anger or succumbing to road rage, spacing out while speeding along a rural highway or remaining anxiously alert, feeling the shame that comes from owning an old beater or the inflated self-worth that comes from a sports car—it is also shaped by film, television, and video games. Cronenberg eschews the cinematic clichés of car crashes entirely. Rather than slow-motion collisions (a trope evident in the safety test VHS Vaughan's crew watch at his house), the crashes in *Crash* are abrupt, emphasizing speed and naturalism. In the first, in which James (who is looking at papers while driving, which is the nineties equivalent of texting while driving) crosses the median, the perspective comes from his driver's seat. It's not quite his point of view, but it offers the terrifying feeling of being inside the car.

    Similarly, Vaughan's build-up to the reenactment of James Dean's fatal car wreck is far longer than the crash itself. In his speech, Vaughan emphasizes, or draws out, the last syllables of words—"Donald Turnup*seed*"—rather than obeying the conventions of Amer-

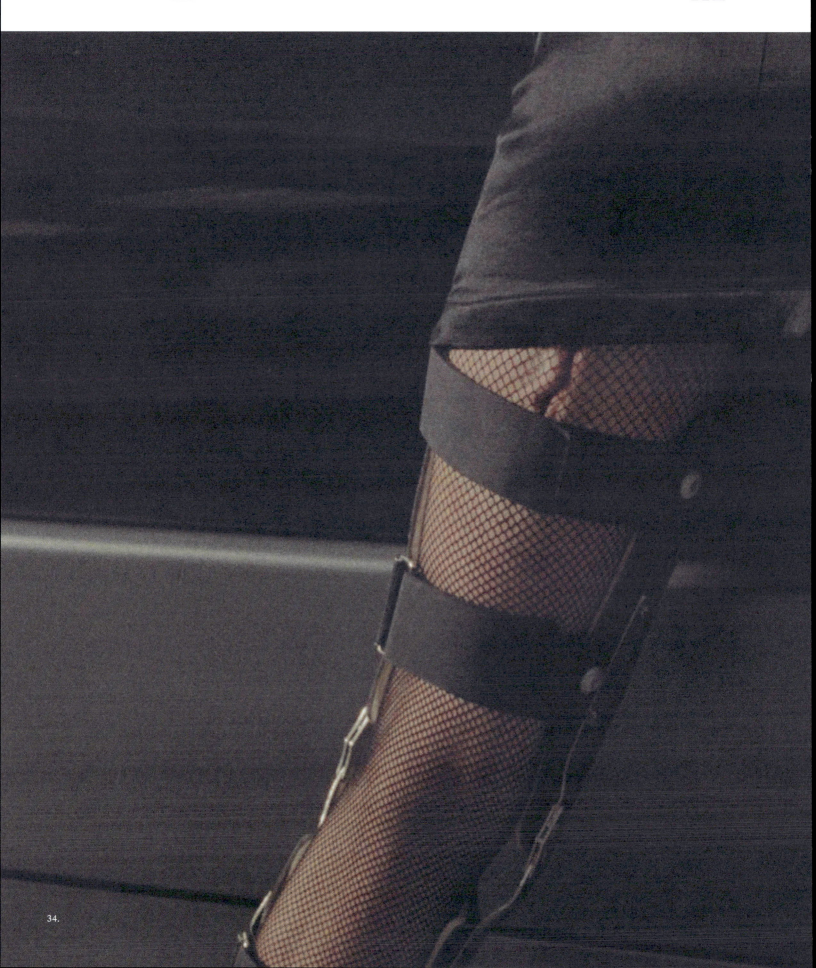

113 PART I. INDIVIDUATION

35.

ican English; he draws attention to his own performance, the staginess only heightening the shock of what comes next. (You have to wonder: What happened to all the other spectators in the stands that night?) When Vaughan and the Ballards survey Seagrave's reenactment of the Jayne Mansfield crash—his blonde wig tossed off his head, landing upright, just as hers did—it gives the sensation of being inside a museum. Vaughan snaps photos of the things he likes, including Catherine, and the people inside the cars, either dead or in shock, are frozen; all time has stopped. This destruction exists for the three of them to gape at (and they exist for us to gape at). This obsession with the past, or a very particular pop past, is also evinced in references to and Alfred Hitchcock's *Rear Window* (James with a broken leg with binoculars on his balcony, accompanied by Catherine, an icy blonde) and *Vertigo* (Vaughan following Catherine in her car, James following both of them). The crashes anchor us, along with the sex, in our own world, our own bodies; we are watching a film, in our own bodies. It contains a kinetic sense that's uncomfortable and rare.

This, coupled with the film's formally radical approach to narrative, is, per Teresa de Lauretis, a queer text. There are multiple sex scenes in a row, deep internal changes are expressed visually, and the Ballards' satisfaction is denied at the end. In thinking of a three-act structure as the mirror of a man's sexual experience (build, climax, ejaculation/conclusion), *Crash* is a film that doesn't let you cum. It's not a porno, after all. (Notably, Ballard thought his book was; he believed the genre was "the most political form of fiction, dealing with how we use and exploit each other in the most urgent and ruthless way.") Although James follows Catherine in Vaughan's car and runs her off the road, following the path that was set for them by Vaughan, Catherine survives. Just as when she was being pawed at by Vaughan in the back of his car, Catherine looks away from James as he kisses her on the grass. She whimpers "I think I'm all right" twice. In these brief seconds, it's hard not to wonder if she actually wants this for herself. But then she begins to cry. James comforts her by repeating what she said to him at the start: "Maybe the next one, darling. Maybe the next one." It's a strange, terrible dream, made worse by our knowledge that it's something that will be repeated—like a traumatic memory or a paraphilia. They aren't any closer to becoming whole human beings.

---

iv.
THE SELF

SHIVERS [1975]
RABID [1977]
THE BROOD [1979]
THE FLY [1986]

WHAT IS THE SELF?

The term *self* can, rather confusingly, refer to the innermost core of the psyche, the colloquial meaning of self, as well as this boundless, unknowable thing with parts that include the unfathomable. It is god-sized, outside of morality. Even more confusingly, it can carry two or more of these seemingly distinct meanings at the same time. But the first is straight-

36. Like the world's ugliest dildo, the parasite mechanically swims up Betts's pipes and into her body.

37. Nola Carveth reveals her new emotionally and biologically self-sustaining body to her husband.

38. Cronenberg, who switched his major from biology to English twenty years earlier, plays the doctor in Ronnie's nightmare.

forward enough: The goal of individuation (see page 26) is to reach the self, the inner core of the psyche. It contains consciousness, the personal unconscious, and the collective unconscious, and as such, it is unique to every individual. It is the source of our individuality, and of our larger purpose.

This self is at once connected to everything in the universe, but also the experiences of a person's day-to-day existence, which carries the concomitant influences of language, culture, and historical period. It is represented by the central point of a mandala, a circle or figure encircled by other objects that are contained within a rectangle or square; it is at once the holding of opposites in this center and the entirety. This composition appears across cultures, be it church frescoes, representations of the zodiac, sundials (or other ancient timekeeping methods, like the Aztec calendar), oriental rugs, dream catchers, and Buddhist and Hindu religious art (where the term "mandala" derives). Mandalas also frequently crop up in drawings made during active imagination, a meditative practice developed by Jung, or in art therapy—we're wired to make and remake this design. Whatever lies at the center of a mandala represents wholeness and balance. And just as in art, holy or otherwise, the self can take many different forms in dreams: an old, wise figure, a vigorous youth, an animal, or an object. Its malleable manifestations evince its transcendence of time, of consciousness.

Part of its function is to maintain harmony between the push and pull of different conscious and unconscious aspects of it. This conflict takes many forms, such as those between our baser instincts (hunger, sex, etc.), what society expects of us, and our own egos. While Freud argued that our existence is driven by these instincts, Jung maintained that our inner life is guided by a larger purpose: to simply be human, and to explore that inner mystery. "Only if I remain an ordinary human being, conscious of my incompleteness, can I become receptive to the significant contents and processes of the unconscious," wrote Marie-Louise von Franz, Jung's longtime student and collaborator. "But how can a human being stand the tension of feeling himself at one with the whole universe, while at the same time he is only a miserable earthly human creature? If on the one hand I despise myself as merely a statistical cipher, my life has no meaning and is not worth living. But on the other hand, if I feel myself to be part of something much greater, how am I to keep my feet on the ground?"

Seeking and maintaining that balance is perilous, which of course opens up the opportunity for exploitation. Throughout history, there have been plenty of grifters who, with the conviction of Christ on the cross, declared that they alone hold the key to wholeness—and they'll teach you how to obtain it too, in exchange for a pile of cash and worshipful attention. Then there are those who firmly believe in the expensive answers they proffer but have succumbed to the darker side of the self—New Age-y types who've become so entrenched in a feeling of a higher power that they've become arrogant and divorced from the real world. Therefore, the self carries a potential for darkness, just like the shadow; true unity is more difficult than either camp let on. Jung believed that reaching the self through individuation was a biological process—one "by which every living thing becomes what it was destined to become from the beginning"—and included not only humans but animals. (Eventually, he extended this to inorganic matter as well.) This view points toward the fraught field of evolutionary psychology—or, more hearteningly, the role of genetics on our bodies and minds.

Jung also described the self as an individual's subjectivity and as the final product of larger psychic development, namely individuation. Consider how Jung argued that mental illness is an independent creative act, one that arises from individuation under flawed or atypical circumstances. Symptoms, which Jungian scholar Anthony Stevens termed as "growing pains of a soul struggling to escape fear and find fulfillment," are manifestations of that process gone awry. Illness is the unconscious pointing us toward a sticking point or sticking points—be it childhood trauma or landing on the wrong solution to life's problems (say, overvaluing money or attention from others).

Illness is a common feature of David Cronenberg's work, as is his interest in identity. Does our self change along with illness, or is our illness shaped by our self? Often Cronenberg's films depict men who have confused their ego for their self, false messiahs who wreak havoc upon women, who in turn allow the darkest versions of themselves to run wild. However, his films also depict the self's innately destructive power, and what happens when the ego, all that is laid on by society and propriety, is destroyed (or badly mangled) by it. In *Shivers* and *Rabid*, scientists whose belief in their magnificent surgical innovations unleash biblical plagues upon, respectively, a high-rise apartment block and the entire city of Montreal. The victims of these epidemics haven't been saved by a messiah, rather they were ground down into bloodthirsty and/or horny beasts, with any deeper essence of their humanity shorn away. Yet these diseases also carry a kernel of the self of the women from whence they were germinated: full of fury, delightfully unleashing violence and contagion. In *The Brood*, Dr. Hal Raglan (Oliver Reed), pioneer of psychoplasmics, attempts to show his patients the way to exorcize their demons and become whole again, but his method instead leads to a high body count and unleashes psychic trauma upon a whole new generation who'll definitely need therapy. By contrast, *The Fly*'s honorable doofus Seth Brundle (Jeff Goldblum) believes that his teleporter not only moves matter but achieves alchemy of the soul. His painful deterioration into something far from human is harrowing to witness—yet even at the worst moments of his transformation, elements of his humanity express themselves. More than the perils of hubris, these films explore the dangerous business of getting to know oneself and pose questions about the immutability and transcendent function of the self.

ON *SHIVERS*, *RABID*, *THE BROOD*, AND *THE FLY*

Starliner Towers is the place where human warmth goes to die. This fictional high-rise, located on an island just twelve minutes away from Montreal, is populated by wealthy people who are profoundly unhappy: lonely Betts (Barbara Steele); neglected Janine Tudor (Susan Petrie) and her cranky, unfaithful husband Nicholas (Allan Kolman); and tortured Annabelle (Cathy Graham). Annabelle, who has the least amount of screen time, drives the painful apocalypse of 1975's *Shivers*. After a cheery ad for Starliner (narrated by Cronenberg regular Ronald Mlodzik), a tour of the grounds with a young couple (whose surname is Sweden) is intercut with Dr. Emil Hobbes (Fred Doederlein) viciously murdering Annabelle and then slicing his own throat. It is later revealed that the doctor—suitably named after the misanthropic philosopher who wrote that life is "solitary, poor, nasty, brutish, and short," and a "war of all against all"—had been sexually assaulting Annabelle since the age of twelve and was using her as a guinea pig for his parasite experiments. Dr. Hobbes had set out to create a parasite that, contrary to what he claimed on his grant proposal, was "a combination of aphrodisiac and venereal disease that will hopefully turn the whole world into one beautiful, mindless orgy." This insane quest was motivated by his belief that "man is an animal that thinks too much, an over-rational animal that's lost touch with its body and its instincts."

Dr. Hobbes's unrestricted, longtime access to Annabelle's body was clearly why he chose her as patient zero. However, the way in which the half-penis, half-turd, half-leech parasite manifests is all Annabelle. The parasite, which succeeds in turning everyone in the Starliner into a raving sex fiend, causes serious pain before it forcibly generates pleasure. It burns its victims with acid-like excretions, agonizingly pokes around inside their abdominal cavities, causes blood to spew out of their mouths, and prompts violent outbursts. But would Hobbes's experiment have turned out the same with another patient—perhaps one who could've given consent, one who hadn't been subjected to years of abuse? The parasite's behavior, outside of its aphrodisiac properties, is a manifestation of Annabelle's mental state. It was incubated inside a truly powerless person, feeding upon her years of pent-up rage and sadness, and therefore becomes a terrifying force rather than a carefree, free-lovin' hippie dick. (Even the parasite's shape—a hideous, malevolent penis—

suggests that's the case.)

Annabelle's parasite is seeking revenge against the world that allowed this to happen to her, and for the most part, couldn't have picked more deserving victims. The denizens of the Starliner have elected to isolate themselves and live in tedious complacency with every amenity imaginable—from an indoor pool to a restaurant to a clinic—and staff to tend to their every need. Despite living inside an expensive security blanket, they mostly appear restless and ungrateful. Consider Betts, who only appears lounging around her apartment in the middle of the day and slurping wine while taking a nice hot bath, not even lifting an eyebrow at a news report about a violent murder of a teenager in her own building. The film's ending, in which a calm, orderly motorcade of sex-crazed residents heads toward the city, suggests that, despite unleashing ferocious polymorphous perversity in everyone (including prepubescent children), this sexually transmitted infection has some sentience, some sense of control. As a radio announcer explains, a rash of sexual assaults have been reported across Montreal. Perhaps this is the last little bit of Annabelle, who knows exactly what she's doing.

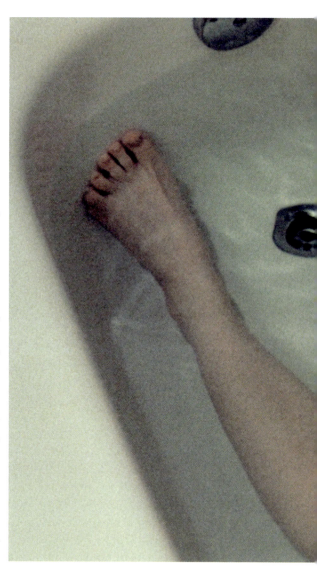

This line of cars, with drivers and passengers dressed to the nines, underscores the carnivalesque nature of *Shivers*. In a literal sense, it reproduces the festivities and parades of actual carnivals, such as those in New Orleans or Rio de Janeiro. In a metaphorical sense, the parasite does what such celebrations have historically done, breaking down social and economic barriers—the on-site estate agent, a waiter, the well-heeled residents, and Dr. Roger St. Luc (the last person in the building to succumb to the chaos, named for the patron saint of doctors and artists)—all join together in a violent, sexual frenzy. This inversion and obliteration of norms is also explicitly stated in a dream that sylphlike Nurse Forsythe (Lynn Lowry) recalls before attempting to infect her boyfriend, Dr. St. Luc, in the Starliner's parking garage: "I found myself making love to a strange man. Only I'm having trouble, you see, because he's old and dying, and he smells bad, and I find him repulsive. But then he tells me that everything is erotic, that everything is sexual. You know what I mean? He tells me that even old flesh is erotic flesh, that disease is the love of two alien kinds of creatures for each other. That even dying is an act of eroticism. That talking is sexual. That breathing is sexual. That even to physically exist is sexual. And I believe him. And we make love beautifully." This is a premonition of the destruction of the sterile, late-capitalist order of the Starliner—a new dystopia that is dirty, disgusting, and not far removed from necrophilia. Though the idea of yuppies terrorizing each other and being dragged down into the dirt they'd so assiduously avoided is inherently comic—and there are many funny moments in *Shivers*—what they're bringing to the mainland is not.

Cronenberg has described 1977's *Rabid* as a "companion piece" to *Shivers*, which takes the bleakness of the latter to devastating new lows. During an idyllic motorcycle ride around the countryside, Rose (Marilyn Chambers) and Hart (Frank Moore) crash into a quarreling family's van in front of a cushy plastic surgery clinic that's about to franchise. Rose is pinned beneath the bike and requires urgent medical care. Rather than take her to a real hospital, the lead surgeon, Dr. Dan Keloid (Howard Ryshpan), decides to treat her at his facility with an experimental skin-grafting technique. (One he seems to be making up as he goes along.) This intervention saves Rose's life but causes her to develop a thirst for blood and a small, sharp penile organ in her armpit to suck it through. (Again, on a certain level, this is comedic—a woman who gains a penis and jumps right into sodomizing and castrating men.) People she uses as blood bags catch a variation of her malady, foaming at the mouth, biting others, and spreading the infection. This soon blossoms into a grim pandemic that requires the city of Montreal to go under martial law.

Though the carriers of her disease are essentially mindless zombies, they gain a crucial aspect of Rose's self: her carnality. When she's not craving blood, Rose is soft-spoken and effortlessly sensual. This is clearly a nod to the adult films that Chambers was known for, playing with her star text, but it also suggests that Rose is a truly free individual,

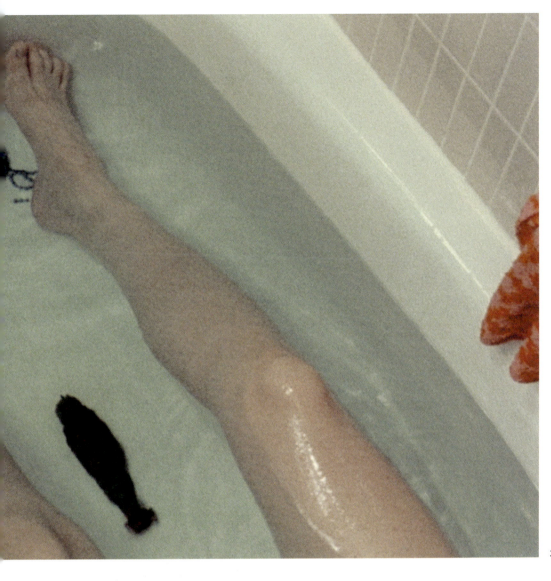

36.

unburdened by ideas of how "good girls" should act, a model of a liberated woman of the seventies. She is unafraid to hitchhike, ride on the back of a motorcycle, or pull out her IV and attempt to escape the Keloid Clinic multiple times. Unlike the doctor's other patients, who are riddled with complexes about their appearance (one Freud-reading young woman has returned for another nose job per her father's request), Rose is comfortable in her own skin—until it's not her skin anymore. Her aura of eroticism also allows her to prey on many different men after her bodily autonomy has been destroyed by Dr. Keloid, including one who tries to pick her up at a porno theater. Her new organ allows her to be the predator, reversing the power dynamic and inflicting violence upon a variety of creepy men—just as Annabelle did. Though most of the people who have contracted her disease are apoplectic zombies, a notable exception is a middle-aged woman on the Montreal subway, who exhibits a twisted version of Rose's joie de vivre. After expelling some greenish goo from her mouth, the woman smiles ghoulishly and attacks a random man, sating her hunger for blood—and, perhaps, reveling in the fact she too has flipped the patriarchal script. As she laughs, the people on the train nearly trample one another to get away from her. As in *Shivers*, the old order has been replaced with chaos, a new burden rather than a new freedom.

Government attempts to regain control via martial law are even more chilling—the infected are shot down and immediately dumped into garbage trucks by men in hazmat suits. But it's when Hart is finally reunited with Rose, after searching for her the entire film, where *Rabid* shifts into far more unsettling territory. Hart catches Rose sucking her friend Mindy dry, and immediately puts it all together. "You carry the plague! You've killed hundreds of people!" Hart shouts. Rose sadly protests, "I'm still me! I'm still Rose." "You're not Rose!" he snaps, growing angrier. Finally, she explodes: "It's not my fault. It's all your fault!" She pounds her fists on him, marking the first time we see Rose become furious. She wants him to accept her personhood, that she isn't an abstract concept or "Typhoid Mary," but a victim (of circumstance, of bad driving, of malpractice), and that this havoc wasn't her intention. Her own body has betrayed her while her mind has remained the same.

When he forcibly attempts to take Rose to the police, she throws him down a flight of stairs and settles things on her own terms, an attempt to restore her agency: she picks up a guy in the apartment's lobby, sucks his blood, and then locks herself in a room with him. She tells Hart about her "little experiment" over the phone, and he hears her being killed by this newly minted zombie. This scene foreshadows what will happen between the two lovers in *The Fly*: one experiencing a loss of control, while the other is unable to help and is forced to bear witness to their partner's death. The final moments of *Rabid* underscore this devastation: Rose's body lies in a pile of trash, her eyes still open; a hungry dog pulls at her leg. She's then tossed into the back of a garbage truck and crushed along with the piles of junk already inside it. Her worst fear has been realized: she's no longer Rose. She's nothing.

A very different lovers' spat defines *The Brood*, one that is prodded on by a very different type of doctor. More importantly, Nola Carveth (Samantha Eggar) is very aware that she's unwell—and is absolutely livid about it. She's livid about everything, really. Nola is in the middle of a divorce from her husband Frank (Art Hindle), and resides at the Somafree Institute of Psychoplasmics, a New Age-y therapeutic center founded and presided over by Dr. Hal Raglan (Oliver Reed). The first moments of the film show Dr. Raglan's method, which involves role-play and heavy doses of castigation, reminiscent of the kind cult leaders use to break their initiates. A clearly disturbed man named Mike is the target of this "treatment," and breaks out in hives as the session progresses. This takes place on a stage before an audience, who, save for Frank, watch reverentially. He's only come to retrieve his daughter Candice (Cindy Hinds), who was visiting Nola for the weekend. When he returns home and gives Candy a bath, he discovers bite marks and scratches all over her back, and assumes it was Nola who hurt their daughter. He turns to his lawyer, who informs him that his options are limited, as courts tend to side with mothers. It's soon revealed that it wasn't Nola, but rather the deformed, childlike creatures that have spawned from her rage—as the demonstration showed, psychoplasmics have the ability to manifest psychic trauma physically. Nola's "brood" goes on a murderous campaign against those who have harmed her: her alcoholic, abusive mother Juliana (Nuala Fitzgerald); and her inert father Barton (Henry Beckman). In the film's second-most infamous scene, the broodlets bludgeon Candy with toy hammers in front of a class of whimpering kindergarteners.

The most infamous scene, of course, is when Nola lifts up her white, flowing smock and reveals to Frank how the broodlets are germinated: inside large gestational sacks that are scattered across her torso. Her arms are raised above her head, like an avenging angel, and she smiles wickedly. Frank, who had been playing "the role of apologetic lover and husband" per Dr. Raglan's instructions, cannot hide his disgust. Nola is enamored with motherhood, and while she doesn't know what her brood gets up to, she adores them, lick-

37.

ing her freshly birthed "baby" clean before Frank. Unlike Candy, who is half Frank's, the brood is entirely hers, each a virgin birth that will never side with anyone else but her—a perfect companion for the paranoid. They carry her self, and all of the complexes and malevolence of her conscious and personal unconscious. There's no other influence.

But Nola is right to be paranoid. What little we see of her mother—who goes not once but twice to "freshen up" her tumbler of brown liquor (no ice) while Candy is visiting her in the afternoon—shows a completely self-absorbed person who can't take responsibility for her actions. Barton (also probably a boozer) is more sympathetic but did nothing to stop his wife from harming their daughter. And, most importantly of all, Frank does want to take Candy away from her; he hates her and is disgusted by her. He feels victimized by her. "You got taken in. You got involved with a woman who married you for your sanity, hoping it would rub off," he grumbles to Candy's teacher. "Instead, it started to work the other way."

Under such circumstances, it's unsurprising that the one person Nola unquestioningly trusts is Dr. Raglan. He's made himself a god who perpetuates her paranoia, demonizing any character in her life. He operates with the reckless disregard of Cronenberg's other scientists, eager to take his patently dangerous hypothesis to its conclusion. (As he often says during sessions, "Go all the way through it. Go all the way to the end.") Though he ultimately does the right thing by releasing his other patients and going into the brood's nest to rescue Candy, it takes him quite a while to get there. His actions—or rather, lack of action—result in Candy (as well as her classmates) being permanently damaged. In the final scene, after Frank chokes Nola to death, he drives Candy back home. She's silently crying and has a thousand-yard stare, barely blinking. The camera pans down to her arm, revealing two small bumps. As the daddy-seeking Mike explains to Frank, Dr. Raglan believes that Nola was "born to prove that psychoplasmics is the ultimate therapeutic device." Nola persists in Candy, both mentally and physically. The long, wintry road Frank and Candy are riding down represents a much longer one ahead of them.

The Fly dares to take you down that road, all the way to the end, without any redemption in sight—which is precisely why it's so excruciating to watch. At its center is Veronica "Ronnie" Quaife (Geena Davis), an intelligent, beautiful, and funny science reporter who should have the world at her feet. Despite these gifts, Ronnie finds herself stuck in a series of increasingly impossible situations. Her ex-boyfriend (and ex-professor!) Stathis Borans (John Getz) is her editor, and has no qualms about letting himself into her apartment unannounced, following her around at night, interfering with stories she's working on, and taunting her new romantic partner, Seth Brundle (Jeff Goldblum). Though in 1986 journalism wasn't in as dire straits as it is today, publishing has always been a particularly small world, one full of cronyism and nepotism, and Ronnie's ability to easily find a new job on the same beat—let alone stop this asshole from essentially stalking her—would've been difficult. Seth seems to offer a way out of her personal and professional entanglements—unlike Stathis, he's very sweet and adorably nebbish. Following a meet-cute at a cocktail party worthy of a top-tier rom-com, Seth takes Veronica back to his place and shows her his functioning teleporter. (Alas, it only works on inanimate objects.) He offers her exclusive rights to document his radical new invention—and to his heart. Their connection is genuine, and we're treated to the excitement that comes with a blossoming new romance.

But Seth is still a man—or, at least, he starts out as one. After Ronnie abruptly leaves in the middle of the night to confront Stathis about his mind games, Seth deduces that

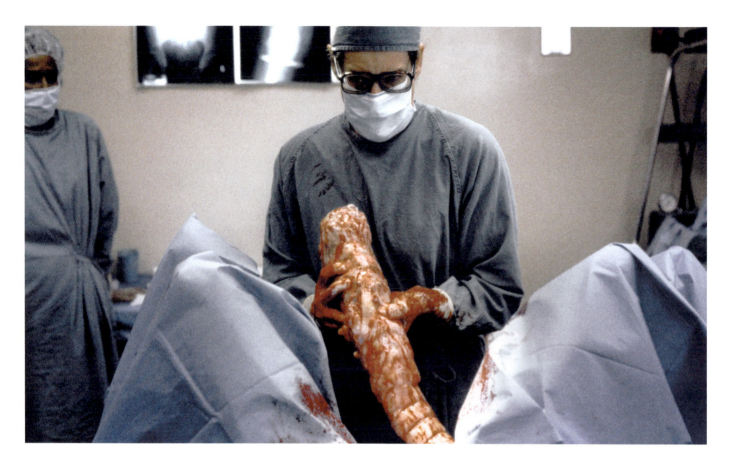

38.

Stathis is her ex-boyfriend, and starts to catastrophize. He gets drunk on the celebratory champagne he was sharing with Ronnie and decides to test his invention on himself—a fatal act of hubris fueled by jealousy. A housefly enters the telepod shortly before he does, but he fails to notice it. Because, as Seth tells Ronnie, computers are dumb and only do what you tell them, the computer fuses Seth's DNA with the fly's. This is what Jung would call synchronicity—a meaningful coincidence. Save for a handful of cultures, the archetype of the fly (just like the centipede of *Naked Lunch*) represents death and putrefaction, closely associated with evil—the Philistine deity Baal-Zebub, Lord of the Flies, became another name for the Christian devil. While the ascension of our souls to a higher realm is represented by butterflies, the fly is a reminder of the decay of our earthly bodies. They spread disease and filth, contaminating us physically and mentally. And this is precisely what befalls Seth.

However, in keeping with Christian symbology for a bit, the devil lies. At first, Seth sees incredible changes to his body and energy levels, swinging around his apartment and engaging in marathon fuck sessions with Ronnie. He also experiences newfound mental clarity and quickness, incorrectly assuming that teleportation has purified him, allowing him to achieve "the personal potential I've been neglecting all of these years." In a manic sugar-fueled rant, Seth tells Ronnie: "Not to wax messianic, but it may be true that the synchronicity of those two events might blur the resultant individual effect of either individually." (The high point of his career and the act of teleportation are what he believes to be his meaningful coincidence.) His evangelizing soon takes on a more aggressive, malicious form, and he attempts to force Ronnie to purify herself and "dive into the plasma pool" by undergoing teleportation. When she refuses, he becomes uncharacteristically irate. He also attempts to forcibly teleport a woman he picked up at a bar after he horrifically snapped her beefy boyfriend's wrist during an arm-wrestling match; she wisely runs away. Then the deformation starts. Bits of Seth's body begin to fall off, and he struggles to use his legs. Despite this, Seth retains his upbeat scientific curiosity. He has confused his ego for his self:

the grand scientist who must see it through. If the self is the sun and the ego is the earth, Seth has developed a geocentric worldview. Ego inflation makes one believe that you're Galileo, when in reality you're not the daring scientist but the dogmatic church. "I seem to be stricken by a disease with a purpose . . . Maybe not such a bad disease after all," he tells an aghast Ronnie. "I'm becoming something that's never existed before . . . I'm becoming Brundlefly," he continues, insisting that she document his transformation. True to form, as Ronnie hesitantly sets up the video camera to record how Brundlefly eats (by vomiting up a corrosive enzyme onto the food), he cheerfully says, "Hey kids, watch this!"

Then Ronnie discovers that she's pregnant. This unexpected turn of events is even more fraught than other unexpected pregnancies: Is she carrying a monster, the seed of Brundlefly, or the last little bit of Seth's humanity? Her dreams offer an answer: In a nightmare, she painfully gives birth to a giant larva that writhes in the doctor's hands. When she visits Brundlefly on her way to get an abortion, she's so upset by his corpselike degeneration she can't summon the strength to tell him. He warns Ronnie that she must never return as "insects have no politics. They're very brutal . . . I'll hurt you if you stay." She flees in tears to Stathis, who suggests she wait to have the procedure until she's calmed down. It's here that she lets out feelings that should be very familiar to those who've had an unwanted pregnancy, a tumor, a cyst, and/or gender reassignment surgery: "No it's now. I want it out of my body now. 'Cause I don't want it in my body. Do you understand me? I don't want it in my body!" In a rare move, Stathis actually respects Ronnie's wishes—but Brundlefly sees them leave together. Despite his warnings to Ronnie that his flyness is taking over, Seth's jealousy reappears, and he follows them to the clinic.

After getting drilled by the doctor who will perform the abortion (played by Leslie Carlson, who also portrayed the shady Barry Convex in *Videodrome*), she informs him that she'll do it herself if she has to. He relents. As she readies herself for the procedure, Brundlefly kidnaps Ronnie and asks her why she wants to kill what's left of "the real me." Back at his lab, Brundlefly tells her that, in order to restore his humanity, he is going to use the telepods to fuse himself to Ronnie and the fetus, assuring her "We'll be the ultimate family. A family of three joined together as one." Ronnie is horrified at the prospect of this hideous trinity but fails to fight him off. It's an insane gambit that, though seemingly motivated by his new ruthlessness, also shows the rationale and planning of a scientist—the true Seth. Brundlefly fulfills another of Seth's subconscious wishes by dispatching Stathis, dissolving Stathis's hand and foot with his digestive enzyme. (Perhaps Seth's initial inklings that being dissolved down and reassembled to the molecular level brings out the true you were right.)

Though reeling from the shock, Stathis manages to free Ronnie from the telepod, and the computer initiates the gene-splicing sequence as Brundlefly is half-in, half-out of the chamber. Again, the computer merely acting upon instruction and available physical material, has fused Brundlefly with the pod itself. This new creature howls as it comes into existence, and slowly, painfully crawls towards Ronnie. With some unknown limb, it positions the shotgun that she's holding toward its head. Ronnie refuses at first, but carries out Seth's last wish, and puts it out of its misery. She falls to the floor, sobbing. The film fades to black, just as it did when Seth first realized that his DNA had been spliced with a fly's.

Though the film originally had an epilogue where Ronnie gives birth to a butterfly (again, a symbol of the soul ascending, of the redemptive element of existence), the final version doesn't. It's just blackness. There's nothing left of Seth.

DAVID CRONENBERG: CLINICAL TRIALS

DAVID CRONENBERG: CLINICAL TRIALS

PART II

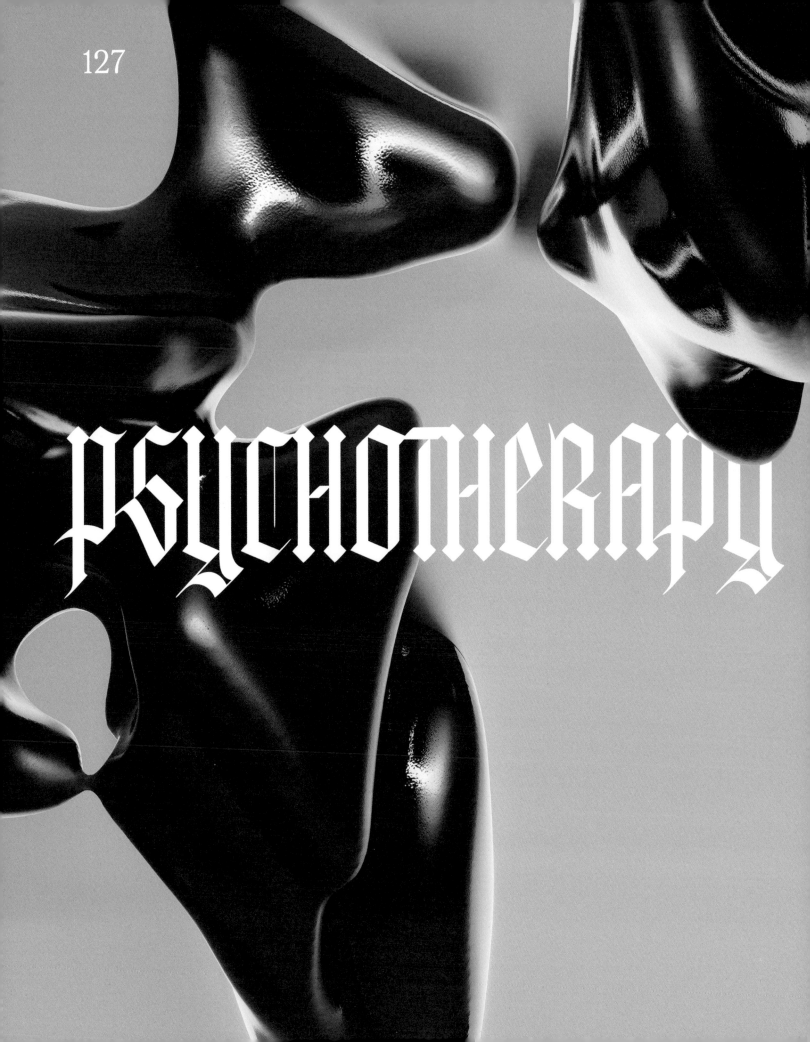

espite the number of journalists and horror fans who openly wondered "What, no exploding heads?" in the early aughts, it's best not to believe the hype about "Late Cronenberg." The preoccupations of his films—the permeability of identity, the ravages of illness and death, the folly of emotionless hyper-rationalism, the problems of elevating men of science to messiahs, an abiding suspicion of shadowy corporations and government, and non-missionary sex—have remained the same. The choice to divide this book into two parts is to reveal this symmetry: though it isn't total, it is, like the human body, striking enough to evince a certain beauty.

Exact doubles (the Mantle twins in *Dead Ringers*, the dueling Joans in *Naked Lunch*, Becca and Terry in *The Shrouds*) or personified shadow selves (Cameron Vale and Darryl Revok in *Scanners*, Seth Brundle and Brundlefly in *The Fly*) also abound in Cronenberg's filmography. Disease or medical intervention cleaves the lives of characters in two, such as the psychic denizens of *Stereo*, Rose in *Rabid*, Nola in *The Brood*. There is no return; a permanent change has come, and how they deal with this new reality speaks volumes about the human condition. (Or, in the case of René Gallimard in *M. Butterfly* or the Ballards in *Crash*, this before/after is sparked by extreme horniness.) These characters wrestle with the various stages of individuation—the shadow, the anima/animus/animum, and the self. They mostly fail to become their best self. This shouldn't be understood as a refutation of Jung's notion of salvation, but rather an acknowledgment that individuation is a struggle not everyone—regardless of how conventionally intelligent they may be—can overcome

In this second half of the book, I pair Cronenberg's films with the different stages of Jungian psychotherapy. This approach is also premised on transformation: not simply from sickness to wellness, but to becoming someone who can better function in society. Though Jung dedicated less time to laying out his therapeutic methodology than to subjects like individuation, alchemy, and the collective unconscious, it also contains four stages. The first stage is confession, in which the patient divulges to their analyst what they've previously kept hidden from the world, unburdening themself and achieving a degree of catharsis. The second is elucidation, in which the analyst educates a patient about archetypes, the unconscious, active imagination, and their maladaptive behaviors. Next comes education, in which the analyst helps the patient to put into practice what they've learned and change their behavior. The final stage is that of transformation, in which the individual begins the process of individuation. Again, this final step is not for everyone—unlike his onetime mentor Sigmund Freud, Jung envisioned therapy as being finite and reaching a terminus.

The pairing of films with stages of therapy is largely associative, not literal; only a few of the films feature actual psychologists in them. Nevertheless, this is meant to offer new ways to think about these complex and often overlooked films. The risible term "body horror" doesn't cut it.

DAVID CRONENBERG: CLINICAL TRIALS

130

PART II. PSYCHOTHERAPY

V.
CONFESSION

A HISTORY OF VIOLENCE [2005]
EASTERN PROMISES [2007]

WHAT IS CONFESSION?

Carl Jung's approach to analysis, which he viewed as an experience rather than simply a mode of learning, was different from Sigmund Freud's in several key respects. Along with drawing from Jung's model of the psyche, archetypes, collective unconscious, and the practice of active imagination, the Jungian analyst differs from the Freudian analyst, in the broadest terms, by abandoning the couch and embracing transference and countertransference. The former is less daunting to explain than the latter. Jungian analysts sit face-to-face with their patients in order to dispel the feeling of being in a clinical setting and to connect the experience of analysis with regular life. There is also the intention of breaking down the power dynamic between analyst and patient (rather than imperiously looming above a patient who's lying on a couch, they literally see eye to eye) and allows the analyst to better see their expressions as a patient speaks, and vice versa.

This leads into the second element, which involves the seemingly scary psychoanalytic terms "transference" and "countertransference." This also eschews classical notions of doctor as infallible and all-knowing. Transference refers to the phenomenon of patients projecting positive or negative feelings from a past relationship onto their analyst—treating them as, say, a parent or a lover rather than a doctor—and countertransference is when an analyst does the same to their patient. (It should be noted that this dynamic occurs in nearly every relationship but is complicated by the fact one party is undergoing treatment.) Whereas Freudians assiduously avoid transference (or at least try to), Jungians perceive it as part of the alchemical nature of analysis: one element fusing with another, being purified, and forming a new whole. Jung wrote extensively about the parallels between alchemy and psychoanalysis, which was not simply mixing chemicals, but also a philosophical practice; synthesis of opposites runs throughout his work and practice. Acknowledging and examining how transference and countertransference unfolds allows a deeper insight into the patient and is based on a simple truth: doctors have feelings too.

Jung outlined four stages the analysand progresses through during therapy, the first being that of confession. This involves the patient telling their analyst about their problems and detailing the parts of their personal history that seem relevant. (Emphasis here on seem; understanding how someone sees themselves is just as important as seeing who they really are.) By doing this, the patient experiences a certain amount of catharsis, a relief from their guilt about something they've kept secret. This can be a specific incident or a hidden aspect of their personality. The analyst helps the patient to confront their

1. Billy, a stock criminal, as the epitome of cool.
2. Billy, a stock criminal, as proof crime doesn't pay. He's fallen through the door, reminiscent of James Cagney at the end of *Scarface* (1932).
3. It runs in the family: Tom Stall/Joey Cusack looks at his son, Jack, with a mix of pride and fear (for his own life) after Jack's first kill.
4. Tom/Joey stares up at his wife, Edie, who's left him at the bottom of the stairs after rough sex. The power dynamic in their relationship has shifted and leaves him longing for the past.
5. A throat for a throat: Ekrem gets his comeuppance mid-pee. Rather than covering the wound with his hands, Ekrem pulls his Arsenal scarf down and lets the blood spurt.
6. The vor stripped bare by his bachelors: the erotic spectacle of a tortured male body, inseparable from the action genre, becomes explicit.

shadow, which comprises the repressed elements of their psyche—traits, tendencies, or behaviors the patient and/or the patient's culture deem undesirable. Through this process, the patient is then able to integrate their shadow into their conscious mind, expand their worldview, and continue down the path of wellness.

What does this have to do with a group of films that, save for 2011's *A Dangerous Method* and 2014's *Maps to the Stars*, aren't explicitly about therapy? I'm arguing for a broader view: that the characters in much of David Cronenberg's cinema undergo similar transformations in their psychic lives that patients in Jungian analysis would over the course of their therapy. These films don't necessarily have an analyst figure, nor any unambiguous signs of healing. Rather, these metaphorical patients encounter others who spur such changes within them.

While all of David Cronenberg's films deal with shadow (and are oftentimes dominated by them) both 2005's *A History of Violence* and 2007's *Eastern Promises* feature men (both played by Viggo Mortensen) who confront their shadow publicly—their darker side comes to light, kicking and screaming. Confessions are a mainstay of the gangster genre, though these two films aren't standard issue. For *A History of Violence*'s Tom Stall, who is first introduced as a mild-mannered family man, his brutal, instinctual response to a robbery garners national acclaim, and leads him back to the man that he's kept buried for so long; his former family (mafia and brother) threatens the one he's created (imaginary yet flesh). In *Eastern Promises*, "Nikolai" commits to his undercover assignment to the point that he's threatened with being taken off the case, contributing to the vory v zakone's (Russian mafia's) body count. Yet even the moments when he pulls back and acts like an FSB agent are, in retrospect, only ambiguously acts of goodwill. Is Nikolai's resistance to leaving the Russian mob's London arm motivated by his shadow? Or has he integrated his shadow and is on the verge of his life's greatest achievement: weakening and taking down a malicious, continent-spanning criminal enterprise? The final moments of both films suggest the possibility of redemption, but also the potential for descending further into darkness.

1.

ON *A HISTORY OF VIOLENCE* AND *EASTERN PROMISES*

Any number of points in U.S. history could be connected to *A History of Violence*. Or it could be a list, which would certainly start with the genocide of indigenous peoples or slavery, include more than one mention of Henry Kissinger, and "end" with the ongoing bloodshed in the Middle East. These sins—motivated by white supremacy, greed, stupidity, religion, fantasy, or the need for "a show of force"—are well known and widely discussed, perhaps more so than in any other moment in the world's history. Violence by an individual, group, or state is not a uniquely American trait, but we've really redefined it. This can be understood both literally and metaphorically, as U.S. support for any number of plainly evil regimes has included not only funding and weapons, but military and torture training. (And then there's Hollywood!)

Noting this isn't to diminish or ironize these very real horrors, but rather to acknowledge how fathomless American violence truly is. This sick mystery is embodied by Tom Stall (Viggo Mortensen), who is at once an impossibly good and evil man.

Tom, longtime resident of Millbrook, Indiana, emanates calm and has a lovely home life—he passionately loves his wife after many years of marriage, and is patient with his two kids, even while they're being obnoxious. He is, however, not universally liked. After savagely dispensing with two would-be robbers, Tom becomes a celebrity—which leads to Philadelphia's Irish mafia seeking to collect an overdue debt from the man he once was: Joey Cusack, a hitman with a reputation for being (according to his own brother) "the crazy one."

We see Tom first, which perpetuates the narrative that he's created—and it's a very convincing one. Even after he's been caught out, Tom refers to Joey in the third person: "I never expected to see Joey again." As his wife Edie incredulously (and rightly) shoots back, "What, was [Joey] in hiding?" It's possible that Tom never "stopped" being Joey, even beyond the display of precise, instinctual killing at his diner. Understanding him as the pioneer in the prairie, standing his ground, is far too easy. It plays into Joey's performance of how society works, an image that the town and the media greedily eat up while ignoring the gaping hole in one of the crook's cheeks. The extent to which Tom believes his own lie and steadfastly sticks to it—without any signs of guilt, irritation, or abnormal behavior—suggests a kind of compartmentalization that is the hallmark of sociopaths. Is Tom, sparkling exemplar of a caring husband, father, and citizen, a purified form of the criminal he once was, or merely a masterful performance of what those things are supposed to be?

2.

One could argue that, when the mask starts to slip, such as when Tom smacks his son Jack (Ashton Holmes) across the face during an argument about Jack beating up a bully, this is proof of Tom reverting back to Joey, that there has been some change. But Jack's acceptance of the slap, running away from Tom in tears, could just as easily imply that this isn't the first time his father has hit him. (He doesn't protest, and Tom doesn't seem surprised that it happened.) Similarly, a scene between the two that precedes this outburst—when Tom runs back to his house and grabs a shotgun, afraid that the mobsters are going to murder his family while he's away—suggests that Jack knows a side of his father that we haven't seen. "I guess they don't like this guy they think you are," Jack nervously asks Tom. "And I guess they want to kill this guy they think you are?" "See, that's the losing my mind part. I have no reason to think that," Tom says; Jack uneasily looks at his feet.

Likewise, Tom and Edie's rough fuck on the stairs, which starts like a rape and then transitions into something consensual, is also ambiguous: Is she turned on by the idea of Joey, the cold-blooded killer, or have they

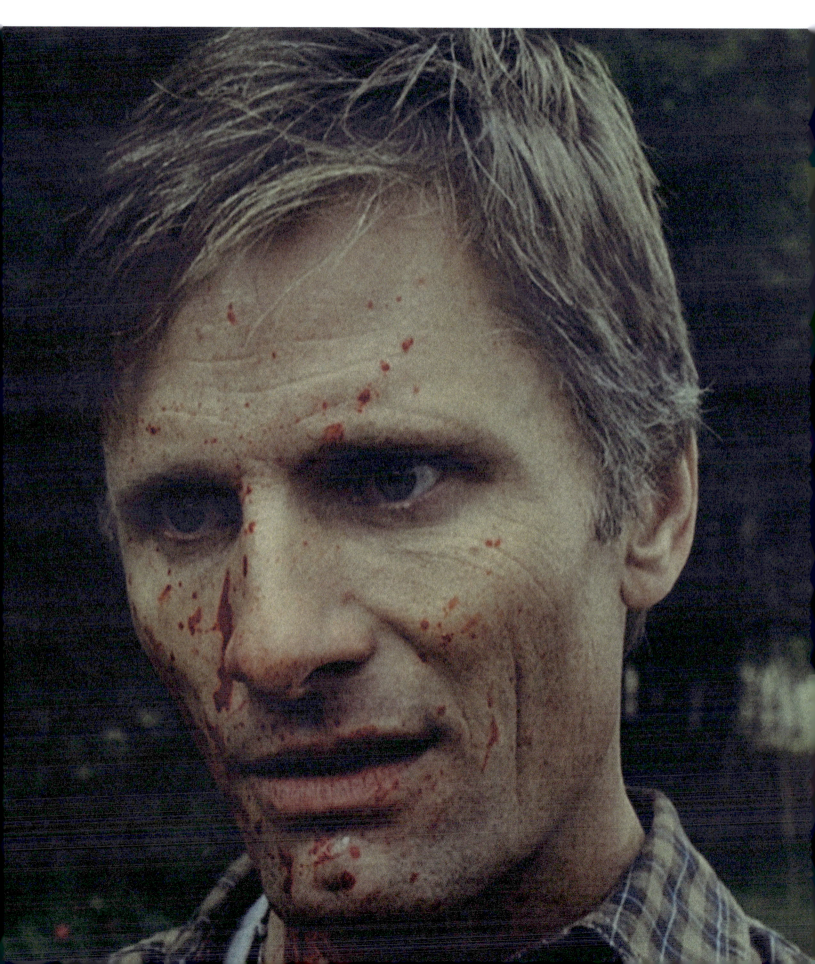

played this game before? Putting on her high school cheerleader outfit and doing a little dance—another little fantasy common to American life at the time, which would widely be understood as something incredibly fucked up in recent years—hints that they might role-play sometimes, and that those indulgences might be dark ones.

3.

Despite their differences, real or imaginary, Joey and Tom are united in one aspect: they both want to kill Joey's older brother Richie (William Hurt). Tom's idyllic life is threatened by Richie, while Joey's querulous sibling has always been an existential threat. (During their reunion, Richie tells Joey that he attempted to strangle Joey shortly after their mother brought Joey home from the hospital; Joey matter-of-factly responds, "I've heard that story.") Joey and Richie's final showdown narratively and thematically mirrors the fight between brothers Cameron Vale and Darryl Revok in *Scanners*. Both occur as the final climax to their respective films (featuring each film's most impressive special effects), and depict a younger brother triumphing over their single-minded, power-hungry sibling. Joey effortlessly dispenses with four of Richie's goons and then puts a bullet through his brother's head.

Yet Cronenberg denies us the sense of satisfaction that should come with Richie's death. As with all of the violence in the film, the camera lingers on the aftermath, the blood pooling underneath Richie's skull, uncomfortably showing the reality of what gun violence is. The speed of action and editing in these fights is crucial, and tussle with the elegant, gliding tracking shots that appear throughout *A History of Violence*. In his 2008 monograph on the film, author and academic Bart Beaty connects the scene near the opening of the film (where the two scumbags who meet their end at Tom's diner finish up slaughtering everyone at the motel they happened to be staying at) to the long opening shot of Orson Welles's *A Touch of Evil* (1958), which also balletically follows two criminals and their victims. It's clear that Cronenberg is playing with Hollywood genre conventions, particularly those of crime films and westerns, and teasing out the contradictions in the process. *A History of Violence* is often at war with itself—as it should be—deconstructing the myth of the good settler, the man who, despite his darkness, restores order.

4.

But more than mere reference, these aesthetic choices turn the film into a legend unto itself, one that carries the complexities of the messier ancient ones. After executing Richie, Tom staggers to a small pond outside of Richie's castle-like home, undresses, falls to his knees, and splashes water on himself. The dawn suggests that he has come out of the night, and that everything is well. Our man made it! He killed the evil king! And yet, when Tom/Joey returns to Millbrook again, it is dark out. His family are eating at the kitchen table, and silently exchange looks when he pushes the door open. Edie looks down, but almost seems to be suppressing a smile. Who is at the table with them? They accept him, whoever he is.

The Stalls' farcical chirpiness during a breakfast scene toward the start of the film has been destroyed. And yet, there's hope—a hope for realness, of healing. As Jung wrote in *Problems of Modern Psychotherapy*, "How can I be substantial without casting a shadow? I must have a dark side too if I am to be whole; and by becoming conscious of my shadow, I remember once more that I am a human being like any other." Whoever's eating dinner with the Stall family is a more fully realized person than Tom Stall ever was. Tom, half man that he always was, is dead.

Eastern Promises also looks westward, though from a viewpoint pickled in millennia-old ethnic tensions, traditions, superstitions, and suspicions. And we see the West gazing back, projecting its shadow onto the East—an evil empire dominated by strongmen, crony capitalism, violence, tribalism, secret societies, and other retrograde beliefs. (Russia, a part of Europe that is also undeniably part of the "mysterious east," has long been subject to Orientalist fancy and disdain.) Even without considering the critique (and hidden psychopathy) of Western life laid out in *A History of Violence*, *Eastern Promises* makes clear that these hemispheres aren't so different. This isn't established through a clash of civilizations, but by collapsing the two, such as when Ekrem (Josef Altin), a Turk, is murdered by two Chechens amidst the post-game crowds of an Arsenal/Chelsea match. After all, football fans are tribal too—they just happen to be a much newer, less stylish variety.

On December 20th, a disheveled and shivering fourteen-year-old Russian girl walks into a London pharmacy. Her name is Tatiana, and she once had dreams and talents and family, but is now hollow, a dehumanized mess that makes others uncomfortable, something they instinctively look away from. The pharmacist, no doubt jaded by years in an uncaring Western metropolis, assumes she wants methadone—until she starts to miscarry in front of him. She dies soon after at Trafalgar Hospital, but her baby survives. Anna

5.

Khitrova (Naomi Watts), a half-English, half-Russian midwife who recently suffered a miscarriage, names the baby Christine and takes on the challenge of tracking down Tatiana's family. A card inside Tatiana's diary leads her to the Trans-Siberian Restaurant, which is owned by Semyon (Armin Mueller-Stahl). This cuddly grandpa graciously offers to translate the diary for her and personally reach out to any relatives he can find—after a brief, sinister pause in their conversation. Anna, who might not have caught that brief flash of evil, is unaware that Semyon is the boss of the London branch of the vory v zakone. Her noble quest eventually leads to his downfall: Semyon fathered the baby, as part of his criminal empire involves human trafficking. (Per the diary, he yelled, "If you never break a horse, it will never be tamed" before he raped Tatiana.) But two men in his service are waiting to pick up Semyon's mantle: Kirill (Vincent Cassel), Semyon's drunk, closeted son, and Nikolai Luzhin (Viggo Mortensen), a skilled fighter who's the object of Kirill's affection and an undercover FSB agent working with the Russian desk at Scotland Yard.

Despite protecting Anna, her family, and Christine, Anna never learns who Nikolai really is. "How can I become king when king [sic] is still in place?" he quips when she asks him why he's been so helpful. He nuzzles Anna, blesses Christine, kisses Anna, says goodbye, then goes to catch up with Kirill, who's ready to party down after almost drowning an infant in the Thames and agreeing to fuck over his beloved Papa. Nikolai chooses not to confess. His commitment to the role is total, and the toll it is taking on his soul is only hinted at in the final shot of the film. Sitting in the dark of the Trans-Siberian Restaurant with a bottle of vodka on his table, he flips a chetki, Eastern Orthodox prayer beads made and used by Russian prisoners. Nikolai's expression is stoic and inscrutable—an image you might see photo-realistically tattooed on someone's leg, a person who uncritically idolizes movie tough guys and their sacred codes of honor. But there's an inescapable feeling of sadness that radiates from him, a sense of being trapped. This comes from the scene that immediately precedes it: Anna, dressed in white, feeds Tatiana's baby in her mother's back garden on a sunny afternoon. This heavenly image is undercut by lines from Tatiana's diary, ones we've heard before, which Tatiana reads from beyond the grave in voiceover. "My name is Tatiana. My father died in the mines in my village," she quavers. After a cut to

Nikolai sitting alone in the restaurant, she continues: "So he was already buried when he died. We were all buried under the soil of Russia. That is why I left, to find a better life."

On the surface, it seems that everyone has returned to their right place and order has been restored. Anna and Christine are once again amongst—as Anna's uncle Stepan would call them—"regular people," and Nikolai is back in the underworld. The brief moment in which their parallel worlds intersected seems to have passed. But Tatiana's presence will always loom over Anna and Christine, and Tatiana's sense of being buried—while also hoping to escape—is likely shared by Nikolai. Nikolai was presumably once a regular person too—and even if he wasn't, he's chosen to spend his life with the mob. Anna, or someone like her, is inaccessible to him, as is her variety of bliss. This might be what he's thinking about as he flips the rosary, a prayer for what he's lost and will continue to lose. Or maybe he's just planning his next move and dreading the prospect of what he'll have to do next as part of the organization, be it kill, traffic more girls, or finally have sex with Kirill. That the chetki and the vodka are his only companions imply that it could be all of the above. Even as we dwell on one of life's hardships, other thoughts will inevitably pass through our minds.

And yet, the dedication. How much regret and inner turmoil can be attributed to a man who so wryly jokes before cutting up Kirill's ex-bestie's carcass, and then repurposes the remains into a progress report to Scotland Yard? To ingratiate himself into the mob, Nikolai has no choice but to go along with Semyon's demands and Kirill's erratic behavior. But he does so with such fleet-footed style. He's a comedic genius; even installing Kirill as head of the vory v zakone, the surest and the fastest way to destroy the enterprise, is incredibly funny. While the darkness of his particular brand of humor is arguably cultural—one shaped by the cold, the dark, deprivation, and shock-therapy economic policies—there's clearly something else burbling under the surface. Is it that he loves the law so much that he has to constantly break it, or is he motivated by some ancient wrong done to him or his family? Or is he grasping at his prayer beads and seeking forgiveness for how much he enjoys doing his job? Certainly, there are moments when Nikolai does good things, though we can only infer that he's informed the police about the sex worker Kirill forces him to screw in order to prove he's "not a fucking queer." Saving Anna's uncle Stepan (the Polish director Jerzy Skolimowski), who also provides a lot of classic Russian humor (and racism!), could be viewed as merely a way to ensure Anna's cooperation and get closer to her. Perhaps he didn't tell Anna who he really was because he'd already used her as much as he needed and felt that it was best to end their transaction with a princely kiss. (After all, him checking out her ass when she first rides up to the Trans-Siberian Restaurant on her vintage motorcycle wasn't a requirement of his assignment.) As with many who undertake undercover work, Nikolai might've completely lost his sense of self, and lives in a state of perpetual confusion. Perhaps he's praying to god not to balance out his misdeeds, but to beg for clarity.

6.

But there's another form of dark comedy at work in *Eastern Promises*. Revealing that Nikolai is an FSB agent and not a vor foot soldier twelve minutes and twenty-one seconds before the end of the film simultaneously indulges and betrays audience members who enjoy gangster films strictly for unhinged brutality and sticking it to the feds. (Yes, you've been rooting for a cop this entire time, but you also got to see a bunch of killing beforehand.) Nikolai's naked knife fight in the sauna similarly rewards and punishes those who are in it for the macho bullshit, giving them exactly what they want but in a way that's explicitly subversive. Even—or more accurately, specifically—the most staunchly heterosexual viewer's eyes will drift downward, attempting to get a peek at Viggo's junk. For even the most desensitized, this movie violence is disconcerting (and, if you're an asshole, unpleasant only because of the nudity). Similarly, other moments of violence are framed and edited in a way that doesn't hide what gangster films typically do. When Ekrem gets his throat cut while pissing on a gravestone, he pulls down his Arsenal FC scarf to better show the blood spurting out, a move that's more typical of horror than a crime drama or action film. (In either of the latter genres, the character would clutch their throat to stem the flow or immediately collapse and fall out of frame, therefore denying us the opportunity to see their fatal wound.) Such choices stand in stark contrast to Martin Scorsese's efforts to make clear that his criminal protagonists, be they *Goodfellas*'s Henry Hill or *The Wolf of Wall Street*'s Jordan Belfort, are awful and should not be idolized nor imitated. I'm not pitting the two directors against each other, but rather drawing the connection between them: Cronenberg was responding to Scorsese's genre-defining films, as well as their more deranged fans.

As with Tom Stall/Joey Cusack in *A History of Violence*, we don't really know who we're dealing with. All we know for certain is that they're very good at fighting. That ambiguity is what makes both films all the more inestimable.

vi.
ELUCIDATION

COSMOPOLIS [2012]
MAPS TO THE STARS [2014]

WHAT IS ELUCIDATION?

Following the catharsis that comes from confession, a Jungian analysand will progress to the second stage of therapy: elucidation. As the name suggests, the key characteristic is insight. Here, with the help of their analyst, elements of a patient's personal unconscious come into view. Previously buried attitudes, attributes, and abilities enter their conscious mind. The analyst also works with the patient to generate new interpretations of the patient's history and present state—a new story, if you will. Psychoanalysis, regardless of its stripe, fashions the random and (debatably) intentional experiences of life into a narrative. (Even if you dislike or disagree with the tale, it's still interesting to hear it told—unless you're working with a terrible analyst.)

In addition to their complexes and projections, the analysand also becomes familiar with the different parts of the psyche: the persona (page page 26), the shadow (page page 82), the anima/animus/animum (page page 92), and most importantly, the self (page 114). The analyst will use their knowledge to impart how these elements, along with the collective unconscious and cultural context in which they live, has shaped both the problems that brought them to therapy and their functioning outside of those issues. This is achieved through dream analysis and discussions about their daily life (their reactions in particular). The analyst will also pay close attention to how transference

7. Amidst a protest, the protesters' slogan (the reworked opening line of *The Communist Manifesto*) appears on a twenty-four-hour news chyron. In the death-centric context of the film, "specter" suggests the demise and unnecessary lingering of the old system.

8. Brutha Fez, who was so pious he moved out of his mansion and into a minaret, lies peacefully in his coffin. Like capitalism (and Eric's wealth), he's passed on.

9. Chaos breaks out in shiny, obnoxious ad-drenched midtown Manhattan. The protesters' symbol is a rat—an animal that spreads disease, eats garbage, and proliferates when unchecked.

10. Eric's haircut from his childhood barber doesn't turn out the way he thought it would—not unlike his marriage to Elise or shorting the yuan.

11. Benjie chokes the life out of a dead girl.

12. The late Clarice Taggart is a true star of old Hollywood, and her spectral image appears as a paranoid projection to her narcissistic, D lister daughter, Havana Segrand.

manifests—whereby the patient imposes a past relationship, role, and/or unconscious thought or feeling onto the therapist. The analyst also begins to interrogate how their countertransference (the same thing, but in reverse) operates. The importance of this dynamic for the analyst underscores how Jungian psychoanalysis is always collaborative, a means of discovery and growth for both participants.

For the patient, the most important part of elucidation is awareness of the self. Naturally, understanding how the other parts of a person's mind influence their behavior, and digging up what they've repressed, is extremely beneficial. But the self, that precious inner core, submerged in the collective unconscious as well as the conscious, that thing that Jung described as being at once "'smaller than small'" yet "as the equivalent of the cosmos . . . 'bigger than big,'" is the ultimate destination. Reaching the self allows us to become the best version of ourselves, of who we are meant to be. However, it's important to note that this knowledge is just knowledge—the patient can be seen as simply information-gathering rather than making significant changes based on it. They're only aware of the self, not fully integrating it.

A pair of 2010s Cronenberg works, *Cosmopolis* and *Maps to the Stars*, are both set in thoroughly vapid worlds: finance and Hollywood. They run on self-perpetuating fantasies that have high-stakes consequences and ruin people's lives. The stock market is fiction, just like the blockbusters and fame peddled by the Industry. Money and notoriety are ephemeral human creations, but they are increasingly viewed as the only things of any value. They're the success of their own marketing—another fantasy. These milieus seem to attract only the greediest, most self-involved idiots one could imagine, and are depicted in a highly stylized yet highly realistic manner. Both feature pale protagonists who are at once at the center and periphery of these weird microcosms that dominate the globe. Eric Packer (Robert Pattinson) and Agatha Weiss (Mia Wasikowska) seem irredeemable: the former because he's a multibillionaire asshole who can get what he wants, the latter because she's the pyromaniac black sheep of a famous family. Through the course of their journeys, they come to an understanding of who they are, and return to their source, to childhood. *Cosmopolis* and *Maps to the Stars* are strange, cold films that are steeped in allegory and archetype. Allow me to elucidate.

ON *COSMOPOLIS* AND *MAPS TO THE STARS*

Despite the novelty of being a Wall Street titan, there have always been men like Eric Packer (Robert Pattinson). A boy king who's reigned into adulthood, he, like Alexander the Great before him, has conquered most of the known world but still wants more: more money; the Rothko Chapel; a haircut. Eric first appears, emperor-like, before a white building with columns and informs Torval (Kevin Durand), one of his security guards, that he must get a trim from his childhood barber. Over the course of this journey—ill-advised because of the nature of cross-town Manhattan traffic and the U.S. president's motorcade—his financial kingdom falls. Eric shorted the yuan, which he believed couldn't go any higher. Its rise defies the hallmarks of a downward trend, such as increased consumer spending and static Chinese interest rates. The market has not behaved as it should, or at least not in the manner that those who rule over this calamitous abstraction believe it does. There's no coming back from this. He's fucked.

Eric remains firm in his desire for a fresh cut, riding in his "Prousted" (cork-lined) stretch limousine as the repercussions of his bad bet approach. As it crawls through the streets, he is visited by members of his modern court inside of it, including his chief of theory (Samantha Morton); a doctor, who examines his prostate; his MILF art dealer Didi (Juliette Binoche), whom he screws after being asked his age by a younger man; and a member of another court, Kozmo (Gouchy Boy), who informs Eric that Brutha Fez (K'naan), Eric's favorite musician, is dead. When Eric briefly ventures outside of his stretch, he encounters a sex worker, a jester (a performance artist who pies the powerful), and his icy queen, Elise (Sarah Gadon). Eric's union with Elise is compared to the marriages of ancient European monarchs: he's new money, she's Connecticut-boarding-school old money. And, just like a royal of old, Elise refuses to have sex with her king—the alliance between their two nations has quietly and catastrophically failed. When Eric finally gets to the barber, he doesn't even finish the cut, opting instead to kill Torval with his own gun and venture into the apartment of Benno Levin (Paul Giamatti), a former employee who's been issuing the credible death threats Torval had been warning him about all day.

Cosmopolis ends in a tense limbo: Benno has his gun pointed at the back of Eric's head and will almost certainly shoot Eric. However, as his freakishly pale complexion suggested all along, Eric is already dead. His decision to short the yuan killed him; the money is done, which means his company is done, which means he is done. We've been watching his long journey to the underworld and his final judgment. Rather than Saint Peter, King Yama, or some panel of posthumous arbiters, it's Benno, head covered by a wet towel, who will issue the latter—and his mind seems made up. The seat of Eric's limo is not a throne but merely part of his burial chamber, and like the pharaohs, he's got drinks, entertainment (the many screens around him that monitor the market), and his servants with him.

Subtle visual cues alert us to this disconcerting reality. The framing of shots, the majority of which are close-ups or extreme close-ups of Eric's face while sitting in his seat, obscure the actual amount of space inside the stretch. His visitors are also often shot in close-up, and most position themselves in front of or close to him, further shrinking the space. However, none of them sit right next to Eric, not even Didi, despite the fact there are three seats in the back of the limo. This imbues an intense sense of claustrophobia—not unlike the tight fit of a coffin. (The muffled sound of the outside world, even as rat-wielding anarchists deface and pound upon the vehicle, also suggests a subterranean tomb.) The streets of Manhattan have become the River Styx, with the other vehicles that pass him by containing souls on their way to the same terminal destination. If you think this interpretation is, like Eric's ride, a stretch, consider Brutha Fez's funeral procession, with the rapper lying peacefully in his open casket at the center, which causes one of the many delays along Eric's route. As Brutha Fez glides past Eric, the lyrics of his song "Mecca," with the chilling chorus "Coming from the streets to Mecca / Death no matter where you go, come 'n getcha," echo through the night.

The haircut, Eric's stated objective for this long ride, is rooted in a desire to go back to his childhood. "A haircut has what? Associations. Calendars on the wall, mirrors everywhere," Eric tells Shiner (Jay Baruchel), a tech guy who's been with Eric "ever since the itty-bitty startup" that set off their rise. Even before he learns of his fatal miscalculation, and despite his infinite wealth and exalted position, Eric realizes that he has lost his way. He can't sleep; he drinks brandy and reads books instead. (Then there are his marital problems, which his wry Noo Yawk charm can't fix—what one might call a failure to integrate his anima.) In *The Special Phenomenology of the Child Archetype*, Carl Jung wrote that the child archetype represents the Self, the innermost core of our being. Rather than believing that babies start off as blank slates, Jung argued that they are at once "born out of the womb of the unconscious," imprinted with all that has come before it, and individual human consciousness. A child thus "symbolizes the pre-conscious and the post-conscious essence of man. His pre-conscious essence is the unconscious state of earliest childhood; his post-conscious essence is an anticipation by analogy of life after death." (Wherever we may be before we're born might be the same place we go when we die.) As part of growing up, lived experience and the development of ego (and shitty things like complexes) distance us from that connection to the unconscious.

7.

8.

Jung identifies that a child also represents something that's in the process of growth, working toward independence. By seeking a return to his childhood, Eric is attempting to not only reunite himself with who he really is, but to liberate himself. With this understanding, the seemingly capricious self-destruction that he's been engaging in all day is cast in a very different light. When he finally gets into the chair, that old, familiar place, all that remains of his tidy Gucci suit are a dirty, untucked shirt and pants. Everything else that makes him important has been stripped away—his wealth, his marriage, his special limo. Only the bits of pie cream stuck to his head are a testament to his former prestige. (The performance artist who pied him has also pied Bill Gates; getting to Eric was harder than getting to the president of the United States.) At first Eric tells the barber, "I woke up this morning and knew it was time." But then he abruptly stands up and leaves before the man can finish, leaving Eric looking like a doll that got a haircut from a kid. His new asymmetrical style is the perfect representation of the fusion of opposites that are the archetypal child, and also extremely childish. He is aware of his self, but he's not ready to change fully. On some level, Eric also understands that this change is death. The ritual of a haircut is also comparable to the preparation of a body before burial. In fact, across many cultures, stiffs get groomed before they're laid to rest—the living want the dead to look their best.

In myths, the extreme vulnerability of children comes to the fore: they often get stolen away or abandoned. This is part of what connects these stories to the real world—children are indeed at risk and preyed upon. But these mythical children also often triumph over this adversity via supernatural powers, precocious intelligence, sheer resilience, or divine intervention. When Eric answers Benno's call and enters the dingy apartment, he's like a small boy wandering into the woods. The only difference is that, mere hours ago, he used to be the big bad wolf.

9.

Maps to the Stars, meanwhile, isn't a satire of Hollywood; it's a documentary of a hell where it never rains, and nobody feels fulfilled. The residents of both of its circles—divided into celebrities who own $12,000 couches and their covetous servants—have been condemned for their egregious sins of greed and vanity.

10.

Despite the perpetual sunshine, they are marked by pale flesh, the same eerie whiter-than-whiteness of *Cosmopolis*'s Eric Packer. And just like Eric, they can't stop sinning. When confronted by the contents of their unconscious, they believe them to be hallucinations or apparitions. These people are so consumed by their personas, never thinking twice about mentioning their film's box office gross or awards haul regardless of the situation, that they don't even realize that they're dead.

Agatha (Mia Wasikowska) travels to this underworld by bus in order to sort out her issues as well as her family's. (All the other passengers who travel with her are asleep, and therefore look dead.) This modern-day Electra defies the order of Los Angeles and is considered insane: though also pallid, she's not vain, as she looks as if she cuts her own hair and is branded by burns sustained during a previous attempt to destroy her parents' incestuous union with fire. Upon arriving at the dream factory, she meets a snoozing Jerome (Robert Pattinson), a limo driver and aspiring actor/writer. He will go on to fuck Agatha in the name of "research," as Jerome's easygoing demeanor hides the fact that he's a fundamentally uncreative "creative" who's hungry for experiences he could use in a script that could potentially sell for millions and, more importantly, make him famous.

Agatha quickly becomes the personal assistant of Havana Segrand (Julianne Moore), a woman who holds the twin dishonors of being a nepo baby and a D-lister. Aside from being too old to be useful in Hollywood, Havana is tormented because she was molested by her mother, the (actually talented) starlet Clarice Taggart (Sarah Gadon), whose premature death by a fire on Christmas 1976 only served to enhance her legendary status. (As this is pre-#MeToo, the sexual abuse hasn't diminished Clarice's popularity.) Or at least Havana *believes* that she was molested—Clarice repeatedly returns to gaslight and taunt her daughter, at one point telling Havana that it was her stepfather who was the abuser. Havana seeks to heal from this trauma, real or imagined, by turning to Stafford Weiss (John Cusack), a best-selling self-help guru whose therapy requires his patients to receive vigorous massages (while partially undressed) and repeat every line of bullshit that comes out of his mouth. Stafford has not only sired Agatha with his sister Cristina (Olivia Williams), but also Benjie (Evan Bird), a volatile child actor who's fresh out of rehab. (Like many of those in early recovery, Benjie is never far from an energy drink.) After learning of her presence in Los Angeles through Havana, Stafford demands Agatha leave immediately and gives her $10,000 to do so. However, he's unsuccessful, as she goes on to bludgeon Havana to death with her lone gold statuette and convinces Benjie to end their cursed family line.

It's a strange victory in a thoroughly strange film, one that blends Greek myth with Nathanael West's *The Day of the Locust*. Everything is laden with meaning: its title references both fate and fame. Agatha, who was previously committed at a facility in Jupiter, Florida, seeks to find and kill her big-name little brother, and proves that her destiny rests in her own hands, not in the stars. (This runs counter to the narrative offered by Greek tragedy, but wholly in line with those peddled by Hollywood.) Mentions of death and excrement frequently pop up throughout, even in the most casual of conversations. These interjections are often jarring: while making a list of items for Agatha to buy (which includes American Spirit cigarettes), Havana asks Agatha if she knows of the acclaimed Dr. Stafford Weiss. When Agatha claims she doesn't, Havana snaps, "Of course not! I'm getting information from a fucking dead person!" Similarly, Benjie's agent is named Arnold Kubler-Ross, who shares a name with the psychiatrist who outlined the stages of grief and whom Benjie mockingly calls "the Great Rabbi of Death and Dying." ("I got a new nickname for you: Museum of Tolerance," Benjie spits afterward, a reference to the city's Holocaust education center.)

Stars, in the words of celebrity news rag *Us Weekly*, are "just like us," but only because they shit. Their death is not just corporeal, but also experienced through irrelevance and the end of fame. They live on through their performances, in both ontological and reputational terms, making career death no less existential than mortality. (Actually dying could offer a career boost.) Clarice, with her far-superior star power, has always haunted Havana. When Clarice rises from a bathtub to tell Havana that she has "shitty tits" and a "used-up old hole [that] stinks worse than I do," she ventriloquizes Havana's worst fears about herself. It's something that makes Havana question her sanity, but more importantly (to her, at least) makes those beliefs real and inescapable. (Unfortunately, they seem to be shared by other denizens of Tinsel Town, such as the two girls Benjie and his friend hang out with at a club, one of whom says Havana's so old that "she's not menopausal. She's dead!") Neither her "work" with Stafford nor the act of playing her mother's role in a remake of Clarice's most-beloved movie, *Still Waters*, helps Havana to process her mother's abuse or her self-loathing. (Both acts are fundamentally rooted in ego and performance.) Although she doesn't live to see it, the new *Still Waters* almost certainly won't revive Havana's career, let alone allow her to approach Clarice's renown. Agatha eventually opting to kill Havana seems almost merciful.

It certainly is for those who live outside of Havana's head, as she's unrepentantly self-obsessed and vile. Havana only landed the role because the actress originally cast suffered the loss of her son, Micah, who drowned in some luxe backyard pool. Upon learning of this, Havana cheerfully bounds outside and dances with Agatha while singing, "Na na na na, hey hey, goodbye," at one point breathlessly adding, "Thank you, little Micah!" between verses. Dead children abound in *Maps to the Stars*. More than a cult of youth, fame, or money, Hollywood is depicted as a cult centered on incest and child sacrifice. Again, this is literal and allegorical. Two powerful families in *Maps to the Stars* break the universal taboo of incest. Meanwhile, we also know (and see in the film) how the industry operates in a wildly provincial, cronyistic fashion, and unceremoniously consumes and disposes of young talent. Studio executives meet with Benjie just to see that he's "bright-eyed and bushy-tailed" (a cute euphemism for gauging his sobriety), they mention the exception, not the rule, to the all-too-common instance of child actors turned addicts: Drew Barrymore, a member of another multi-generational star family.

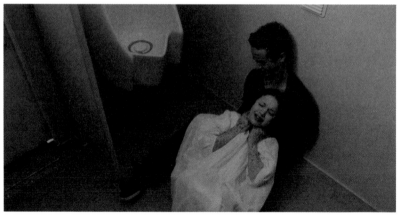

11.

Incest and sacrifice often blend into each other, with the repercussions of incest being a Gehenna only ended by death—hence Agatha's mission. Benjie is ill-tempered not only because he was making $300,000 a week at the tender age of nine, but because he's so inbred. The dead children who visit him—Micah and a girl with non-Hodgkin's lymphoma he met at a hospital as part of some make-a-wish program—are ostensibly products of his incest-scrambled brain. Benjie's cavalier attitude quickly fades after Agatha, whom he believes to be a "psychotron," tells him that she also saw dead children before she set their old house alight. But who's to say that the dead can't surprise those who don't know that they've croaked? In an attempt to rid himself of the sick girl (who, like Clarice, is always clad in a flowing, virginal white dress), Benjie strangles her inside a bathroom trailer—only to realize that he's actually killed his younger, freckle-faced co-star, whom Benjie loathes for constantly upstaging him. This scene-stealing prowess is glimpsed in the only part of the film they're making, *Bad Babysitter II*, that's included in *Maps to the Stars*, a bit where Benjie's character cuts a hole in a wall and the boy exclaims, "I wanna see her vabina!"—something that suggests the kid's star power might also be one of Benjie's many delusions. While discussing the attack with Benjie's therapist, Cristina initially believes that the production will replace the boy and not her son and is incredulous at the prospect of Benjie being prosecuted. ("He didn't take a gun to a school!" she shouts, alluding to another great fact of American life, the mass shooting.) His career is dead, and very soon, he will choose to die alongside Agatha after "marrying" her by exchanging their parents' (and aunt and uncle's) rings. Rings are a gift, as is the choice to sacrifice oneself. He's learned of his family's terrible secret, of his true and terrible self, and finally does something totally selfless, without any ego.

There is another child in the film, not unlike Benjie, who bears discussing: Havana. She's a puella aeterna, or what we might call the female version of a manchild. She pouts and stomps around when she doesn't get what she wants and has a wildly infantile understanding of the world. Like a child, Havana treats Agatha, a fully grown woman, alternately as a toy, playmate, punching bag, and servant. Havana has Agatha dragging around giant potted plants ("You're already wearing gloves," Havana snaps) and filling in for her actual maid on extremely short notice. Like a true narcissist, Havana views employing Agatha as a form of community service, because Havana regards Agatha with pity—a burned girl who cannot trade on her looks. Thus, Agatha also serves as a mirror of herself as a victim. These two sentiments are intertwined and expressed during a particularly cringeworthy moment during their initial meeting/job interview. "I think you're beautiful," Havana tells Agatha. "And you know who looks just like you, inside? Havana Segrand." To pity Agatha is to pity herself. "I get the sense that I'm working through something by hiring her," Havana proudly tells Stafford. "Two women marked by fire," he murmurs in his well-rehearsed guru voice.

Yet Havana is not undeserving of sympathy, and therefore deserves a much better healer than Stafford. She was molested, either by her mother or her stepfather, so her arrested development (and the fact that it remains untreated) is a legitimate tragedy, one that's rooted in something very horrible and very real: a child's innocence being sacrificed for an adult's pleasure. (This again evokes the actual crimes of Hollywood: victims of documented abuse by powerful people and the victims of its industrial complex.) What compounds her childishness is the fact that others cannot see her as anything other than the child of a famous

12.

actress, and not an actress worth knowing otherwise. Like many bad therapists do, Stafford encourages her to go even deeper into her illness. After he therapeutically pummels her, Stafford tells Havana about "the imago deity." (He even cites Jung—incorrectly.) "We call it the magical child. And that child will not fail," Stafford assures her.

However, it's Stafford's own daughter/niece who is the magical child, not Havana. It's Agatha's persistence, as well as her unhinged quirky charm (which pulls in Carrie Fisher, Havana, and Jerome), that allows her to right Stafford and Christina's wrongs. This duality is perfectly encapsulated by Benjie when Agatha surprises him in his trailer: "You know, for a disfigured schizophrenic you got the town pretty wired." Like many children of myth, Agatha has been separated from her parents, but has extraordinary resolve. Despite the constant gaslighting, she knows herself—and that she and her brother are abominations that must be destroyed. She's the archetype of the unknown maiden, the outcast, and the madwoman with divine visions. Agatha performs the ultimate sacrifice unhesitatingly, acting out the course that had been set for her: ritualistically marrying her brother and slipping into eternal sleep.

Archetypal child figures, Jung (actually) wrote, are often also heroes, and "identified with things that promote culture, e.g., fire, metal, corn, maize, etc. As bringers of light, that is, enlargers of consciousness, they overcome darkness." When Agatha commits suicide alongside Benjie, gazing up at the heavens, she is, in a way, razing Hollywood in the hopes that something far better will rise from the ashes. Or, at the very least, she ruined Stafford's bullshit self-help empire and the *Bad Babysitter* franchise.

vii.
EDUCATION

A DANGEROUS METHOD [2011]
THE DEAD ZONE [1983]
SPIDER [2002]
CRIMES OF THE FUTURE [2022]

WHAT IS EDUCATION?

Using the insights from confession and elucidation, a patient begins to apply these lessons to their daily life, and modify their behavior accordingly. Now aware of how they project their unconscious thoughts, feelings, and experiences onto others, they can move away from repeating negative behaviors. This allows the patient to not only become better adapted to society, but to also advance in the individuation process (page page 26). Though much of Jung's approach to therapy draws from the work of fellow psychoanalyst Alfred Adler (such as doctor and patient sitting face-to-face), this stage in particular is rooted in Adler's ideas about what the function of therapy should be. Adler's theories were centered on social factors and interactions rather than biological urges or deeper spiritual/psychical concerns. While confession and elucidation are rooted in the unconscious, education's focus is a means of getting a patient to a point where they can rejoin the society in which they live in a healthy manner, not harming themselves or others. Thus, the focus during education is on the persona and ego, the conscious elements of the psyche.

13. Sabina and Dr. Jung walk the grounds of the Burghölzli shortly after her arrival. Their conversation is pointless, but her reaction to him striking her coat with his cane (in an attempt to shake loose the dirt) comes to define their relationship.

14. "Suicide! Interplanetary travel!" Sabina spits at another doctor who attempts to engage her by asking what her interests are.

15. The obedient and (to borrow Dr. Freud's phrase) exquisitely Protestant Emma lies waiting for Carl, and wants nothing more than to please him.

16. Sabina, stricken by hysteria, is forcibly taken to the hospital by horse-drawn carriage.

17. Sabina, now fully in control of her thoughts and movements, leaves Carl behind, who is now suffering with the illness he cured her of.

18. Johnny Smith's gift/curse takes on new levels of emotional weight as he sees the scissors wielded by the Castle Rock Strangler as they plunge down into a victim's chest.

19. Young Spider compulsively weaves his twine webs, a passion perhaps sparked by tales of his mother's childhood in the Essex countryside.

Since each individual is different, there are no set parameters for how an analyst should advance a patient through the education stage; however, they must be able to give their patient realistic options for changing their behavior. The individual must remain true to themselves. In recognition of this, some Jungian therapists take the view that, for many patients, education should be the final stage of analysis. For other patients, particularly those who are so sui generis or need to go further, as Jung wrote in his book *Modern Man in Search of a Soul*, "to educate them to normality would be their worst nightmare because their deepest need is to march to the tune of a different drummer." While it may sound exciting to, in the parlance of our times, "not be like the other girls," it's actually quite alienating. Jungian analysis offers room for those who suffer through that reality.

The quartet of films discussed in this chapter—*A Dangerous Method*, *The Dead Zone*, *Spider*, and *Crimes of the Future*—feature characters who exist at different places along the "normie" to "weirdo" spectrum. Yet each finds a way to exist in the vastly different social settings in which they live—or at least get as close to it as they possibly can. At the center of the interlocking love triangles in *A Dangerous Method* is Sabina Spielrein (Keira Knightley), a woman who first appears in the back seat of a horse-drawn carriage heading toward the Burghölzli mental hospital (and toward Carl Jung, Sigmund Freud, and Emma Jung) in the throes of hysteria, and ends the film cured, a talented doctor in her own right, and speeding away from Carl's messiness in the back seat of a car. *The Dead Zone*, an adaptation of a not-very-good Stephen King novel, follows the sad tale of John Smith (Christopher Walken), a New England everyman who becomes clairvoyant after waking from a coma, loses everything he loves, and chooses to save humanity by sacrificing himself. In *Spider*, Dennis "Spider" Cleg's (Ralph Fiennes) transfer from a high-security mental health facility to a dingy East End halfway house causes him to reexamine memories of his childhood—and "replay" events from that time that he couldn't have possibly witnessed. Although the now-middle-aged Spider achieves a terrible new understanding of what actually led to his incarceration, he ends up being sent back to prison, which, tragically, is the best the state can offer a man like him. And then there's *Crimes of the Future*'s Saul Tenser (Viggo Mortensen), an aging, iconic performance artist and government informant, who discovers that his chronic pain—the source from which his art flows—can finally be ameliorated. The film ends with a grainy shot of Saul in a state of pure bliss—he finally knows how to exist in this world.

ON *A DANGEROUS METHOD*, *THE DEAD ZONE*, *SPIDER*, AND *CRIMES OF THE FUTURE* (2022)

We first see Sabina Spielrein (Keira Knightley) as a bundle of crippling symptoms: a compulsively jutting chin, a stammer, a childlike defiance of authority. Her movements are strange, as they're manifestations of a disorder that no longer exists. (Knightley based her hysteria on the paintings of Francis Bacon and photographs taken by neurologist Jean-Martin Charcot of his patients.) Over the course of the film, Spielrein grows into something far greater—first a research assistant to Carl Jung (Michael Fassbender) and then a doctor—all thanks to psychoanalysis. She also begins an affair with Jung, threatens to ruin his life over it, and then drags Jung's professional mentor, Sigmund Freud (Viggo Mortensen), into the fray. But she also gives Freud the idea for the death drive, which, in case you don't know anything about psychoanalysis, is incredibly important to his intellectual viewpoint. She's a thoroughly complicated woman, capable of good and bad, who, at the end, seems to have triumphed. She's got a husband, a career, and a baby on the way; she's over Jung—and then the black title cards roll, revealing that only the gentile in this dynamic love triangle lived past World War II.

13.

20. Spider prepares to bash in the head of Mrs. Wilkinson, the caretaker of the facility he's been moved to, who has transformed into the horrible, braying tart Yvonne.

21. An installation component of Saul and Caprice's show. Its message is the same as Cronenberg's own beliefs: there is no soul, no afterlife, no other extension of our essence. Our body is all we have.

22. Caprice tattoos and removes Saul's newest organ as part of their performance.

23. Saul Tenser and his love/muse Caprice mesh their bodies together in mutual appreciation of their live organ-removal artistry.

Spielrein has been rescued from obscurity, but she also remains unknowable in a way that many wildly influential thinkers of the twentieth century aren't. The debate about the nature of her relationship with Jung, and if she was even his patient or he merely handled her hospital intake forms, continues to this day. Yet it's important to remember that her personal and professional transformation wasn't uncommon for its time. An epidemic of female patients falling in love with their newly minted male analysts led Freud to identify the phenomenon of transference, a concept that became a crucial pillar of understanding all types of talk therapy. (And, of course, this led to the establishment of rules that forbade this kind of ethical trespass.) Women were always at the forefront of this burgeoning field in messy, exciting, tragic, and influential ways.

In the nineteenth and early twentieth centuries, asylum admission criteria were overwhelmingly weighted toward "pathologies" experienced by women, and as such women made up the majority of these institutions' intake. During this era, the number of asylum residents swelled. For the middle and upper classes, an asylum was the perfect place to hide away an unwanted wife; for the poor, sending a female relative to an asylum because she suffered from, say, postpartum depression and could no longer work, was a financial relief and more humane than just leaving her out on the street.

Despite the often questionable reasons for their admittance, a great number of women were in very real, very terrible pain. Aside from the potential traumas associated

DAVID CRONENBERG: CLINICAL TRIALS 154

14.

15.

with the rigid role of motherhood (miscarriage, childbirth, losing multiple children to illness), repeated incidents of incest, rape, and assault were meant to be taken in stride. The Victorian woman was to be seen and not heard—a facile statement, but one that's nevertheless true. That Sigmund Freud sat down and actually listened to women was a fundamentally revolutionary act that threatened the social order. Maybe women weren't fundamentally irrational creatures? Maybe they had a good reason to be angry or sad or both? These earth-shattering hypotheticals were paired with the creation of a new kind of relationship: one where a person could discuss their deepest miseries and everyday problems with a non-judgmental conversation partner/helpful authority. The analyst's couch was not a confession box; it was a secular treatment for spiritual problems. This new kind of relationship endured, and has fundamentally changed society. However, what made Freud's new treatment truly radioactive—beyond the idea of a man alone with a woman who's lying on a couch, for about fifty minutes, a few times a week—was the number of Jews in the profession. Anti-Semitism is baked into Western societies, from food to language to work schedules to customs; the level of outright hatred that, in large part, defined the era cannot be overstated. (It's also worth mentioning that Anti-Semitism is a German word.)

Constantly beset by attacks from all quarters, the fact that psychoanalysis survived—and became as influential as it did—is not only a testament to its efficacy, but the

16.
17.

force of will required to withstand such vitriol. The stern image of Freud with his cigar as an old man and Jung as an authoritative yet mystical grandpa is burned into our minds, even if we don't know that much about psychoanalysis. They wanted to project that level of sturdiness to, in the parlance of our times, fuck the haters. In the film, Freud's stated refusal to even countenance Jung's brief discussion of synchronicity, or meaningful coincidence, comes from that fear of being ridiculed—but also from his need to remain the powerful, not-killed-by-his-son father in this relationship. (Even Otto Gross, the anarcho-psychoanalyst who pushes Jung to have sex with Spielrein, is more acceptable to Freud.) The power of *A Dangerous Method* comes from complicating these "great men" in a variety of ways: Freud and Jung are shown as young, vibrant, and self-important—something that the film sometimes plays for laughs. (Freud always had killer zingers, even if his book about jokes kinda sucks.) More than simply dramatizing their lives, reiterating their greatest hits, it digs into what the men who sought to unleash the repressed had themselves repressed: that great minds often engage in petty, juicy drama.

However, *A Dangerous Method* maintains a degree of visual fracture. The actors are often blocked in a way where they aren't looking at each other, or are obscured in some way. Part of this comes from the way dialogue scenes are typically shot (one character speaking, then the other), but also mirrors the way psychoanalysis was originally performed (the patient looking away from the doctor). This framing also underscores the massive cultural, class, religious, and philosophical divisions between Jung, Freud, and Spielrein. More importantly, it highlights our fundamental inability to really know Spielrein, who, until 1980, was just another name in one of Freud's footnotes. The film can do whatever it wants to Freud and Jung, and there will be an army of outraged analysts hooting and hollering about what actually happened. (Even a whiff of something not being entirely accurate has been met with hostility by various psychoanalytic publications.) But because she was a woman, because she was Russian (writing in the wrong language can condemn a brilliant mind to obscurity), because she specialized in child psychology (which was considered a "less important" field), and because she and her daughters were killed in the Holocaust, Spielrein can only ever be partially reconstructed. And though it is firmly her film, Cronenberg embraces this gap. (A film actually about Jung would've probably started with his apocalyptic dream and definitely involved Toni Wolff, the mistress who, as Spielrein cheekily notes, shares many traits with her.) Even Spielrein's most intimate moments, such as the Edwardian BDSM scenes, retain a distance and involve reflections in mirrors. Tragically, she likes to see herself—something that we cannot do.

In this film about epic breakups and history's bias toward men, it's worth spending some time considering Emma Jung (Sarah Gadon). Emma, who was the second-wealthiest heiress in Switzerland, funded her husband's career, and granted him a degree of independence and stability to grow that would've otherwise been impossible. (It wasn't only first-class stateroom steamer ship tickets.) In addition to essentially being in a throuple with Carl and Toni Wolff, Emma became a renowned psychoanalyst in her own right—something that the film ignores. (The screenwriter Christopher Hampton, who authored the play on which the screenplay is based, has since expanded Emma's role.) Instead, poor Emma simply serves as a counterpoint to Spielrein not only because she is Jung's pale, Aryan wife, but because she's stuck in the role of loving, ever-pregnant helpmate. Emma is the one who does as society commands, even when she knows her husband is fooling around. Gadon brings an air of ambiguity to the role: Is Emma really happy, or is she just pretending? She remains a cipher, an incomplete woman to set off how open, defiant, and complicated Spielrein is.

Spielrein isn't punished for this courage; instead, the world she healed herself to be a part of ultimately, violently rejects her. (Freud was right to be wary of these gentiles.) As she cries in the back of a car speeding away from Bollingen, the Jungs' massive lakeside home, it mirrors the opening scene where she's brought to the Burghölzli by horse-drawn carriage. The change in transportation signifies not only the passage of time, but of personal progress. Perhaps, instead of crying because it's bittersweet to see Carl, she too has had a vision of the future.

Although it's present in much of Cronenberg's work, *The Dead Zone* has the most pronounced tension between its absurd or fantastical elements and outright tragedy. It's often funny when things are deadly serious. The many places the film goes—unsurprising given that it's based on a 428-page novel of the same name—at times makes it feel as if it's three separate films, shifting genres and styles, yet united by tremendous sadness and dark comedy. *The Dead Zone* begins with Johnny Smith (Christopher Walken) half reading, half performing the final lines of Edgar Allan Poe's poem "The Raven" for his elementary school class, and then assigning them "The Legend of Sleepy Hollow" for homework as the bell rings. Johnny, though sometimes referred to as "John," lives in a perpetual happy boyhood. "You're gonna like it," he says mischievously above the din of the kids gathering up their belongings and rushing out the door. "It's about a schoolteacher who's chased by a headless demon." Christopher Walken, who can only ever be Christopher Walken, is wearing an unconvincing "normal guy" costume (sweater vest, corduroy jacket, tie, big eighties wire-frame glasses), with his trademark bouffant combed down into awful bangs. Again, the man's name is John Smith—comical mundanity is inextricable from who he is.

But that hyper-normality, however strained it may seem, is precious. Later that evening, after politely telling his fiancée Sarah (Brooke Adams) that he'd rather wait until they were married to have sex, Johnny is hit by an eighteen-wheel milk truck, and goes into a coma. When Johnny emerges from it five years later, he has the ability to see the future. Now, the punishment begins. His job is gone, Sarah has married someone else and had a child, and his legs, atrophied by years of inaction, force him to rely on a cane even after months of physical therapy. Things get worse: after seeing her son on television being grilled about his newfound abilities, Johnny's deeply religious mother suffers some kind of attack and abruptly dies in the hospital. Bereft, Johnny vacillates between cursing god and being a vocal atheist. From the moment he wakes up from that coma, the Walken bouffant is in full effect, as is his suffering.

Rather than seeing something auspicious, like winning lotto numbers or the outcome of the Super Bowl, all of Johnny's psychic visions are of intense pain and fear from past (a mother sacrificing herself to save her son from the Nazis), present (a little girl trapped inside a burning house), and future (a group of boys falling through the ice while playing hockey). Along with the agony of actually experiencing the visions, which he describes as feeling like he's "dying inside," his insights more often than not lead to pyrrhic victories—something else that clearly torments Johnny. After seeing the hockey players drown, Johnny warns Chris Stuart (Simon Craig), a wealthy and well-connected man, not to let his sheltered son Roger (Anthony Zerbe) go out on the ice as part of a scheduled play date. Though this is deadly serious, his warning is delivered with Walken's distinctive cadence: "THE ICE IS GONNA BREAK!" While Roger believes Johnny—since Johnny has been his tutor and successfully drawn him out of his shell—his father doesn't, furious at the suggestion of canceling his plans. And when the other boys go out to play, two of them drown. The last time we see Chris, he sits alone, surrounded by his mansion's finery, wearing a thousand-yard stare and slowly sipping a crystal tumbler of whiskey. Despite having the right information, people ultimately behave the way they want to. Omniscience can't change that.

Then there's the aforementioned tragedy of Johnny's personal life. Not only is everything he once cared about gone, Johnny is set apart by his clairvoyance. Though Sarah comes to visit him one afternoon (with her toddler in tow!) and they finally consummate their relationship, she makes it clear that their rendezvous is a one-time thing. Johnny, his father, Sarah, and her son eat dinner together afterward, a happy family scene that shows what could've been but can never be. It's not bittersweet, just bitter. Even if he were able to find a new girlfriend—which he has no interest in doing—what kind of life could he have with her, with the constant threat of premonitions intruding any time he touched her? He can't pick up his old life, nor fashion a new one.

After successfully identifying the Castle Rock Strangler (who turns out to be a cop who's been "investigating" the case), Johnny moves out of his father's home and to another town. He isolates himself and stuffs the endless letters from people desperate for his help into a large closet, unopened; he knows that he can't give them what they want. His solitude is broken by the students he tutors and his doctor, who has no real method of treating his physical or emotional problems. (Johnny's doctor is played by Herbert Lom, best known for playing the chief inspector in the *Pink Panther* movies; although it's not a comedic role, Lom's presence alone adds an odd frisson to the unfolding tragedy. The push and pull never really ends.) Johnny's situation is hopeless, a living death that has no end in sight.

Then, another man comes into Johnny's life: Greg Stillson (Martin Sheen).

Stillson is a figure who's come to dominate politics nowadays: an unscrupulous, fake populist who believes he's on a mission from god. When he's not laying on the cracker-barrel

18.

PART II. PSYCHOTHERAPY

DAVID CRONENBERG: CLINICAL TRIALS

charm and making empty promises about bringing manufacturing jobs to swaths of unemployed, rural white people, Stillson is blackmailing journalists and snapping at his underlings. During one televised rally, he's introduced as "the most successful third-party campaign this state has ever seen" and someone who "represents both the poor and well-off." The contradictions of the latter statement don't matter to his dispossessed fans; he's a political outsider who will right the wrongs of all who came before him—staying true to the dreams of our founding fathers. Before the skating tragedy, Johnny and Chris watch one of Stillson's rallies on TV, and Chris incredulously wonders how people can't see through Stillson's bullshit. But Chris has no idea what it's like to be economically disaffected. He can't even see that he's part of the problem, as Chris is willing to play nice with Stillson in case he wins the election. (Support from the wealthy, and having personal wealth, has always been one of the hallmarks of a fake populist.) Yet Stillson's appeal also leads to Johnny running into Sarah once again—she's one of the rubes who's out canvassing in the cold for the politician. Shortly after, Johnny goes to another rally near his house (complete with a brass band playing "Dixie") and shakes Stillson's hand, which leads to Johnny's most apocalyptic vision yet: Stillson as president. Claiming he's got a mandate from people and god's blessing, Johnny sees Stillson ordering a nuclear strike by gunpoint. His down-home charm and faith in himself, even as he's killing millions of people, never wavers.

This threat—coupled with Johnny's hard-earned knowledge that people will always do what they want—gives him a renewed purpose: he must kill Stillson. After posing the classic "If you could go back and time and kill Hitler, would you?" hypothetical to his doctor, Johnny hatches a plan and buys a rifle. Before he hobbles off to meet his destiny, Johnny sends a letter to Sarah, professing his undying love for her, and writing that "nobody will understand, but I know I'm right." In one of the funniest and darkest moments in the film, Stillson uses Sarah's son as a human shield while Johnny shoots at him—a moment that leads to the complete collapse of Stillson's political career. (Johnny has one last vision of Stillson blowing his brains out over a copy of *Newsweek* magazine, whose cover is a photo of Stillson dangling the boy in front of him while standing before a giant American flag.) Nobody gets hurt or dies except Johnny and Stillson. He's stopped hiding and finally found his place in the world. Johnny's found a cure for more than just his headaches.

19.

Dennis "Spider" Cleg couldn't be less like Johnny Smith—except that, in a few crucial regards, he is. Spider's long boyhood has lasted through middle age, though he lacks Johnny's charm. And like Johnny, Spider is completely alone, and is paralyzed by what's in his own head.

After the opening credits—a series of Rorschach test images made out of the kind of distressed wallpaper you'd see in an under-funded institution or a humble midcentury East End home—the first shot of *Spider* is the film's most action-packed: a train slowly pulling into London's Waterloo Station. The camera tracks forward through the crowd of people rushing toward their next location, parting them by some unseen force. You could (sentimentally, annoyingly) say that this force is cinema itself, but the camera has multiple powers throughout *Spider*, most importantly that of a co-conspirator. At the end of this long, unbroken shot capturing a stream of people comes Spider, a shabbily dressed man who's hunched in a way that doesn't suggest age but severe mental illness. His slow, hesitating movements, prematurely white hair, and indecipherable mumbling confirm our preliminary diagnosis, so it's almost unsurprising when he reaches into his pants and starts digging around. He's reaching for a piece of paper with his destination on it, not his penis, but we're primed to expect the worst of him, and he ultimately delivers on that. But first, we experience the world as he does—more or less, though not always. More than just "experiencing madness," witnessing him reconstructing memories, as well as things he just "knows" happened, we realize that our minds and identities work just the same as his.

Spider has been shipped, unescorted, to a halfway home in the East End from a high-security mental health facility elsewhere in the United Kingdom. It's somewhere out in the country, a place where the most callous among us prefer the mentally ill to reside. Though the time period is never explicitly stated, one can gather from Spider's current age and clues from his childhood memories—as well as the era in which the country, like the United States, started sending mentally ill patients who needed extensive care to cheaper, less specialized facilities—that *Spider* is set in the 1980s. Over the course of the film, Spider revisits the past, sometimes as a boy, at others as a man watching himself as a boy (standing in a corner or a closet), and still other times as a man watching situations he could've never witnessed as a boy. (At one point Spider drinks a pint as he watches his father at a pub—who's also drinking a pint.) As he experiences or re-experiences these events—which, thanks to the representational nature of cinema and the absence of voice-over, can be mistaken as having really taken place—Spider scribbles notes in a cipher only he understands, but still goes to the trouble of hiding his notebook in his new room. Flashing between the past, the "past," and the present—which also has a funny way of shifting into the fabricated—we eventually learn why Spider has been institutionalized for all these years. Believing that his father Bill (Gabriel Byrne) had killed his mother (Miranda Richardson), buried her in their allotment, and replaced her with a cheap sex worker named Yvonne (also played by Miranda Richardson), Spider avenges his mother by gassing Yvonne. However, as the film's concluding moments show, Yvonne was never really there: Spider killed his mother. This revelation comes as he's about to kill this horrible "tart" yet again in her sleep, as Yvonne has now replaced the head caregiver at the halfway house, Mrs. Wilkinson (first played by Lynn Redgrave, then by Miranda Richardson).

Given the nature of human memory, every film has the potential to "change" each time you see it. In *Spider*, the crucial revelation that Spider, not his mean ol' dad, killed his mother, changes your understanding of what you're watching. However, the film is constructed in a manner that, with every rewatch, continuously complicates your perception of the story, putting the viewer inside Spider's head in a way that point-of-view shots alone could never achieve. Yes, Spider is an unreliable narrator. But is this a long-brewing admission of guilt, or is it merely a cyclical occurrence, a mental computer program, which runs and reruns itself every few weeks because the trauma is too great to accept? Has any of this happened at all?

As he's being driven away from the halfway house, away from the places that caused him to realize he—just like William Lee in *Naked Lunch*—accidentally and on purpose killed the person he loved the most, the elder Spider and the younger Spider get into black cars that are similar to the point of being identical. The buildings around Spider are now shot in an ambiguous way that removes any ability to tell if we're in the 1950s or 1980s. The final shot is of the young Spider in the back seat of this car, and the only "witness" to this transformation is Terrence (John Neville), a loquacious, elderly patient who peers down

20.

from a window as Spider/Spider are hauled away. They are one and the same: the older Spider carries with him the memories, beliefs, and paranoid schizophrenia of the boy he once was, and is the same person in a biological sense. Yet the young Spider is also performing the same trick that Yvonne can: supplanting another person physically and mentally, by sheer will alone. Could he ever be the same after realizing that he made this fatal error, assuming this realization hasn't been twisted in some way?

Despite the murkiness that hangs over Spider's life, it's clear why this man with the Samuel Beckett haircut has found himself looming over an elderly nurse while she sleeps, poised to bash her head in with a phallic ball-peen hammer: he not only suffers from schizophrenia, but has a Madonna-Whore complex. Sex and sexual attraction is revolting, which means any woman who isn't a mother is Yvonne, that same damnable whore, and must die. During a flashback to his time at the high-security facility, Spider takes a cheesecake photo out of his tobacco box while eating lunch with his fellow inmates. After covering up the image with his filthy hands, the woman becomes Yvonne yet again.

While this can be attributed in part to the trauma of having his beloved mum not only replaced by another woman, but by one as coarse and uncaring as Yvonne, his murderous hatred also comes from another place. The confusion also arises whenever a woman attempts to control him—taking on a more active, free-thinking role than benevolent caregiver—which is why Mrs. Wilkinson also "becomes" Yvonne. He desires the woman in the photograph, and hates her for making him desire her, her confident look an affront to his power. Sexual freedom, independence, and the refusal to let Spider do whatever he wants are inextricably tied together. His delusion, then, is an extension of the time in which he grew up: women are meant to be compliant and helpful. Rather than defying society's rules, he takes them far too seriously. Even though he often sees himself as a helpless boy, he is an eminent enforcer of order.

The degree of Spider's control—and creativity—is evident in his art. He uses bits of trash he finds on his walks to create giant "webs," which he uses to manipulate his surroundings: locking a door, turning on the gas knob, opening up a cupboard. His notebook, a documentary that's actually an incredible work of fiction, remains obscured to us. As Cronenberg has said in multiple interviews, Spider is the archetype of the artist: he's poor, messy, self-indulgent, and consumed by his need to create. His murder and attempted murder of "Yvonne" are, in a way, a bit of performance art: he must make the same thing, over and over again, until someone understands. But Spider also embodies an artist's greatest fear: nobody understands him or his work. He has no other mode of expression, and is condemned to spend the rest of his life in obscurity—unacknowledged and unheard. Despite being so loyal to society's rules, desperately trying to fit in, society has deemed the only way to deal with someone like Spider is to lock them away, far, far away. Though it's unclear if he'd be happier back at the prison for the criminally insane, it's the only place he can go. No girls allowed.

Crimes of the Future (2022) is another portrait of an artist, one who alternately enjoys and suffers from all that comes with prestige. It's very obviously a self-portrait. Saul Tenser (Viggo Mortensen) is an aging performance artist who specializes in "body art": his body spontaneously—or as some of his fans suggest, subconsciously—grows new organs, which his partner Caprice (Léa Seydoux) tattoos and removes. His influence is so great that the National Organ Registry requires all citizens who sprout neo-organs to tattoo and remove theirs, just like Saul. The N.O.R's goal is to keep humans human: if these extra organs

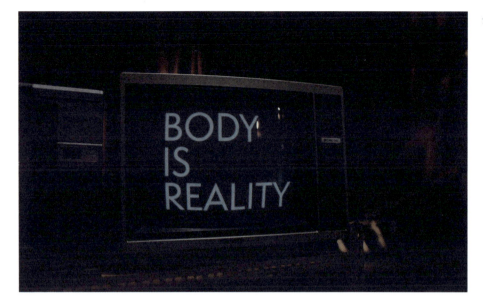

21.

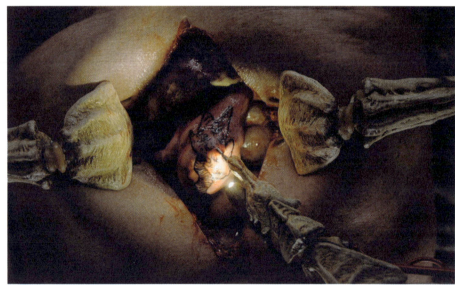

22.

were allowed to remain in bodies, they could lead to further mutations or be passed down through the generations, resulting in something other than human—and therefore something ungovernable. Unbeknownst to Caprice, Saul also works as an undercover agent, infiltrating subversive groups that dabble in Inner Beauty Pageants and modifying their bodies so that they can eat plastic and other industrial byproducts. The leader of the latter commune, Lang Dotrice (Scott Speedman), seeks out Saul and proposes a concept for Saul's next show: a live autopsy of Lang's son, Brecken (Sotiris Siozos), who was born with the ability to digest plastic. The show goes on as planned, but once Caprice and Saul open up the boy, it becomes clear that Brecken's body was posthumously altered. In his last meeting with his police contact, Detective Cope (Welket Bungué), it is confirmed that the government hacked Brecken up to suppress the plastic-eaters' movement. Saul, now committed to the plastic-eaters' cause, leaves early. In the film's final scene, Saul eats one of the plastic bars the commune had been making, and feels relief he's waited a lifetime to experience.

Despite its deeply self-referential nature, *Crimes of the Future* is never cloying. Saul is Cronenberg himself, performance art is cinema, "body art" is "body horror" (the questionable subgenre Cronenberg supposedly invented), the National Organ Registry stands in for TIFF and Telefilm Canada, and Timlin (Kristen Stewart) and Wippet

(Don McKellar), the jittery geeks who work at the NOR, are a heady mix of film fans and people who work in film (critics, archivists, programmers, publicists, or whatever). However, the way in which these parallels are drawn—and Saul's succinctly croaked objections to the various interpretations of his work, the state of performance art, and to the state of the world—are commentaries that are just as applicable in our reality as they are in the film's. The government's endeavors to control both art and body are meant to protect those who are already powerful, going so far as to deny nature and very clear biological warnings. Lang is dangerous not because he modifies his body, but because he recognizes the need to feed on our own industrial waste. It's not a government agent who puts a bullet through his head as he weeps following Brecken's autopsy, essentially losing his son twice, but two repairwomen/assassins for LifeFormWare, the company that manufactures special beds and eating chairs for those who suffer from pain while sleeping or eating. Without the myth of a singular form of biological normality, LifeFormWare would go out of business. The women, who'd previously murdered a surgeon who was coordinating an Inner Beauty Pageant and left him in one of their Breakfaster chairs, kick Lang's lifeless body after they put drills in the back of his skull. Nobody can be allowed to imagine a world without an alternative to capitalism, either.

And then there's Saul. Rather than a vibrant living legend who's palling around with fellow luminaries or giving self-important talks to aspiring performance artists, Saul is a feeble old man who's in constant, crippling agony. He rarely ventures out, and when he does, he wears an all-black version of a Renaissance-era jester's costume. This suit—and Saul's demeanor—evokes Jan Matejko's painting *Stańczyk* (1862), which depicts the famous Polish court jester Stańczyk solemnly gazing at the floor in a darkened room while a royal ball rages in the background. Stańczyk, who may or may not have existed, is a powerful Polish cultural figure, as it was said his accessible yet intelligent satire commented upon the past, present, and future. (So Stańczyk was blasting through the high/low dichotomy several hundred years before postmodernism.) This, of course, also serves as an apt description of a film director who used his popular (but never too popular) films to explore philosophy, science, technology, sex, and psychoanalysis, and very often tapped into something prescient. Even if Stańczyk wasn't the inspiration, Saul's outerwear can also be thought of as an inverted version of the Mantles' bright red surgical gear in *Dead Ringers*; Beverly also contemplated inner beauty pageants. (The number of references to Cronenberg's other films in *Crimes of the Future* could fill several pages—Brecken's body is kept in a floor freezer, just like Soyka's body in *Eastern Promises*, and Viggo Mortensen's character opens both of them!—but simply taking inventory of them is more of a Timlin thing.)

When he's out and about, Saul barely moves, usually assuming a squatting position, his face covered. He doesn't want to be stopped; he just wants to retain a bit of normalcy and keep his life as quiet as possible. In short, he has humility. Where this comes from is evident in his surname: Tenser. One of the grosser—and funnier—sequences in *Crimes of the Future* involves a performer who can only be known as "the Ear Man": a figure who's covered in artificial ears with his eyes and mouth stitched shut. "It is time to stop seeing," an authoritative male voice booms over the venue's sound system as the artist's lips are sewn together. "It is time to stop speaking. It is time to listen." As soon as the voice stops, techno music blares and the Ear Man launches into an impassioned modernist dance solo.

The entire spectacle is self-important, meaningless provocation. However, in the context of the film, this performance can be read several ways. The voice's timbre and corny commands, which lead into a sudden burst of frenetic action, are highly reminiscent of a nineties movie trailer. A trailer is fluff, only the best bits of an otherwise indistinguishable two-hour outing; the voice in the trailer is meant to bolster the sense of gravity in a thriller or drama (or be a sassy sounding board for jokes in a comedy), and underscore the ad's basic imperative: go see this piece of shit right now! But what about the message, which seems to be "sit your ass down and listen, straight cis white man"? Rather than

a condemnation of such political efforts, it's proven to be false allyship: another attendee informs Saul, who's been crouching in a corner, that the extra ears don't even work—they can't hear. Thus, this idiot is just making himself the center of attention, and isn't actually interested in doing any extra listening.

Yet there's one more level to go down regarding the Ear Man. The pars tensa is part of the eardrum (or tympanic membrane), specifically the tense part of it. The eardrum is the barrier between the outer and inner ear; it's what absorbs sound and then passes the vibrations on to bone deeper in the skull, making it a crucial component of hearing. Thus, this connects Saul Tenser to the Ear Man in a way that goes beyond the two men simply working in the same medium: Saul is also an ear man. (His work as an undercover agent, keeping his ear to the ground so to speak, makes him a listener, not a talker.) Saul's distaste for the performance therefore comes not only from its crudeness, but from recognizing the crappy efforts of his younger self. (This naturally begs the question: Which terrible late-nineties horror film director was Cronenberg thinking of when he penned this scene? Or was it merely a bad trend?) Later, Detective Cope, a certifiable philistine, tells Saul that he heard the Ear Man's show was "good" and "very disturbing." Saul witheringly responds, "It was okay. If you like escapist propaganda."

Despite his double life, Saul doesn't choose to escape. In a world without physical pain, feeling's role as a way out of obsessional thinking comes into sharper focus. As Wippet reminds us early on, pain is an evolutionary necessity: knowing that it hurts to burn your hand keeps your fingers away from an open flame. The world of the future has, for reasons unknown, become desensitized to or evolved past it. And though Saul may not be able to put into words the physical pain he experiences, he expresses it (and its liberatory potential) through his art—particularly at the Brecken autopsy. Caprice, who is unsettled by the prospect of doing the autopsy from the start, loses it once Brecken's body is opened, revealing the "hack job" done on his insides. (As Cope later explains, it was Timlin, inspired by Caprice, who made the alterations—perhaps she's having her own Ear Man moment.) Caprice's voice quavers as the audience gasps: "So we see that the crudeness and the desperation and the ugliness of the world has seeped inside even the youngest and most beautiful. And we see that the world is killing our children from the inside out ... And we know now why we'll have a second autopsy, and a third." Here is genuine shock. Here is genuine provocation. Here is a roomful of people feeling that something here is grievously wrong. While Brecken's autopsy doesn't serve as the great unveiling that his father had hoped it would, it still becomes a moment of coming together beyond the boundaries of witnessing a spectacle.

And, in the end, Saul chooses not to escape from who he is. After spending yet another sleepless night in his special bed and a frustrating morning attempting to eat in his special chair, he decides to try to eat one of Lang's special plastic bars. Caprice films him taking the leap of faith with a small ring camera. (The bars are fatal unless you've had the necessary surgeries to digest plastic.) And yet, it proves to be the right decision. After taking a bite, Saul begins to cry. Finally, he can eat—one of the basic things an organism does—without gagging or choking. Despite his foresight and intelligence, it turns out that his body wasn't betraying him. The film ends with Saul faintly smiling beatifically, almost like Joan on the stand in Carl Dreyer's *The Passion of Joan of Arc*. Even the unreligious can experience transcendence from the mundane.

23.

viii.
TRANSFORMATION

VIDEODROME [1983]

EXISTENZ [1999]

WHAT IS TRANSFORMATION?

Transformation is a deceptively straightforward concept in analytical psychology. (It certainly confused the hell out of me.) This sublime triumph of the self, the unified whole of that which is conscious and unconscious within the psyche, is a feat few achieve. As M. Esther Harding, a student of Jung's, explains, it exists outside the bounds of conventional morality, religion, and cultural ideals, and puts one into "a right relation to the unknown and unseen powers of the spiritual or psychic world." This sounds like woo-woo bullshit. But the feeling of rightness that emanates from certain people who have achieved transformation, an intangible self-assuredness and ease of being, is also undeniably real. You've absolutely felt it in others. Individuation is one variety of transformation, which is achieving a completeness of the psyche. The process of transformation can be expressed through three component symbols: the circle, the mandala, and the hermetic vessel. Again, this is extremely confusing. A mandala is a circle. Why would Jung invoke the pseudoscience of alchemy, ancient attempts to transform junk into gold that mostly resulted in accidental poisonings?

The apparent strangeness and counterintuitiveness of these steps/symbols comes in part from how divorced transformation is from traditional notions of self-improvement. Consider the Abrahamic religions' notion of cutting off the "bad part" of yourself, physically or mentally. Beverly Mantle in *Dead Ringers*, who, mind hazed by drugs, does both as he carves up his identical twin Elliot in the hopes of finally separating them once and for all, only to destroy himself in the process. The circle represents fully understanding the distinction between what is and is not the self. It requires the individual to bring into consciousness previously unconscious components of themselves. The central struggle of *Dead Ringers*—the act of distinguishing between the I, not-I, and projections, such as the anima/animus/animum—shows that this is incredibly difficult, even for the highly intelligent. The mandala, as Harding explains, is the bringing together of those opposing forces within the self, containing them, and then bringing them together in a way that maintains their distinctiveness. Think of the end of *Scanners*, where, after self-immolating, Cameron Vale defeats his murderous older brother Darryl Revok and fuses with him; their new body retains elements of both men. Finally, there's the stage represented by the hermetic vessel. Jung wrote at length on how depth psychology and the individuation process was akin to alchemy: not a desire for a Midas touch, but rather the concept, the historical act, and the philosophical school of thought. Alchemy, the Hermetic Art, was not simply transforming something into gold; rather, it was divine knowledge, ascertained through experimentation, analogic symbols, and practices intentionally kept secret amongst practitioners. In the most practical sense, alchemy required one to know what kind of container could hold such intense pressure required for a transformation, and prevent any seemingly unrelated materials, such as smoke, from escaping. It is in this stage when, within a secured psychic

24. After watching a tape sent from the office of Brian O'Blivion—in which O'Blivion is strangled to death by a masked executioner, who turns out to be Nicki—Max desires to physically merge with television.

25. Max's new orifice. Barry Convex inserts a cassette which orders Max to kill his partners and hand over Channel 83 to "us." Max retrieves the handgun he'd previously stored in his stomach and goes on a rampage.

26. The giving anima: Nicki Brand (Deborah Harry) is down to be tied up and whipped or do the whipping herself.

27. The special at the Chinese restaurant: the two-headed amphibian Allegra saw at the gas station. Ted experiences a "genuine game urge" to wolf it down, revealing the bone gun.

28. A mutant amphibian splashes around one of the breeding pools in the back of the Chinese restaurant. Its mutability is not unlike our own.

29. Cronenberg's satirical depiction of modern immersive gaming as a leisure and pleasure activity extends to throbbing, glowing consoles that resemble sex toys.

30. A young Jude Law reveals hidden depths as wide-eyed intern-turned-corporate raider Ted Pikul, his performance echoing the layered narrative of *eXistenZ*.

31. Cronenberg's final gift to the audience in *eXistenZ*: Heidegger's "being-towards-death."

container, a person who has done the immense work of reconciling their component parts can then begin wrangling and gaining control of the nonpersonal elements of their psyche. *The Fly*'s meek scientist Seth Brundle fails horribly at this. After entering the crucible of the telepod, neither his body nor his mind can withstand reconciling the opposing elements of his being. What he believes to be a form of purification, of advancement, is quite the opposite.

You may be thinking that this all sounds like drivel. Its relationship to cinema is opaque at best. It kinda seems more like a David Lynch thing.

But he's not the only director who's catching the big fish. *Videodrome* and *eXistenz*, whose protagonists fight against reality-bending technological forces, ones that accept and expand upon the assumptions of anti-violence, anti-pornography, and anti-entertainment crusaders, and turn the story and the medium back on itself. Their self-reflexive plots demonstrate the expansive, mystical, and fundamentally unknowable aspects of transformation. Like parts of the individuation process, whereby we integrate different components of the psyche into our consciousness, transformation requires temporary or persistent loss of control—which is evident in these films. Across cultures, there exist myths about dragon-slayers, who triumph over a primordial force that threatens society as a whole. Some of these heroes are part wyvern themselves, which gives them the ability to triumph where others have failed. This is the case with *Videodrome*'s Max Renn, an unabashed smut-peddler who, like the malicious *Videodrome* signal, exclusively broadcasts softcore porn and violent garbage on the TV channel he co-owns. When the reality-bending, all-encompassing *Videodrome* signal calls to and attempts to subsume him, he is able to fight back. In other fables about those who slay the dragon, the heroes consume the blood or heart of the dead beast and gain special powers, again setting them apart from the rest of humanity. The protagonists of *eXistenz*, anti-game zealots Allegra Geller and Ted Pikul, shape the nested realities of a game they're playing in order to assassinate a star game creator. By fusing opposing components of their surroundings (mutant amphibians that become game pods) and their psyches (a skin-flick master growing a vagina on his stomach), they transform physically and psychically, mastering what is and is not a part of them. Although these films seem to end with violent deaths, they are ultimately hopeful. Their narratives raise questions about the nature of what we know, or what we think we know. They've tapped into something powerful, like the cathode ray, the collective unconscious, other unknowable parts of the psychic realm, and mastered them. They've transcended. And that we can't pinpoint exactly where they've gone is exactly the point. The abrupt cut to black, so often read as death, is not the end, but the end of possible representation.

But what if it is death? On an episode of *Face to Face*, shot at his home, the Bollingen Tower, in 1959, Jung was asked whether he believed in life after death. Jung stated that death, which we can empirically know nothing about, could also be such a transformation: "There are these peculiar faculties of the psyche, that aren't entirely confined to space and time. You can have dreams or visions of the future, you can see around the corners . . . only ignorance denies these facts. It's quite evident that these do exist, and have always existed. These facts show that the psyche, in part at least, is not dependent upon these confinements. And then what? If the psyche is not under that obligation to live in time and space alone—and obviously it doesn't—then to that extent, the psyche is not submitted to those laws. . . . And that means a psychical existence beyond time and space."

ON *VIDEODROME* AND *EXISTENZ*

Consciousness is what modern, supposedly advanced societies demand we exclusively center our lives on. If we focus hard enough, and put our mind to use in the right way, we will maximize productivity and, depending on which stage of life we're in, get better grades, make more money, produce more content. Just produce more of whatever it is you produce. Few among us worry about a dreamless night. An unproductive day, however, is cause for serious self-recrimination. *Videodrome* excoriates our narrow focus on conscious experience.

It also probably would've been a better place to begin this book. An exemplar of Cronenberg's thematic concerns, dramaturgy, and visual style, the film also serves as a synecdoche for the writer/director's career. What was once a profane cult hit has not simply moved into the mainstream, but become a sign of refined taste. It's cinematic alchemy.

Videodrome begins when Bridey James (Julie Khaner) instructs Max Renn (James Woods), snug as a bug within his dark, filthy apartment, to "slowly, painfully ease yourself back into consciousness." Bridey, who self-describes as his Girl Friday (a professional superego), assures Max that she's not a dream. If you choose to believe her, the film approximately begins when Max reaches consciousness—that nameless experience we all share but cannot properly define.

And if Bridey isn't a dream? It's quite possible that Max dreamed of money or peach-shaped asses or other aspects of work before being exposed to the *Videodrome* signal, what appears as a live torture and execution TV show but is actually a weapon designed to eliminate North American perverts and art-house film fans. We'll never be certain what is or is not real, as we're bound to Max's perspective throughout the film. He's in every scene, a quick-witted detective who's still always one step behind. The visions and dreams that intrude on his conscious experience are horrible to him because, as a modern man, he has no schema for dealing with them. This is often understood as a sign of our hopelessness in the face of technology that we don't fully understand—a late capitalist subject subsumed by the idiot box. Yet, as the film progresses, Max not only learns to navigate hallucinations, but to use them to work against the dark forces behind *Videodrome*. When Harlan, a video pirate and alt-right 8kun user avant la lettre, attempts to insert a new tape into Max's stomach, Max turns Harlan's hand into a pipe bomb and blows him up—a reversal of fortune that would make the Unabomber proud. Later, Max doesn't simply shoot Barry Convex, a businessman and intelligence agent who's been testing out *Videodrome* on Max, but renders him a burbling pile of goo, and ruins the moronic, bourgeois pageantry of Spectacular Optical's "Medici Line." It's not simply revenge but revolution. Max pierces the heart of propriety and order in a way that Civic TV, the softcore porno station he co-owns, never could. Max embraces his true darkness to defeat the shadow of the American Century: a CIA cutout that, as Barry proudly proclaims, makes "inexpensive glasses for the Third World, missile guidance systems for NATO, and *Videodrome*."

So where does Max "go" at the end of the film, when angelic Nicki Brand (played by Debbie Harry) appears to Max in a derelict boat on a Toronto dockside and instructs him not to be afraid to let his body die? As in the beginning of the film, Max seems to obey the command of the woman on the screen before him. The screen goes black before we hear the sound of a gunshot. But Max, who has ceased identifying with his persona of unrepentant smut peddler and gains power over the other parts of the self—his shadow, the feminine (of Nicki, of a stomach vagina), a sense of justness (his horror at Nicki's death, of the killings he's perpetrated under *Videodrome*'s sway), and his personal and the collective unconscious—is transformed into something else, something that is no longer limited by consciousness and the physical. He's gone beyond the grasps of what our reality can handle, and proceeds to the video arena to continue the battle. (Arenas more often than not resemble mandalas: squares contained within circles, circles within circles.) While the Hollyweird Ballards from *Crash* miss orgiastic mutilation in a car crash by a hair, Max actually becomes the new flesh. He's no longer physically unrecognizable, but he's entirely unknowable.

What makes Max so different? Returning to that opening scene: rather than falling asleep to the sound of the television, Max is awoken by it. The TV turns him on, not the other way around. This juvenile double entendre is the point—Max is not only a professional chauvinist, but a kind of inverted man in all respects. He eats the crusty remnants of last night's pizza for breakfast. His business meetings take place at 6:30 AM in seedy hotel rooms instead of inside an office between 9 and 5. In this respect, he's an animal who merely acts on impulse, making him more susceptible to influence. As Masha (Lynne Gorman), a sexy, Eastern European GILF who works as producer and distributor in the international softcore TV racket, tells him, Max has no philosophy—unlike *Videodrome*, a plotless marathon of torture and death set inside an offal-pink, windowless room. He's someone who openly deals in sexual desires that others seek to hide from the world, but, because his job is to be led around by his dick, his problems ultimately arise from getting led around by his dick. (Put another way: "death by chocolate.") It's in everything he doesn't do, and everything he does. The test pattern of Max's ironically named Civic TV— an illustrated image of a large, smiling man sitting in bed with a small TV set resting in his crotch—underscores this *symbiotic*, not symbolic, relationship. This television isn't just an orgone accumulator; it's replaced this man's cock entirely. A soothing male voice intones, "Civic TV: the one you take to bed with you."

Of course, this cartoon is a small detail. Yet it's a delicate stitch in a film whose fabric is made up of the physical connection between technology television and the body, one that takes a step beyond Marshall McLuhan's notion that technology is an extension of the human mind, sex organs, and appendages. This is where *Videodrome*'s horror lies. It's not simply that this technology has the ability to physically transform and control us, giving a pornographer like Max a vagina in his stomach in some goofy "well, how do *you* like it?" role reversal. Rather, the horror comes from the reality that TV has possessed this ability for its entire existence, and we haven't noticed because we've been stuck in some gooey mental state between sleeping and cumming. As Brian O'Blivion, a media prophet who's a cross between McLuhan and Sigmund Freud, explains on *The Rena King Show*: "The television screen is the retina of the mind's eye. Therefore, the television screen is

24.

part of the physical structure of the brain. Therefore, whatever appears on the television screen emerges as raw experience for those who watch it." This statement frames common warnings about television's dangers as a positive development: sitting too closely to the TV will hurt your eyes, representing instances of weird sex or heinous violence are, necessarily, endorsements and will lead to copycat acts. The film bears both of these assertions out when, in one of *Videodrome*'s most iconic scenes, Max buries his face in the heaving, stretching TV screen with Nicki's lips on it, not penetrating its skin but being subsumed by it; a make-out session during his reverie that ends with the set exploding and discharging actual viscera. This notion of being somehow damaged or blunted by watching television is nothing new, a belief shared across the political spectrum. These gripes are inevitably extended to new televisual technologies, such as TikTok, which is mostly evil because it's made by a Chinese company, but also because the infinite scroll of its interface is somehow more addictive and deleterious than any other social media company.

The specifics of TikTok's "badness" speak to many different fears—many of which are present in *M. Butterfly*'s unflinching dissection of Orientalism. But the recurrent paranoia of invasion by technology taps into something deeper. It's not merely the act of stopping and watching something—for pleasure, or boredom, or exhaustion, or horniness, or with belief that it's actually good—and then being taken in and deranged. In 1919, Victor Tausk, a psychoanalyst whom Sigmund Freud anointed as his successor after cutting Jung off (only to later lose the crown), published a paper on the phenomenon of what he termed "influencing machines" among paranoid schizophrenics. The afflicted believed that these machines were the source of all of their persecution and suffering; many said that their influencing machine had the ability to implant and remove memories, ideas, images, and feelings through invisible means, either man-made (X-rays, radio waves) or magical. One patient described his multipurpose torture device as "a magnet as well as a gun." Unsurprisingly, influencing machines were always incredibly technically complex and had extreme influence over the "inventor's" sexual desires. "All the discoveries of mankind are regarded as inadequate to explain the marvelous powers of this machine," Tausk wrote. In his analysis, Tausk argued that these devices were narcissistic projections, an external explanation of their loss of agency, built by the patient as they slowly lost touch with reality. (As depicted in *Scanners*, part of the experience of schizophrenia can be understood as losing the boundary between self and the outside world.) While some patients believed that their doppelgangers were operating the machine that was tormenting them, Tausk proposed that the machines themselves were their actual doubles: a mechanical, mystical, and all-powerful device. In a more nihilistic view, this can be understood as what happens to Max, the childish pornographer who fuses with various bits of technology (a tape, a television, a gun) and then leaves his body behind at the film's conclusion. But even if it's all a paranoid delusion, and *Videodrome* is just something built by Max's diseased mind, his engagement with this wild unconscious, and his eventual control over it (rejecting *Videodrome*'s programming), suggests some hope. He becomes the dragon and all its darkness in order to achieve justice.

eXistenZ, alternately an advertisement for the joys of anal sex and a warning about the dangers of blind technological optimism, has many parallels with its CRT predecessor. Cronenberg's first original screenplay since *Videodrome*, *eXistenZ*'s elliptical, matryoshka-like narrative structure, legitimately exciting action and sex-ish sequences, and ambiguity make it an equally prescient statement on technology.

DAVID CRONENBERG: CLINICAL TRIALS

174

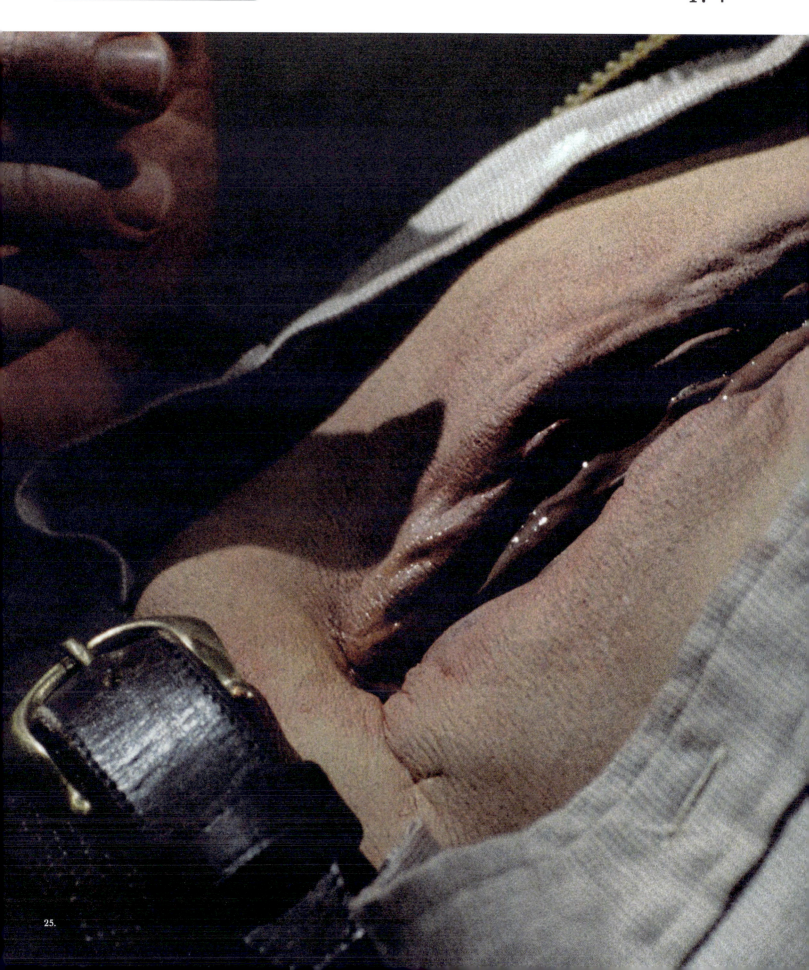

25.

26.

DAVID CRONENBERG: CLINICAL TRIALS

The most efficacious summary of *eXistenZ* begins with its final shot: Allegra Geller (Jennifer Jason Leigh) and Ted Pikul (Jude Law) stand with their guns pointed directly at the camera. They're part of the Realist underground, and have managed to get into a pre-release test run of a new immersive virtual reality game, tranCendenZ by PilgrImage. They've just killed the game's creator, the star designer Yevgeny Nourish (Don McKellar). Now that this deformer of reality is dead, they're aiming their guns at a fellow participant, who stops staring at his portable device, gets out of his seat, and nervously asks, "Is this still part of the game?" This poor man is right to ask, even if he proves Allegra and Ted's point about the dangers of recreationally separating oneself from one's body. *eXistenZ*, and the game that this focus group have been playing, begins with Allegra as a star game designer who's attacked by a Realist at a special preview of her latest immersive video game, eXistenZ. Ted is the dozy, hapless marketing intern who tags along on a quest to save her precious creation. Though Allegra and Ted remain committed to their roles, they both manage to lay bare the problems with abandoning oneself to technology: Allegra plays the feckless, selfish lover of destruction and chaos, while Ted prudishly resists to a point (espousing Heideggerian gripes along the way), and inevitably pays a price for giving in to Allegra's demands. The characters and the technology that they use, as well as the film's deconstruction of our notion of time and ontology, and constant folding back onto itself, represent transformation.

Cronenberg, a lifelong lover of gadgets, identifies that this desire to explore and break free from consciousness, to extend ourselves, runs throughout human history. *eXistenZ*'s opening credits emulate cave drawings, which are understood as proof of humanity's evolutionary split from other primates, the first examples of a higher cognitive function. Of course, the exact function(s) of these paintings in their respective ancient societies are lost to time. Consider "The Sorcerer," a drawing found in Trois-Frères, Ariège, France. The figure—a humanoid figure with deer antlers and a tail—can be interpreted as being part of a religious ritual, a representation of a fantasy, or simply entertainment. Or all three at once. By firelight, some cave drawings move—an early precursor to film; combined with psychedelic plants, they could become immersive in a way that even the most innovative 3D movies can only faintly imitate. Apart from their culturally distinct characteristics, cave drawings also represent a break from material reality. These early humans were compelled to create something more than the world they saw around them, and these drawings offered a way to transcend and transform. By opening *eXistenZ* in this manner, Cronenberg points out that we've been at the nexus of art, entertainment, and reality-bending, heightening our self-representation, for a long time. Despite its seeming sophistication, virtual reality is an extension of our ongoing desire to do exactly that.

Games, just like art, are also universal and have been a constant throughout human history. They not only help us build skills—teamwork, strategy, etc.—but they also offer us a chance to engage with our shadow. We can be malicious, angry, and selfish in a playful, safe way. In the same volume in which McLuhan wrote that technology is an extension of the human body and mind, he argued that games—long before gamer chairs and video poker were destroying brains, postures, and bank accounts—are "a machine that can get into action only if the players consent to become puppets for a time . . . for individualist Western man, much of his 'adjustment' to society has the character of a personal surrender to the collective demands. Our games help both to teach us this kind of adjustment and also to provide a release from it." In order to fire up her game pod (which has the only copy of eXistenZ on it) and see if her game was damaged in the attempt on her life, Allegra has to play with someone friendly. She asks Ted twice, "Are you friendly, or are you not?" This repetition is not unlike the repetition of dialogue Ted and Allegra find in her game: the NPCs (who later turn out to be real people) they encounter get stuck in loops, waiting for one of them to say the right game line. Knowing what to say is made more

27.

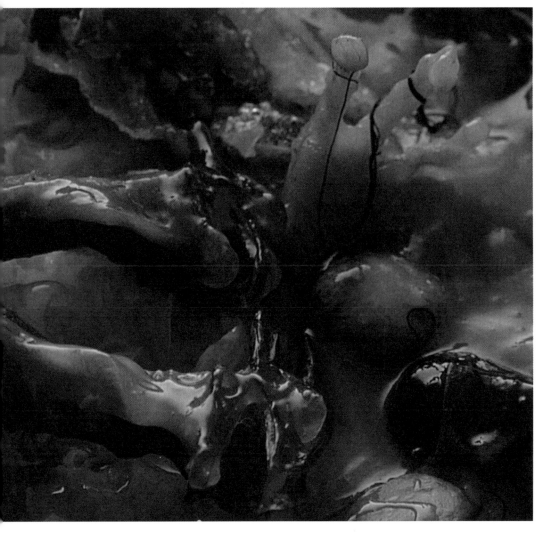

complicated by virtue of the fact that Allegra's game is essentially like life, as it begins at a video game store where they choose to play the game Trout Farm. (Other titles at the store include Hit By a Car, no doubt a tongue-in-cheek reference to *Crash*.) At this point, the viewer of the film *eXistenZ* is at least three layers of unreality deep: the outermost being tranCendenZ, then eXistenZ, then Trout Farm. As Ted struggles to play the latter, "I don't know what's going on. We're both stumbling around together in this unformed world, whose rules and objectives are largely unknown, seemingly indecipherable or even possibly nonexistent, always on the verge of being killed by forces that we don't understand."

Allegra, who's always dressed to the nines, flirtily tells Ted he's just got to get used to it. Like Nicki in *Videodrome*, Allegra is the strong, sexually liberated guide to the world of *eXistenZ* (the film) and eXistenZ (the game). At many points, she's in total control, pushing Ted to open up both physically and mentally. Allegra gifts him with the pleasure and burden of being penetrated, and repeatedly, gleefully jams penis-like objects inside his new, second asshole, a universal bioport, which is located on his lower back, slightly above his first anus. Like Nicki, she shows Ted that there's more to life than predictable, missionary-style sex, inserting a bejeweled dildo (or butt plug) into his new hole to fight an infection. (For anyone who knows nerds who are also into Lifestyle, this dynamic should be familiar: those who play Dungeons and Dragons also like to play sexually.) Though Ted envisions himself as Allegra's archetypal male protector, she's the one who's saving him from a life—sexual and otherwise—prescribed by patriarchal Western culture.

28.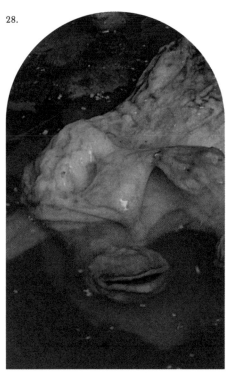

Yet, also like Nicki, Allegra's confident familiarity with the world she initiates Ted into is sometimes overtaken by the realities of that world. Allegra is in constant danger, as is her precious creation, eXistenZ. Ted isn't entirely unhelpful, such as when he gives into the game urge to gobble up a questionable "special" at a Chinese restaurant, uncovering a tooth gun, one identical to the one the Realist threatened Allegra with outside of the game. The satirically xenophobic Chinese restaurant—strange, disgusting food that's unfamiliar to the Western palette—represents the fears and promise of the East, which is at once totally incompetent and poised to subsume us. Similarly, the odd, thick accents of the alternately helpful and harmful figures they encounter along the way—Kiri Vinokur (Ian Holm), Allegra's mentor who lets the pair crash at his chalet; D'Arcy Nader (Robert Silverman), a proprietor of a video game store; and Yevgeny's character, a factory worker who claims to be a real Realist—signal these conflicted feelings about the broadness of the West's fascination with the East. Meanwhile, Ted's willingness to submit to Allegra's whims alternately save and endanger both of them. It's a crapshoot, another lovely idiom derived from the urge to game.

29.

The special—a two-headed mutant amphibian, caught in the stagnant waters behind the restaurant—is more than it seems, not only in the virtual world but in reality. It's the same breed of creature Allegra encounters at the Country Gas Station, where Ted is fitted with his first, unregistered bioport by the grinning bumpkin Gas (Willem Dafoe). (Country Gas Station is at once reminiscent of corny locations in games and actual corny North American chains, familiar to anyone who's eaten at Country Kitchen, Texas Steakhouse, or any number of shitty fifties-style diners.) Allegra caresses the surfaces of the gas station and sniffs the pumps, seeming to revel in the world of the game she may or may not be in. And then, in this reverie, comes the two-headed mutant. In alchemical terms, this mutant represents the final stage of alchemy: Rebis, a Latin term that means double matter. The Rebis is frequently represented as a divine hermaphrodite, the final product of having undergone putrefaction and purification. It literalizes what Allegra and Ted are: two heads, united by a singular purpose. Possessing male and female elements, this strange, beautiful creature signifies that unification of all things. And, inside Allegra's game, it is from other mutant amphibians that all game pods abound, the devices that allow humans to access another, fantastical plane of existence. As Yevgeny's character in Trout Farm says, "Seems like most everything used to be something else, yes?"

Allegra's game pod—fleshy, full of blood, is somewhere between a placenta and external sex organ. (Allegra and Ted are inevitably splayed on beds, very close to each other, as they play or try to play eXistenZ.) In this world, players connect their ports (which, again, are clearly anuses) to their bodies via umby cords. The name (and look) is clearly a play on umbilical cord, as the player is the game pod's battery, literally feeding off of them. Inside eXistenZ, technology and biology have entirely fused; when Allegra and Ted emerge into the "real world," they're wearing bright blue plastic headsets and using handheld controllers. A more conservative reading of this big reveal would be that flesh will inevitably be replaced by technology; it's just the way of the world, and the Realists are wrong.

However, it's important to remember that neither the characters nor we the audience are done stepping out of the narrative just yet. Ted and Allegra's killing spree takes place without any headgear, which implies that they aren't playing a game and are actually killing people. However, given the insane barrage of hackneyed twists at the end of tranCendenZ, and the continuation of the anti-game theme, the man who wonders if he's still in the game is right to do so. But the film *eXistenZ* ends with Allegra and Ted glaring at us, the audience, and we're left with our own devices: our totally organic minds. Our interfacing with technology has ended, and we must now go out and play the game of life— one not unlike Allegra's creation. This confused man stands in for us, the audience—one who's presumably spent years watching (or playing) equally gory and violent nonsense.

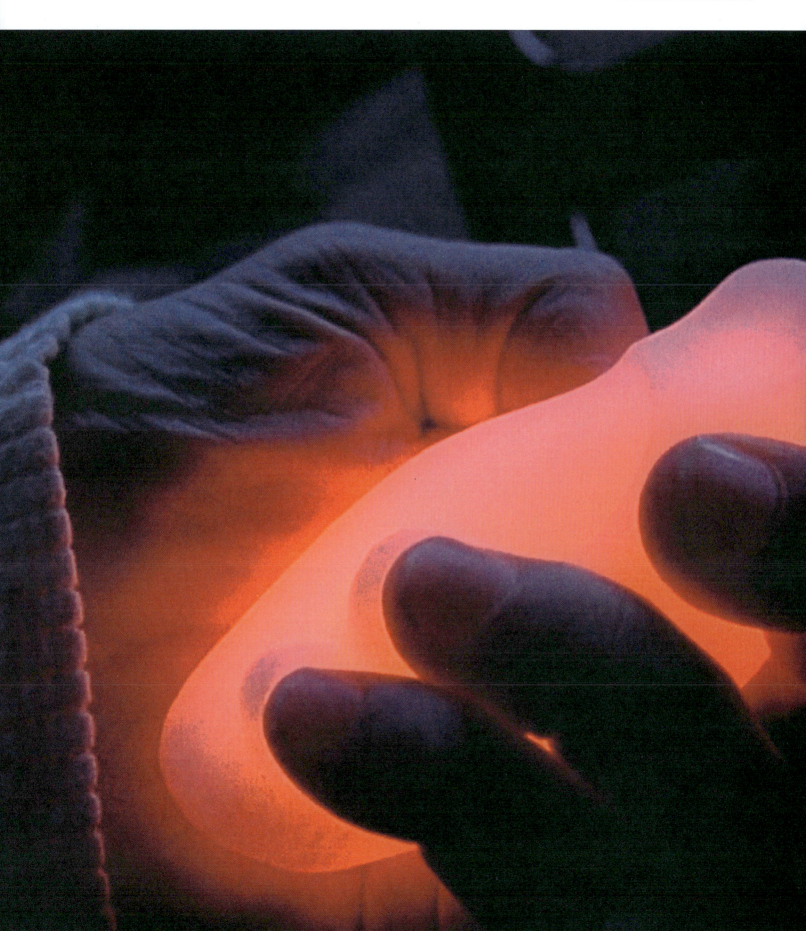

DAVID CRONENBERG: CLINICAL TRIALS

180

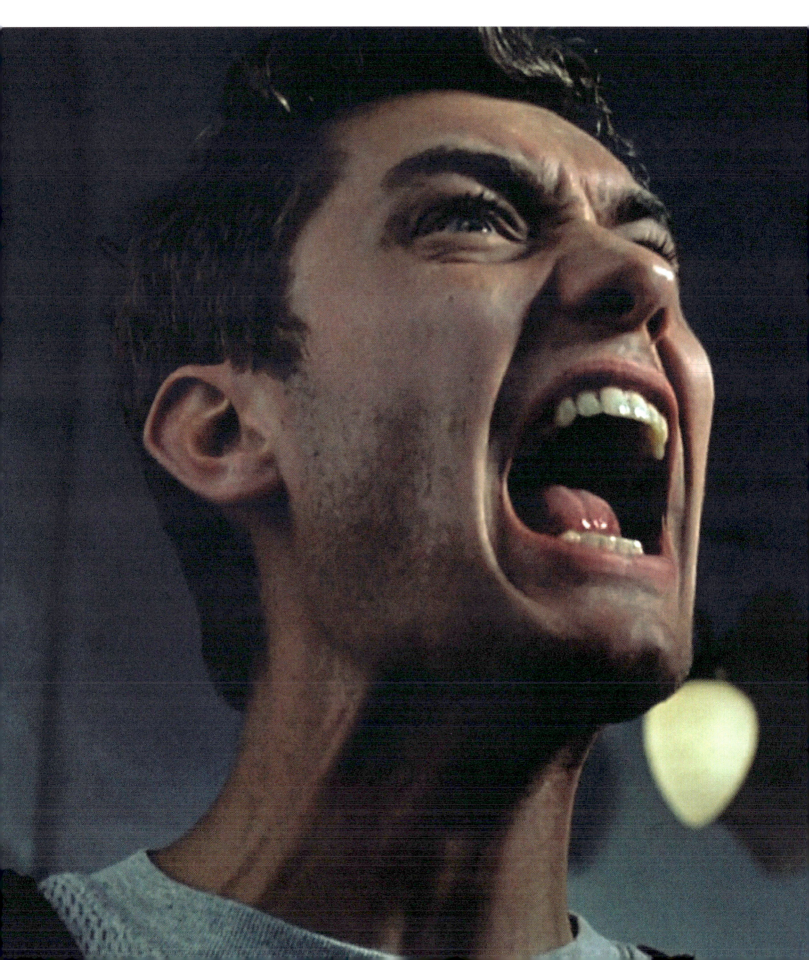

After Allegra and Ted murder our surrogate, who's left for us to be? We've been similarly strung along, allowed to indulge in alternately cliché and realistic violence and explosions. We've been entertained, just like this man, and now that entertainment is at its end. Drawing attention to these parallels jolts us awake in our seats, making us aware that we too have been sitting, putting our life on pause. Though Cronenberg demonstrates throughout his filmography that technology and its excesses are inevitable, it doesn't have to replace everything about us if we don't want it to.

And, once we glimpse the conditions of this pre-release playthrough of tranCendenZ, we see that Allegra and Ted might have a point. This isn't a love letter to cinema; it's hate mail. PilgrImage, a corporation run by people who create nothing yet insist on using their name in every mention of the game Yevgeny made, cares nothing about art but does the bottom line. And then there are the idiots who played it. Each one brought their own expectations to this experience, and though they seemed to enjoy the ride, they delivered facile thumbs-up/thumbs-down reactions to what would be considered a vast, transcendental experience. D'Arcy Nader's first reaction to the time-bending potential of tranCendenZ—where twenty minutes feels like days—is to say, "Just think about it, man. If you stayed your whole life in the game world, you could live about, uh, 500 years." (Allegra reaches for Ted's hand as he says this, perhaps to squeeze away her disgust as couples often do.) After a few more weak jokes, the assembled players almost immediately begin fucking around on their handheld devices, eager to be plugged into something else. By contrast, Allegra and Ted's reaction, which is to murder the game's creator, the "greatest deformer of reality," is more nuanced. The couple have not simply played the game correctly, but played a game in real life: they successfully deceived the press team behind the game's developers and smuggled in real guns—not a tooth gun—with the help of their giant dog. The film concludes shortly after they have achieved what they believe to be their ultimate purpose. After killing Yevgeny, they've become heroes, at least in their minds. And by shooting the ungrateful, unthinking test audience, they might've become heroes to artists, too.

30.

31.

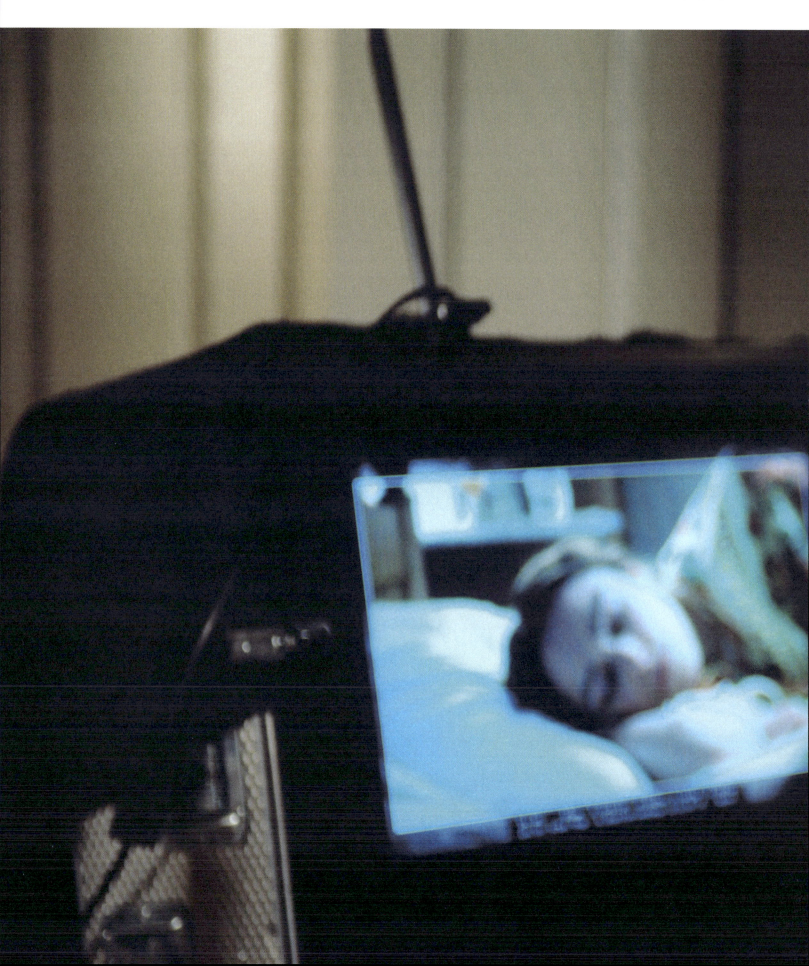

Interviews

CAROL SPIER
Production Designer & Art Director

HOWARD SHORE
Composer

SIR CHRISTOPHER HAMPTON
Playwright & Screenwriter

JEREMY THOMAS
Producer

PETER SUSCHITZKY
Cinematographer

Production Designer & Art Director
CAROL SPIER

It's hard to tabulate just how much Canadian production designer Carol Spier has contributed to the concept of what a David Cronenberg film both looks and feels like. Her work comprises a sense of precision, whether that means helping develop an aesthetic route for a film, finding locations that connect with the stories, or building faraway worlds from scratch with often-limited resources. Spier has worked with Cronenberg since his early, genre-inflected days, and across six decades and sixteen films, she has become one of his most trusted and iconic collaborators.

✱

i. You've been working with David Cronenberg since *Fast Company*. What sorts of conversations do you have when you first get the script from him?

I think at the beginning it's more conceptual. It's more what direction is he going in it, who the characters are mainly, because it's storytelling. It's about characters and every script has a new set of characters and they all have a new background. Where do they come from, who are they, and how do we make their characters come alive on the screen? How do we help the actors to develop their characters by what we put around them or give them as props? So it's basically a character development thing at the beginning.

ii. When you're thinking about those questions of character, how much of the feasibility is determined at that script stage?

At the beginning you try not to apply the budget to it. I mean, you've always got that in the back of your head, but there's always ways around it. Like, if a character comes from a well-bred background with lots of money, which you don't have, you figure out ways to do it or get around it, or you beg, borrow, and steal in order to do it. You don't think of that at the beginning until you sit down and you do your budget and realize, oh my gosh, I've only got $5,000 to do that set, and I need $20,000.

iii. Walk me through the scouting process.

We start out looking for locations. Sometimes I do a breakdown at the beginning, about what the locations are, whether they're location or studio, or what could possibly be studio, what could possibly be location. Some things you know ahead of time—you definitely know what will be in the studio. So in which case, you're maybe looking for an exterior that you like that has attractive elements about it, like the windows, the style, the period. So you look for an exterior knowing that you can design something for the interior. You can do what you want, but you keep those elements, like the windows, doors, or style, so that people realize that they're the same place, and not that when a character goes through the door, they're going into something that's totally different—unless, of course, you want it to be that way.

You also have to keep a certain amount of logistics in mind. You obviously want to make sure if you're shooting it as a location that it's not in a heavy traffic area or that you're near an airport. So keeping sound in mind, knowing that people can get to the location without any—well, sometimes you can't, if it's on a mountain, you have to take that in consideration. You have to consider how far away the base camp is gonna be. You find a place that you love, but it's not great for those reasons. So you then have to somehow compromise between the production and the look. You want to figure out some way.

iv. **What sorts of conversations do you have with cinematographers like Mark Irwin, Peter Suschitzky, or Douglas Koch during pre-production and production? Obviously you want what you've designed to look good, but as a production designer, you have to amend or alter your approach to accommodate their needs of where the camera has to go.**

With all DPs, one of the main conversations you have with them is the light sources. They want to see all the practical lamps that we're putting on the sets, all the overhead lights that we're putting on the sets, what kind of lights, whether they are incandescent, fluorescent. Or if you're building a set, they want to know where the window placement is, or if there's windows. If there aren't any windows, can you please put a window somewhere? The exterior of the restaurant in *Eastern Promises* was a location, and the interior was built in the studio. But it had quite a bit of expanse of big windows on the front. And we didn't want to worry about what was outside those windows and what world was out there when we were in the set. So I came up with the idea of doing a decorative Russian-style grid on the windows, so that the light was diffused through the windows and you couldn't see what was out there. But it still wasn't a great light source, so I incorporated a skylight into the domed ceilings in the restaurant set. That could either be a skylight that goes to a lighting shaft, or it could be just a fake light, so then they could light from above whenever they needed to.

You always try to accommodate where their light sources are coming from rather than talking about color and showing them the colors that we're using. You know, most DPs like darker colors and most hate white. Not so much now with the digital, digital seems to be easier to work with the white than before, but still . . . it's something they've always hated. They still don't like white.

We know that everything is gonna be crisper and cleaner with digital, so we can't cheat as much with some things. We just take it all into consideration about what the look is gonna be. It hasn't really changed from our point of view. It certainly affects makeup on the actors.

v. **Which lens is used, and the length of the lens, changes how images look on-screen. Cronenberg's more recent films tend to use the same lenses. Do you design with that in mind, knowing that this three-dimensional space you've created is going to be represented in a particular way?**

Yeah, definitely. Also the aspect ratio, whether it's 1:85. Most of David's films have been 1:85. So if you're designing a tall room, you're never going to see the top of the room. So if it's anamorphic, it's always going to be cut off. So you always keep that in mind when you're designing what lenses certain views. David tends to use wide angles a lot, which I like, because then you see what's behind the actors, as opposed to those tight close-ups—we might as well hang all the set dressing from the actors' ears because you'll never see it.

vi. **The sets of *Dead Ringers* use these bruise-like colors. When did that color palette emerge during the creative process?**

We kind of fell into the bruise colors. When I was first talking to David, we wanted that picture to have a very hard-edged, clean, very cold look. So we were thinking steel and metal and lots of various tones of grays—blue grays, green grays. And then as we started getting fabric samples for furniture and costumes, we started to realize that the colors that we were leaning towards almost fell into this bruise color thing. Those shades of grays then led into the purples and then into the greens. If you've ever had a bruise, you can see how your bruise colors change as the bruise develops.

vii. **Where does the eerie non-space of the *Videodrome* set, where the torture happens, come from? There's this texture and this wetness that also extends to the special effects, like the hand-gun.**

Well, there was this video within the film that had to be made, and there was a torture set. And I thought, *That's not something I'm all that familiar with.* So as I do with every film, I did a lot of research.

I read a lot of reports from Amnesty International, which were very depressing, about what people did to torture people. And one of the things was color. That's why we went with that kind of bright, orangey-red color, because apparently that color is a color that gets—I'd be tortured if I had to spend a lot of time in that room. I think the clay wall was, again, something I read where it was a combination of water and mud where they had tortured people. And we thought, *Well, let's see if we can figure out how to make this clay stay on the wall and run electrical currents through it.* It took a lot of trial and error and research and development to get that working without the clay falling on the floor all the time.

viii. **I have to ask about *Naked Lunch*. Because of the Gulf War, the entire production was forced to recreate Tangier in Toronto. You'd build one set, and then re-dress it, so the bazaar would become the mugwump factory. You can kind of tell that they're the same place, but also they're not, which gives the film an even more surreal, hallucinogenic quality. Did you speak with Burroughs about ideas for how to create a sense of Tangier, or even just the room in which Bill is writing?**

I wish I had spoken to Burroughs at the beginning. Unfortunately, we didn't talk to him until almost three-quarters of the way through the film, when he came to visit us on set. By then, everything was pretty much built and together at that point. But it would have been fascinating to talk to him about this space. We did go to the space where he actually did the writing while we were in Tangier. We didn't copy it exactly, because it was just a room—we had to make it a little more interesting. So the feel of that, like the view out the windows, was a little different. We visited a house there that could have been the Frosts' house, and some of the stuff we were planning to build in the studio anyways, like the Frosts' apartment and his room in the hotel. Some of the things that we weren't going to build were much bigger in scope. There was one location, a leather-dying factory, which had all of these huge vats. It was gorgeous. But unfortunately I couldn't recreate that; it was much too big.

While we were in Tangier, we spent a long time photographing details—you know, texture, all the doors and the windows, everything. James McAteer, the art director, stayed behind for a few more days after we left just to take more photographs. And then when we got back, we found out that we couldn't shoot there. So now what do we do? We thought about other places we could maybe go that were similar in look and really couldn't come up with anything. So David sat down and made a list of everything that he could change in the script, I made a list of everything that

I thought I could build, and we put those together. I think in the end, because we had already found a location that we were going to use for the exterminator's, we thought, *Well, let's turn that into the drug factory.* And the Frosts' apartment, which we were building anyway, turned into the New York restaurant. As we were building one section of the casbah streets that the actors had to walk through, they'd film it, then go and shoot something, and while they were away we'd build another section of the street. Then they'd come back and shoot that new part we'd built. A little bit of that corner of the New York bar was part of the casbah streets. If you're walking by it, you don't really realize it, but you're actually walking by the New York bar. And when you're in the New York bar, you're looking out into the casbah streets.

In the end, I think it was better because he really never did go to Tangier. I mean, he was on a drug trip. So, using places that he was familiar with and turning them into Tangier made it part of what's in his head.

ix. **I read in an interview that one of your favorite films to work on was *M. Butterfly*. The interiors and the exteriors are just really incredible, as they span a different variety of styles and feelings. How much did you want these spaces to cohere or contrast with each other?**

We spent a long time, maybe a week or two, scouting locations in China. I also spent a lot of time, again, taking photographs. And I also spent a lot of time with our Chinese art director, Mr. Wong, because I had to do a crash course in Chinese architecture. I got every book I could find and everything I could find on Chinese architecture because we had to design Song's courtyard in the studio in Toronto. We did quite a bit of Chinese stuff in Toronto because we couldn't do it there in China, mainly because of the subject matter—it was against the law in China. We shot on the Great Wall of China, on the older section, but we had to build the interior of the tower for one of the scenes, which I think might've even been cut from the film. We also started shooting on a train there, and then the train took off before we finished shooting, so we had to finish the scene in Toronto. So I had to rebuild part of the railway station. And then there's another scene in the Chinese theater, which got flooded out, so I had to build that in Toronto. So, it's a good thing between Tangier and China that I take a lot of photographs.

x. **You began working on *Eastern Promises II*, but the money never came together. How far into that process did you get and what** sorts of elements did you want to include? From what I read, it was going to be a bit different, in terms of location . . .

Yeah, there was going to be a lot more in Russia. They wanted to shoot in Toronto. So I spent a lot of time—all on my own time, I wasn't being paid to do any of this—going through my files and the files at the film office, looking at what locations were out there that might work for us, and finding some locations that might work for some of the houses. I was kind of excited about redoing the restaurant because, okay, the original restaurant was done for the father. It was a very traditional-looking restaurant. But what's the son going to do? I mean, he's going to want something a little more upscale, a little more modern. That was going to be the fun thing for that one. But then it just didn't happen.

xi. Costume designers work closely with production designers. Do you have a favorite memory of working with Denise Cronenberg?

Well, I have one favorite memory, but I can't tell you because it involves an actor. And I don't think that actor would like to know. He wouldn't want to put it in a book anyways.

But I have a lot of memories of Denise. I mean, Denise was fabulous to work with. We both knew David so well, we knew what he liked, what he didn't like. We would sit with him at the beginning and talk about the characters and who they were and what they were—the whole thing, down to, "Did they brush their teeth twice a day?" Then she would go off and do her thing, and I would go off and do my thing. We would also discuss color palette. And then we wouldn't talk for a while. Then we'd get together and go, "Okay, what have you been doing?" And luckily we'd both be going in the same direction because we had worked on so many things with David. Denise used to say I was like David's second sister.

★

Composer
HOWARD SHORE

David Cronenberg's 1979 film *The Brood* is the second composer credit on the CV of famed Canadian movie composer Howard Shore, and he has since become one of the director's most trusted collaborators. Yet Shore's eclectic range and musical interests have served to enhance the director's work in a variety of different ways, from the jazz-inflected score to *Naked Lunch*, the work with loops and samplers for *Scanners*, incursions into opera with *M. Butterfly*, and even melding with modern indie-rock sensibilities for *Cosmopolis*. Shore has just completed work on Cronenberg's most recent film, *The Shrouds*.

◼

i. You're one of the first people David Cronenberg sends his scripts to. To create the score, you read the script, its source material, and then discuss the ideas of the film with him. Can you break down that process?

Well, it's linear. The discussion with David generally comes a little later. That has to do with spotting the film [where the composer and the director meet and discuss each scene during postproduction]. We do that. But before the spotting, I'm working on the ideas from the story without too much of David's input other than his brilliant writing. I'm reviewing, as you mentioned, the screenplay and the research material, which takes me far and wide depending on the source material. Music to me is not necessarily what I'm hearing. It's also what I'm seeing on the page. I compose with pen and paper, so it's also visual. Once I have the composition that I want to use for the scene, then I think about orchestrating it.

ii. You create folders of research to help you compose. What are in those? Are there parts of the text that you're drawing from, little phrases of music, or music by other composers or musicians?

They're notebooks—I write music every day. The folders are really just timestamps of ideas from that particular day. I'm the type of writer who writes and then moves forward the next day, but also keeps an eye on reviewing the past and updating it. Nothing is discarded. I just save the ideas and then decide later if any of them are good or bad, or where they go in the film. So the folders help me to keep track of the time.

Once I have the composition, the harmony, and counterpoint that I'm interested in using for the film, I begin scoring in the film.

INTERVIEWS

I review the folder, analyzing that music and trying to figure out where to place it in the film. And once I do that, I then think about orchestrating it. How do I play this? Who's going to play it? Where is it being recorded? What are the physics of the room? Who's the recording engineer? All of those questions are parts of the process. Film music is basically the art of recording.

iii. You've said that napping is an important part of the process and that you get ideas from dreams. Typically people laugh at that, but rest and dreams are really important to the creative process—Salvador Dalí, for example, would doze off in a chair while holding a key, and then when he dropped it, he would wake up and paint what he saw in that presleep state or use it for inspiration. So, what are your dreams during the writing process like? Do you see the movie, or do you hear the music, or do you simply dream that you're working on it?

No, I'm not dealing with the film at that point. This is usually early on, when I know the story, I've read David's script, and I've indulged in all of the research for months at a time. Months and months if it's something like J.G. Ballard or William Burroughs. That allows me to start thinking about music, and the napping process is just tapping into the subconscious. I'm just relaxing my body. I'm relaxing my brain, and I'm allowing the ideas to flow from the napping couch. It's an important period because I'm tapping into peripheral ideas about the ideas in the script and the story, not so much the imagery. It's more about the ideas.

iv. Your work gets down to the frame sometimes, matched with specific cuts. What does collaborating with editors such as Ronald Sanders or Christopher Donaldson look like?

I follow their leads often when it comes to how a scene progresses. I'm looking for clues into the filmmaking, into David's idea of that scene, and the rhythms of it through the editors. Sometimes, the editors work from my music. They take a scene and use a piece that I may have written for that scene and shape it.

v. For *Naked Lunch*, you combined the talents of the Master Musicians of Jajouka, the London Philharmonic, and Ornette Coleman. Each was coming from very different musical traditions, and they weren't necessarily using the same tuning, which is challenging. Your original plan was to have Coleman play some Charlie Parker solos that were recorded by a fan, Dean Benedetti, and then also work in some Moroccan music. But then Coleman was like, "No, I'm going to write my own music instead of doing this." How much were you involved with those compositions?

> Was he asking you for input on them? Were you able to observe him working?

Some of the music from *Naked Lunch* came out of my personal library of recordings that I had made, pieces that I had written earlier in my work before I even started on the film. Before I spoke to Ornette about the film, I was working with the Benedetti recordings, which are a series of recordings done by an Italian jazz enthusiast who recorded Charlie Parker in New York clubs with a wire recorder. They're mostly snippets, really—they'd be like thirty seconds, a minute, a minute and a half—and it's Parker live. I was using those recordings, looping them, and then writing another piece for the orchestra to accompany the Parker recording.

I had constructed something through editing and tape looping, and I played that for Ornette. I asked, "Can you recreate these Parker pieces?" And he said that he could, and that he loved to copy Parker, and that it was Parker who inspired him to play the alto saxophone. He actually played the solos for me, from memory, in the hotel in London where we met. And then he said he would rather write his own bebop tunes for himself and the trio [Barre Phillips and Denardo Coleman] that would complement the Parker, Ornette's own album, *Dancing in Your Head*, the William Burroughs book, and the time period. They are fantastic pieces. We recorded those, and then we recorded live with the orchestra. It was really pure improvisation with the orchestra. Ornette would find a player—a violist or a second clarinet player—and he'd just zero in on them the way a jazz musician would play with another person in a small jazz group.

Every take was a completely different approach. After the recording I had tremendous time to work with the recordings and shape them. Then I'd place them into the movie at specific moments, mix them, and do all the technical work that takes place to finish a film.

vi.
> How much were you giving direction during those sessions? How did that process play out?

I conducted the orchestra, and I let Ornette just play the pieces that I had written for the orchestra—pure improvisation. As I mentioned, he was just reacting to different players in the orchestra. He treated it like a jazz gig. Even though there were eighty musicians in the room, he would play with them very intimately. And then I did a bit of editing afterwards to create the pieces. So I had these beautiful recordings. They were done freely, not necessarily to the film. Then I shaped them to put them in the film. It was the "cut-up method." We used those techniques.

vii. You were combining supposedly unrelated musical styles as far back as *Scanners*. Like *Naked Lunch*, there were sounds that the orchestra couldn't replicate in the electronic music that you'd created. You'd been experimenting with tape loops since childhood. How much experimentation with the technology itself influenced the final score of *Scanners*? What was the process of fusing that with the, let's say, more "traditional" instruments?

Those techniques were the reason that I started working in film—the interest was accessing the technology as it developed and expanding it, but also working with a narrative, ideas, and storytelling. Some of the scores I did were more experimental than others: *Scanners* and *Videodrome* were certainly experimental scores for me. *Videodrome* was created with the Sinclair II, which was the first digital computer workstation—very expensive, very experimental instrument. *Scanners* didn't have that technology. It was just using analog technology and recordings that were made using various electronic sources and different keyboards, synthesizers, and then processed and cut up and looped. There were sometimes four or five loops happening at the same time. Then I wrote an orchestral piece to go with the loops.

I'm always moving through different ideas that I was interested in. There were things that I was interested in doing for years, but I didn't really have the opportunity to do until I started working with David. We have a lot of trust in each other. In a sense, we've kind of grown up making films together. If you look at the whole thread of what we've created over the years, one thing led to the other. I was able to try different techniques, different electronic ideas, different tape ideas, different orchestral ideas, and some completely symphonic scores, like *The Fly*, *M. Butterfly*, and *Dead Ringers*.

viii. For *Scanners* and *Videodrome*, you've cited the influence of people like Harry Freedman, particularly *5 Over 13*. Were there other electronic musicians, like Morton Subotnick or Bebe and Louis Barron, that you were also drawing influence from?

Tōru Takemitsu, the great Japanese composer—I was really interested in his electronic music. I discovered a lot of his works at the library in Toronto. I was interested in Subotnick, Kagel, Stockhausen, Cage, Carlos. It led me through a lot of different ideas of what could be done away from the orchestra. Takemitsu was particularly interesting for me because he wrote over ninety film scores. He was a master with the orchestra and acoustic recordings, but he also did all these beautiful electronic works.

ix. You created an operatic score for *M. Butterfly*, and in it you use two harps. Then for the next film, *Crash*, you used three harps with this wailing electric guitar. What was it about that sound of the harp that seemed to fit so well with these two films, forming kind of a bridge between them?

It wasn't so much the sound of the harp as it was of what the harp represented in terms of range, because I'm orchestrating based on range. Yes, on *M. Butterfly* I wrote for two harps. That was the first time I used the counterpoint of writing for two harps with the orchestra. And once I had done that, I was interested in writing a third part. This was purely on a music level, before I was even working on the film. So I was starting to write a third part. When I started approaching the music for *Crash*, I realized that I wanted to record the three harps and base the score on that composition.

That's really the genesis of the *Crash* score, the three harps. You hear the harps all through the film. I transposed the harps to the six electric guitars—so two electric guitars on each of the three harp lines. The harps are set left, center, right, which, in surround sound, is everything that you're creating in the front of the image in the theater. The score was layered with the electric guitars, essentially playing the three harp parts up an octave. And then I added three woodwind soloists: alto flute, oboe, and clarinet. I added two percussionists, mostly playing all metal percussion. Some of it was created specifically for the recordings by a group called Nexus.

x. Speaking of opera, you adapted your own work on *The Fly* into an opera. Returning to your own work is a dream come true for an artist, but it's also kind of a dangerous proposition. Did you feel like you were maybe "correcting" things that you wish you'd have done differently, or were you expanding on things? Or were you bringing new things to it?

The relationship of the film music to the opera was very minimal. There's a piece at the very beginning of the opera that is from the film score—a thematic idea. Once the orchestra plays that, it's quickly put away, and the opera just takes off into a whole different area. So I just tip my hat to the film at the very beginning, and that was really the only connection between the opera and the film, other than the screenplay written by David being the inspiration for David Henry Hwang's libretto. The experience was interesting to me in that I got to write completely on my own for months and months at a time, and I liked the process of the composition and the orchestration of the opera.

DAVID CRONENBERG: CLINICAL TRIALS

198

xi. **I'm tempted to kind of go back and ask about your collaboration with Metric for *Cosmopolis*, because that stands out from other things that you've done. And it has this amazing kind of drive to it that is at once completely in line with what is happening in the film—but also, he's just in the limo, traveling very, very, very slowly.**

Yes, I had a good collaboration with Metric. I'd worked with Emily and Jimmy earlier on another film, and when this came up, I wanted to use some of their sound in the film. We wrote three songs together for the film and they played on much of the score.

Film music was a way to work with other artists, which is what I was so interested in, you know, being in the studio and able to work with really different artists like Ornette Coleman, or Metric, which kind of expanded into things like *Lord of the Rings* and working with James Galway, Renée Fleming, and Annie Lennox. And when you're working in film, you can really pretty much call anybody in; they're kind of interested right away.

xii. **How would you sum up the essence of your collaboration with Cronenberg?**

My contribution is really through music. I'm sure I put things into the film that he might not have thought of. You know, a certain expression or something that he shot—that I could take a little further. I could expand upon it a bit, or I could add something new and interesting to a scene that he might not have thought of that approach musically.

It can be really surprising. One day I was in the dub with David for *Naked Lunch*, and I had written a piece for a scene. At that point it was an earlier version of what I had written. We listened to both. We couldn't decide. So we ended up using parts of both of them, overlapping each other. We created that right in the dub together. He's open to trying things and experimenting. The process is very egalitarian. He's really open to other people's ideas.

Playwright & Screenwriter
SIR CHRISTOPHER HAMPTON

More often than not, David Cronenberg has written the screenplays for the films he directed. With *M. Butterfly* as the early outlier, he started to film other writers' scripts more often in the 2000s, cultivating an interest in Sir Christopher Hampton's play *The Talking Cure* when seeing it in 2002 and eventually adapting it as 2011's *A Dangerous Method*. Hampton is a veteran author, playwright, screenwriter, translator, and occasional director, and prior to his work with Cronenberg he found success with his script for both the play and film version of *Dangerous Liaisons*. He wrote the screenplay for Joe Wright's *Atonement* and Florian Zeller's *The Father*.

✱

i. *A Dangerous Method* was adapted from your play, *The Talking Cure*, which was itself adapted from a screenplay you'd written as a vehicle for Julia Roberts. What was that original screenplay like? I gather it was more focused on Sabina Spielrein.

Yes, it was called *Sabina*. So indeed that's what it was. Julia Roberts's company suggested it. I'd worked with her before on a film called *Mary Reilly* and got on with her very well. Somebody in her company got hold of the story, or got hold of John Kerr's book [*A Most Dangerous Method*], I guess. They then asked me if I'd be interested, and I said yes, not realizing the vast amount of research that it would entail. And I wrote a script that I think Julia liked. However, I don't think they were ever going to let her play the part.

ii. Yeah... I read that Spielrein's interest in the scatological was there, as well as a masturbation scene.

The masochism always disturbed people, but you couldn't leave it out because it was the basic diagnosis. So the script kind of drifted, as film scripts do, into some sort of limbo. And I thought, *Well, it's an awful lot of work to be stuck in a drawer.* I had a friend who said, "Why don't you write it as a play?" So I started again. As I wrote the play, I realized that I made a mistake in this triangle of Freud and Jung and Spielrein. It was really Jung who was the main character, and once I'd made that adjustment and made it about him rather than about her, it all fell into place and was much better. The play ran in 2002 with Ralph Fiennes.

I think David got in touch with me about a year or more later, because he'd worked with Ralph, and he was sort of interested. He had picked up the published play in a bookshop in Toronto and read it. He asked if I was interested in writing a film, and I said, "It's funny you should say that because there is a film script already." I sent it to him, and he got back to me and said, "Well, I think the play is much more successful. I'd rather make a film from the play rather than from your old script."

So then there was the usual trouble of when a studio owns a property, getting it back from them. Julia was very helpful. I think she intervened and said, "Give it back to him." At least that was from her company. Twentieth Century Fox was a little less generous. I think they charged Jeremy Thomas a million dollars for my script.

iii. **Fox chose you to adapt Kerr's book not just because of this relationship with Julia Roberts, but because, like Cronenberg, you were a "Freud guy." You were into psychoanalysis. How did you find your way into Jung and his work? The film/play/film takes place before more of Jung's—to be uncharitable—woo-woo stuff.**

Yes. I was always much more sympathetic towards Freud. I had read a lot of Freud, but I didn't really know much about Jung. I didn't react very sympathetically when I first started reading Jung. Eventually, when I'd worked through God knows how many of those books, I began to realize that I was very interested in the fact that the patients were—of course, Freud had very faithful patients and people who depended on him and so on—but Jung really did make a connection with patients. They loved him, so there was something interesting about that. Then there's Jung's idea about individuation, which, crudely speaking, means when you get to about forty, you start to work out exactly who you are, and you begin to fulfill the promise of that person. I think that is a very attractive idea. I also think that he gave his patients hope, and that is admirable. Freud tended to say, "Well, it is what it is. Get used to it. Get on with it."

iv. **Probably the most fantastical part of your research and preparation is that you went to Burghölzli, the psychiatric hospital where Jung treated Spielrein, and found an orderly who'd worked with Jung. He took you to Spielrein's file and gave you thirty minutes alone in the room with a photocopier. Tell me more about that trip and the process, because that's really incredible.**

Yeah, it is. You just happen to be lucky sometimes and happen upon someone who's going to be cooperative. Inside it were copies of the diaries, as well as the case file Jung had kept. I can speak German, so I was able to see how he wrote about her, and how he clearly became more and more interested in her, and more and more involved in her. That also had her correspondence with him, the letters that she wrote, and so on. A lot of that wasn't in Kerr's book. I met Kerr and got to know him a bit in New York because, like most psychoanalysts, he was slightly crazy and couldn't leave the island of Manhattan. He had come to the conclusion that Jung and Spielrein hadn't had an affair, and that's what's in his book. However, the combination of what I found at the Burghölzli and also stuff that was being published in Germany, which hadn't been published in English, sort of made it clear that they must've had an affair. I mean, he would send a postcard saying, "Tuesday between five and seven."

v.   **Well, Jung's later behavior also suggested they had an affair.**

But I didn't want to make it up. I didn't want to invent it. So it was very good to have made these discoveries in the course of research, to have found these pieces of evidence that helped the development of the drama.

vi.   **How did you attempt to balance the rhythm of the language from these real people with the rhythm of what sounds good for an actor to say?**

One of the things about doing research in a foreign language is that it gives you a certain freedom that you don't have when they're English speakers, so you can paraphrase a little bit more and extract the essence a bit more, without betraying what they actually said to each other. You can just translate it in a more pointed or effective way, I suppose. The other great discovery in the course of all this research was the story of Otto Gross, who was an interesting figure. And it does seem as if the analysis of Otto Gross, who was a patient sent to Jung by Freud, did change Jung's thinking about . . . I mean, Otto Gross sitting there saying, "Are you crazy? Why wouldn't you have an affair with them?"

vii.   **You have to have sex with your patients.**

That was his position. I can see that it made its effect on Jung.

Of course, a lot of people didn't believe any of that and thought I'd made it all up. There was quite a lot of criticism of this fanciful story. The climax of the whole thing was when I had to go and speak to the psychoanalytical society in Hampstead. I was told that the audience was roughly fifty-fifty Freudians and Jungians. So that was scary! I mean, the Jungians, by and large, thought I'd been too kind to Freud, and the Freudians thought I'd been too kind to Jung. Their criticism was that I'd been too soft on the other fellow rather than complaining about what I'd said about their man.

viii. **There's a lot of humor in the script. A particular favorite moment of mine is when Freud corrects Jung by shouting "psych-OH-analysis!"**

There was one review in some psychiatric magazine where there was a great rant about this and that it was a mistake of mine because I thought Jung spoke French, when in fact I knew perfectly well he spoke Swiss-German. The information is actually derived from Freud's letters, where he wrote, "I must discourage this thing of people calling it psych-analysis, because it's in fact psychoanalysis." And then there's a rather pedantic explanation of why that is. Those people, Freud in particular, took themselves so incredibly seriously, probably because of the embattled situation that they found themselves in. But it becomes quite humorous. I think the battle between Jung and Freud is quite funny, really, because they were both great men, and the pettiness of great men is always amusing.

ix. **What was the collaboration with Cronenberg like? He has a tendency to really pare things down.**

During the first meeting I had with him in Toronto I asked, "Is there any particular piece of advice you want to give me before I go back and do it?" He said, "I like a script to be eighty-seven pages." That was his entire advice. So I went back and I wrote the script, which I think came out at 103 pages. Then he asked me to go back to Toronto to discuss the first draft.

I've worked with some very, very good directors but never anyone who is so incisive and so clear about what they wanted. The meeting took about two hours. He went through the script and said "I think you should do this," or "I don't like this bit," and he asked me to do certain things, such as showing Spielrein's parents at the beginning. It was absolutely clear what he wanted, and it was all very logical, so I went back, and it took me a couple of days to do it. I sent back the second draft and he said, "Oh, this is very good. I was wrong about the parents, take them out again." Then there was a short list of notes of additional things to do, which took me about forty-five minutes to finish, and then the script was done—except that it was 103 pages.

Just before pre-production started, I got an email from David which said, "I don't want you to panic"—which of course immediately causes you to panic—"but I like to do my editing before I shoot rather than after, and so I've taken the liberty of making a few changes." He'd cut about fifteen pages. I was horrified at first, but then I saw that they were such skillful changes. There were two or three things that I wanted back in, so I wrote back and asked him to reconsider. A week went by and an email came back from him saying, "I've considered your suggestions very, very carefully ... no."

I really like the film, I'm very proud of the film, and the only criticism I would make of it is that the first ten or fifteen minutes are too truncated. Spielrein's treatment covers about the first third of the stage play, and he's squeezed it down so it does seem like sort of a miracle cure, rather than going through the phases. But that's okay. It's a small criticism, but that would be my only criticism. I wasn't keen on the title either, but David had just made *A History of Violence*, and all the distributors said that if it had a sexier title, it would've done much better at the box office. So that was going around his head a bit and he thought *A Dangerous Method* was a more interesting title than *The Talking Cure*.

x.   You have to sex up your historical dramas.

Yeah, he's quite good at doing that anyway!

xi.   Were you ever on the set?

Yes. It's very interesting with directors, how some of them don't feel comfortable having the screenwriter on set. David was very, very welcoming. I don't think he was planning to take any advice, because I think he figures everything out in advance and somehow communicates it to the actors in a very economical way, just as he did with me when I was working on the script. The actors all admired him enormously and wanted to do what he wanted them to do, so the filming would finish at four o'clock in the afternoon most days. I remember flying out because I particularly wanted to be there when they shot the final scene, for which I think two and a half days had been allocated. I think I got there on the evening of the first day and they'd practically finished it. He finished a week ahead of schedule, which is apparently what he always does.

One of the things I noticed about him, which I'd never seen any other director do, is he sat in his trailer where there was an enormous screen and he'd watch it during the setups. He would engage in dialogue with Peter Suschitzky about the lighting, and he knew where the lights were and what needed to be done. He's a techie and very, very interested in all the technical side of things. I mean, I've directed some films, and I really leave it mostly to the cameraperson because I don't really know enough about it, but David knows everything.

✭

INTERVIEWS

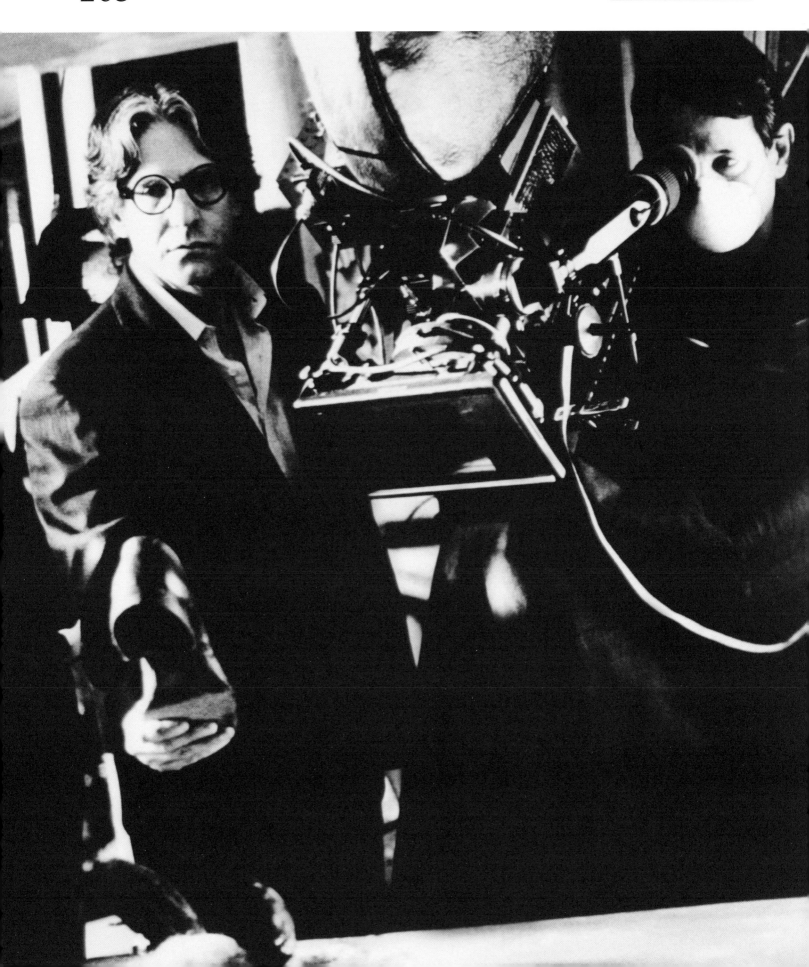

Producer
JEREMY THOMAS

In Jeremy Thomas, we have a rare instance of a maverick producer-auteur whose attachment to a film ushers in more than a measure of intrigue. Having made his name working with Nicolas Roeg, Bernardo Bertolucci, Nagisa Ōshima, and Jerzy Skolimowski, Thomas met David Cronenberg in Toronto and, discovering a mutual fondness for William Burroughs's *Naked Lunch*, an enduring creative partnership was born. In addition to 1992's *Naked Lunch*, he went on to produce 1996's *Crash* and 2011's *A Dangerous Method*.

---

i. **In your work, is there a balance you have to strike between artistry and commercial appeal?**

Of course. I've been at it for fifty years. Really. I'm not kidding. And every project is a bit different, and you have to have some sort of reality in the last, say, twenty years of the size of the film and the ambition of the film to what you can get made independently and in the non-industrialized film business. I have worked just once or twice in the industrialized film business. I work in the non-industrialized area, so that has a certain ceiling, whereas in the old days I drove to make forty-million-dollar movies, which were epic, but you can't do it anymore. So I have to either make minimalist what should be maximalist sort of things or try and find a way of doing the story in a very economical way. That's really different, but it was one of the ways I was making those films with David [Cronenberg], it was really the content that was a challenge. It wasn't to do with the stars. Yes, of course it was *Naked Lunch*. That the film was made at all and we've got such a great thing here with us forever… It's extraordinary, really. I don't think you can think of doing that now. The gatekeepers are influencing what a lot of people watch and how to establish your unusual film as you did in the past by careful marketing manipulation in cinemas. Then it will turn up on DVD, and you find an audience for your film if it was a good one. But now that's very difficult to achieve that or to find support for original and unusual things.

ii. **In Christopher Rodley's *Cronenberg on Cronenberg*, it says that the two of you met during the Toronto film festival, then known as the Festival of Festivals, and you had some Rastafarian friends, and you guys were smoking some weed…**

It's all true. I was particularly notorious that year because I had *Bad Timing* and the Sex Pistols film, *The Great Rock 'n' Roll Swindle*, and they tore the cinema up on Bloor Street . . . the punks stopped the screening. And *Bad Timing* won the Labatt Award. And we were sitting in a bar, which was a reggae bar, and we had cans of Red Stripe. I like smoking herbs, you know, and I was sat next to David. I knew his films very well, and we had a really nice connection for a nice hour or so. And then I asked him what he would like to do because I was hungry to work with him, and he said, "I tell you what, I've always wanted to make *Naked Lunch*." And it was like a lightning bolt. He was the only person in the world who could do that, and I was the only producer in the world that would want to do it. I managed to get the rights from William Burroughs for a very modest amount of money because he really wanted David to make this film. I knew that nobody else could adapt this but David. And then I was very patient because I was busy making this film and that film, but every time I went to Toronto, I would go and see David. I kept the option in the book, and one day he came through with a good script, and then I somehow found the money. Then later we moved on to *Crash*.

iii. **There are very few "middle-brow" films out there now, but what are the rules about how much you can fund those films by filming in a location? Cronenberg got his start with the tax shelter system.**

They're not tax shelters. They're national incentives for countries to stimulate people spending, in the case of the U.K. billions of dollars in production with a huge workforce and a modern employer. But we're not building steel. It's a modern business. These studios in England and what they do here, if you look carefully, it's an incredible trade. People really love that. So they've worked out. And even in America they work in a lot of places. We need to give some incentives for people to bring, say, five million bucks to spend in Norwich, Connecticut. Of course, the financing of my films has been helped by that over the last few years. The producer has to be a good smuggler, you know? And he has to smuggle and pirate. You have to smuggle these impossible ideas into the reality of filmmaking. And that's what we did with *Naked Lunch*. That film was smuggled through Japanese finance and William Burroughs and Cronenberg, and somehow people didn't really understand what it was because they didn't . . . well, because nobody had read *Naked Lunch*, of course, but there was an incredible name and IP [intellectual property]. Yes, and then you had the people, the talent involved, but Burroughs's name was also how the interest was generated.

iv. How much time did you spend on the set of *Naked Lunch*?

All the time. I remember the dreadful weather. I liked Toronto. I stayed there with the film, now I don't do it so much but I was there because I was fascinated watching David work. I hadn't worked with him before and every director I work with is a different sort of director. They all have different methods of doing it, and David has a method. I was enjoying it. I was involved on a daily basis.

v. Do you have any particularly vivid memories?

I'm not a big anecdote guy and the anecdotes are really unspeakable anecdotes. It was a pretty happy film. It's always very serious making films with David as opposed to, say, other directors which are like fiestas with moments of seriousness in them. David's head goes to a very calm, very composed place . . . it's all planned. It's exciting seeing a film being realized, in the moment. I was really interested in seeing David working because I always had such an admiration for his unusual films and his unusual mind and how he translated these ideas into images. He's basically a suburban guy in a suit who was looking after his children when he was widowed, sitting at his typewriter, and inside his brain was all this incredible stuff.

vi. The aftermath of *Crash* is very well known: the fallout and all the controversy. But I'd love to hear a bit about the process of preparing to shoot it.

With *Naked Lunch*, we went to town with it. And we had a nice time at Cannes and it was good. It was nothing like *Crash*. It was good and the film opened. I can't remember how successful it was where and when, but it was well received by those who would do the work and see the world. And for those who wouldn't, it wasn't made for them. And that's my attitude to films on reviews. When you get polarized reviews, I always think, *Well, we didn't make it for you*. At a certain point David said he would like to make another film so I optioned the rights of Ballard's book for years, again like the other one, and I got to become quite friendly with Ballard and I did *High-Rise* (2015) with him. I was working with Bertolucci and him on another idea. I really got to like him a lot and then David decided to make the film. And it was a very difficult film to finance. Telefilm Canada changed their rules so I said I'd produce it with somebody else. I wasn't on the set every day that film, but I was on the set quite a bit. I was going in and out, which was opposed to *A Dangerous Method* where I was on set every day. But *Crash* is an incredible film. We had to get that film through and it really, really made people crazy.

vii.   Yes, yes, it did.

But unexpectedly crazy. I didn't realize how crazy... I had no idea that this explosion was going to happen to us, including to David. It's his most controversial film. We had that a couple times on *Naked Lunch* and on *Crash*—we were censored by the people who bought the film. They didn't know what they were getting. They don't know what to do with it. I mean, people read scripts, and they see different things in the script. When we read a book, people take different things out of a book and what it's about. You read a Henry James book, everybody takes something different.

viii.   **At what point did you realize that it was going to be life-destroyingly controversial?**

Cannes. I had no idea until I saw people going berserk. Hundreds of people, another room put on for the press conference. The reaction of people going crazy. I hadn't seen it before. Famous critics going nuts, shouting. And Ballard loved this. He loved it all. And then we got into it. Because we knew it was a strong film. But we didn't know that it had pushed these buttons and people enough for Francis Ford Coppola [head of the Cannes competition jury in 1996] to say, "I abstain." It means I hated it so much I couldn't vote for it. And he hated it, and it still got that prize. I've heard from people on the jury, and I'm not allowed to say what happened in the room, but this was a particularly polarizing episode.

ix.   **How did you develop your own taste in art and film?**

I'm not an academic. I left school at seventeen and went into the film business in the lab. So I sort of self-educated through Ken Loach, Perry Henholm, and the various people I worked with. I was like a sponge. I got all these ideas and politics from Ken, and then I got to know [Jerzy] Skolimowski's abstract brilliance. And then I got Roeg and his genius about life and people, what goes on inside people's heads. He's obviously the Rolls-Royce of filmmaking—technical filmmaking. And then I went on to [Nagisa] Ōshima, and then I was off to the races because I got Ōshima and Bowie together. I had a big hit. And then I was free to do what I wanted for about twenty years, pretty much. I was free until about 2000. *The Dreamers* was the last film that I did where I could put my hand in the air and there were swarms of people wanting to give me money—enough to make the film freely. And then it slowly became more austere and regulated in taste. Because the audience weren't following their own tastes.

The tastemakers were making the films, the cinemas were closing down, and people suddenly saw that they didn't have enough films for them to make choices. Something happened.

Regarding *Crash*, I think it was quite successful actually. But again, it was censored by the American distributor. Ted Turner. First we had Murdoch and his group at Fox for *Naked Lunch*. Of course it was very stupid of me taking their dollar, because when they really got to understand what it was, they were ashamed of it. And it was the same with *Crash* because Ted Turner was very vocal about it. He couldn't believe that he'd got this film. We got hammered by that. Supposedly he was watching the film with Jane Fonda.

x. **For *A Dangerous Method* you were originally going to have Christoph Waltz and Christian Bale, but they had to move on and, one that you would have to start looking for financing all over again.**

With *A Dangerous Method*, [Christopher] Hampton had written a play and David and I optioned it and commissioned Chris to write a script with David's input. Because David was involved we managed to attach really good actors. We had Vincent Cassel, Kiera [Knightley], Viggo [Mortensen], and [Michael] Fassbender, and yeah, it was incredible. They all were very generous when it came to working with the sort of budget I could find for the film. We stayed in this wonderful hotel near the Cologne studios where we shot the movie. It was unusual for David to shoot outside of Toronto. I don't think he liked it. We shot it in Lake Constance as well. Doubling up. It was very enjoyable. It was a happy film. And it was the problem with that film, as when it came out it wasn't what people thought a Cronenberg film should be. Because there was no glistening and weirdness in terms of body stuff. But it's a film about people, and about a take on Jung and Freud and Sabina Spielrein. Funnily enough, years before, I tried to make *The White Hotel* by D.M. Thomas with Bertolucci, which was inspired by Sabina Spielrein and Freud, but it wasn't to be. So I knew the subject. I think it's a film that's been a little bit unheralded because it doesn't fit into Cronenberg's body of work in a simple way. Like *M. Butterfly*. When people see a Scorsese film, they want it to be like that or about that sort of subject.

xi. **I've looked at all of this different research material for this and two things I've noticed: First of all, there's a definite drop-off in the quality of the writing about his films and the responses to them; and then there is a very clear moment where Cronenberg has this legend behind him. And then everyone starts their review with, "Hey, there are no exploding heads in this movie."**

That is a burden for David.

xii. **People stopped talking about what's actually there.**

I mean, it's like a painter makes a really beautiful photorealist painting. And then he makes abstract paintings, and he's not allowed to make those because the audience wanted him to make the thing he became known for.

xiii. **How would you contrast the experience of fundraising for *Naked Lunch* versus *A Dangerous Method*?**

Raising money for *Naked Lunch* was the most difficult of the three films. Because the text and the material and the legend of Burroughs was more difficult and I was less . . . well, I was pretty successful then and I managed to find the money. But I did find the money and it was a decent budget as well. And I'm still doing it. Can you believe it? I'm still making films.

xiv. **Yeah, do you guys still race?**

No, no, no, but we did. We did race and I used to go and enjoy it. I like cars a lot and he likes cars a lot. He's retired from that. He's a Tesla man now, but he was absolutely a diseased petrolhead with motorbikes and trail bikes and all sorts of restoring old cars. He's also a wonderful conversationalist. But he's a private man, like all of us a bit. I'm really proud to have been involved with him on those films.

Cinematographer
PETER SUSCHITZKY

The British cinematographer Peter Suschitzky had been working at a high level in the film industry for over twenty years prior to his first collaboration with David Cronenberg—1988's *Dead Ringers*. His close creative collaboration with Cronenberg has blossomed into one of the greatest and most distinctive director-cinematographer partnerships of cinema's modern age, and his precise, stark, expressive style has come to define what we think of as the Cronenberg look. Suschitzky has worked on every Cronenberg film up to and including 2014's *Maps to the Stars*.

✶

i. **In numerous interviews, you've said that your love for film began when a friend of your father's came to your sixth or seventh birthday party and he brought a projector and you watched a bunch of silent shorts, including some by Charlie Chaplin. And then you've worked with Kevin Brownlow, who has a deep knowledge of interest in silent cinema, which he incorporated into his films. Have you ever pulled from that visual language of silent cinema for your collaborations with David Cronenberg?**

Yes, but completely differently. Because in silent films, to state the obvious, the camera has to tell a story. And in David's films, it's a different matter. He doesn't do anything just for the sake of showing something. If I suggested a shot that he thought was superfluous, he would just say, "That'll never be in the film."

ii. **Why do you think that is?**

He's very concise. Or, he became very concise anyway. He always kept his films to well below two hours, to more like an hour and a half.

iii. **Ninety minutes is the perfect length for a film. So I respect that.**

Yeah. I think that my love for film started just before the incident that you mentioned; when I was maybe five, I lay down on the floor and built a cinema out of toy bricks. It had space for an imaginary screen. And my father had come back from work with scraps of film. And I put a piece of film there and a flashlight behind it. And then I dreamed myself into cinema. And I kept that image right through my life.

iv. Do you feel like music is an influence on your work as a cinematographer?

It's very difficult to say. If you're practicing a craft, whether it's writing plays or making movies or painting, everything that you see and experience in your life, even if it's just visiting a field in the countryside, might have a subconscious influence on what you do later. Music has entered my soul very deeply. I know most classical music almost by heart. But it's such a different medium that I can't say how it's influenced me. I am aware of rhythm in film, but I think I might have been very aware of that without my knowledge of music. Music has just given me an enormous amount of pleasure right through my life.

v. Within a single setup, do you feel there is rhythm within it?

Yes, through the composition and through the light, maybe through the movement of the actors or through the movement of the camera.

vi. How do you understand that rhythm?

Within the frame, there's always a focal point or, if there isn't, then it's likely to be a mess. But usually, with a focal point, it doesn't mean that it's in the center of the screen; it might well be off to one side. A focal point can be emphasized or minimized according to the light and according to the frame, the composition. But my work is very instinctive. I don't think a lot about it. In fact, I try actively not to think. I used to play a game with myself, where I used to say to myself, "I've never done this before. I've never done this before." Because I've learned to consider repetition and formula to be the enemy of creative thought. So I would walk on to a set saying that to myself, convincing myself that I was innocent of all experience in movies. And that was rather scary. And later years, I forgot to do that exercise and felt a bit calmer at my work.

vii. Do you perform camera tests before shooting? And if so, what are you looking for in those tests?

Well, the tests are rather banal, but very useful. They have to do with the costumes and how the actors feel in the costumes and the makeup. They also give me a chance to familiarize myself with the faces of the actors and how the light behaves on their faces, particularly if I haven't worked with them before. But David has told me several times before the start of a movie, "I don't know what I'm going to do, how I'm going to do this movie."

But the fact is that as soon as you film the first take, it already establishes a style which you have to try to maintain. And I'm sure that what David told me was partly expressing a fear of the unknown, the journey we were going to take. Of course, he'd really thought an enormous amount about the film. He doesn't rehearse before the movie. He doesn't rehearse off set. He only rehearses on the set. He's always worked that way since I've worked with him.

viii. **Do you tend to approach lighting actors you've worked with before in the same way?**

Yeah, I know what I can't and what I should not do. Especially if it concerns an actress, if I'm allowed to use that expression. Especially if it concerns a woman's face.

ix. **When you were making *Dead Ringers*, you pushed Cronenberg toward wide-angle lenses, right?**

I did try to introduce him to the fact that one can use a wide-angle lens, even for a close-up. And we did that occasionally in that film. He was much more traditional in his approach to filmmaking on that movie. You may know this, but his approach was to shoot a wide angle of each of the scenes that we were engaged in shooting, then to shoot a mid shot, which might include two or three actors, and then to do close-ups and closer close-ups. So that all took a very long time. And we would shoot the whole scene on each shot. In the last film that I shot with him, he did very few shots and only one take of each shot, which put the actors on edge.

x. **Are you collaborating with Carol Spier or the other production designers in that respect?**

The production designer is of prime importance to me, of course. They provide the material in front of the camera. And I do talk with them and visit them in their studio to see what their concepts are. It's very important to me. Luckily on David's films, we've always had good designers, mostly Carol Spier.

xi. **Considering that you're mostly working on an instinctual level, what conversations are you having with Carol?**

Talking about color and light sources, that sort of thing. And Carol is particularly talented at producing lovely textures. The walls are always interesting to look at; they're never bland. They're full of texture.

xii. **With the VFX part and the representative on set and then perhaps in postproduction as well, are you talking about color, or what elements of the image are you guys focusing on?**

We'll be discussing color, and they'll probably remind me that there has to be interactive lighting between the live shooting and what they're going to add afterwards. In other words, if there are explosions added afterwards, there has to be a flash on the actor's face. Quite simple things, but important to be reminded of.

xiii. **What do you make of less obvious VFX, like beauty work where an actor might have the dark circles under their eyes removed or a shadow on their face changed to make their nose look a little more appealing?**

Yes, some things should be done. I've made corrections myself without being asked to do it. I worked with an actress who had a lot of small blemishes on her forehead. And I asked the technician I was working with, the colorist, to defocus her forehead.

It's amazing what you can do. And I've no objection to any of that. I am not of the school that believes you have to be totally honest, in other words. As long as the spectator is not made aware of it, I think it's okay.

xiv. **With digital now, Cronenberg watches a scene being set up and led on a screen in his trailer and communicates via talking to you. Do you like that process?**

I'm very, very happy with it. I like for him to see exactly what I'm doing. I don't keep any secrets from him. And he doesn't, as a rule, ever interfere with what I'm doing. We decide on where to put the camera before he goes to his trailer and has a sleep, which he likes to do. Yes. So we choose where the camera is going to be and which lens we're going to use. And then he leaves me alone to light the scene.

xv. **Do you feel like when you're working on a film your sleep or your dreams help inform your creative instincts?**

Yes. But to be honest, I can't answer that question with anything illuminating. I probably wake up not remembering my dreams. Besides, when I get tired towards the end of shooting a movie, I don't know whether I remember any of my dreams. I'm just grateful for all the sleep I can get.

xvi. **You've frequently expressed the importance of the script and that everything flows from that. And you don't do any additional reading if it's based on a book. How do you navigate the transition from script to film?**

I do honestly work very subconsciously, and I find my way into a film. As I said, I have to establish a style in the first scene that we're shooting. People tell me that my style has changed from film to film, but I don't do it consciously. I never decide before we do a film to imitate a particular artist. I don't believe that you can make any photographic image look at all like a painting because in a painting you subconsciously sense the brush and how the paint went onto the canvas. I don't know how I change. I just know that I change a little bit from film to film. I don't like doing the same thing all the time in any case.

xvii. **With *Cosmopolis*, 90 percent of the film takes place inside of a limo. What were the challenges that came with that enclosed space?**

I must say that if the script had been attached to another director, I would never have done it because it's my bête noire to shoot in a car. It's terrible—a really frustrating, horrible experience. But I did it because I wanted to continue working with David. And yes, at the same time, one of the problems of shooting in a car is the lack of space and the lack of variety of angles that you can achieve because there's nowhere to put the camera that hasn't been tried before. I usually encourage the sound department to go in first and place their microphones. The props department has to go in, and nothing can happen simultaneously with a car. But in the end, I think we got enough variety to make it look interesting.

xviii. **Obviously the same with *Crash*, right? I mean, there is less time in cars, but the time in the car is very important.**

Yes. I'm thinking of the big car wash scene, which is a hugely important scene. Looking back on it, there is a lot of use of horrible fluorescent lighting, but when they're at the car dealership and then when she's seducing the car salesman and then also being, you know, it's a very unique scene.

xix. **The night scenes in *Crash* are just terrifying. How did you land on that look?**

I think it was largely through necessity. The budget of the film was perhaps a factor, but it wasn't overwhelming. I never felt truly limited, but I was aware that we had a certain amount of money. And I'm sure that if you noticed the harsh neon lighting in some scenes that I was doing that deliberately, because it felt right for the scene. I hope it still does. I had one of the most fun experiences on that film, although it was one of the very hardest films that I've shot with David. We shot a lot of it outside at the beginning during the Canadian winter in November. So it became very cold. Somehow, because the situations that the script demanded of the actors often had an undercurrent of the comic or the ridiculous, I laughed it out during the shooting of that film.

xx. **And then, you know, the look of *Maps to the Stars* really matches its subject matter in that all the scenes are very brightly lit and it** has almost this mid-'90s rom-com lighting where it's always noon, and it's never raining, it's never dark outside, it's very much like perpetuating all these myths about Los Angeles. So were there any films that you revisited before shooting?

No, there weren't, but one challenge that we had, which was an important one, was all the interior scenes are filmed in Toronto. So the outside had to be dressed a little bit with some foliage that you might see in Los Angeles, and maybe, subconsciously, I wanted to keep it sunny in the sets and the locations that we were shooting, even when it wasn't sunny. It reminds me of another occasion when, in *Naked Lunch*, we were going to shoot the exterior scenes on location in Morocco, and we went to scout the locations and came back, and two or three days after we were returned to Toronto, the first Gulf War broke out, and the insurance company wouldn't allow us to shoot there. So we did everything in the studio, which gave it a great sense of unity that it wouldn't have had. Yes.

xxi. Cronenberg has said that all of his films are comedies in a way. So do you feel like that comes into the composition stage, into the lighting, into how you're presenting these little moments of black comedy?

No, I don't think that affects my lighting. But the fact that he has a gentle sense of humor is somehow always in the background and makes it so pleasurable to work hard with him, even though he might be sleeping half the time. I've always experienced great pleasure, and I've always known from the beginning that it's a privilege to work with somebody who just wants to encourage me to do my best and doesn't try to get me to do things differently, except on a few occasions.

xxii. Do you feel like you helped David maybe become more intuitive as a filmmaker over the years? When you're doing something for that long, you obviously grow as an artist and you learn from mistakes. But I would say the films that he's made with you shift towards more the idea of "let's see what happens." Do you feel like that is part of your collaboration?

I'm sure we both influenced each other, but not deliberately. It's just in the form of osmosis over the years. Spending a lot of time together and having done eleven movies together, I'm absolutely sure that we've influenced each other in many ways and some ways which I don't realize until I'm working with somebody else. Then I realize, hmm, what a shame I'm not working with them if they talk about that. I don't know if you'd say the same about me, I have no idea.

INTERVIEWS

DAVID CRONENBERG: CLINICAL TRIALS

DAVID CRONENBERG: CLINICAL TRIALS 222

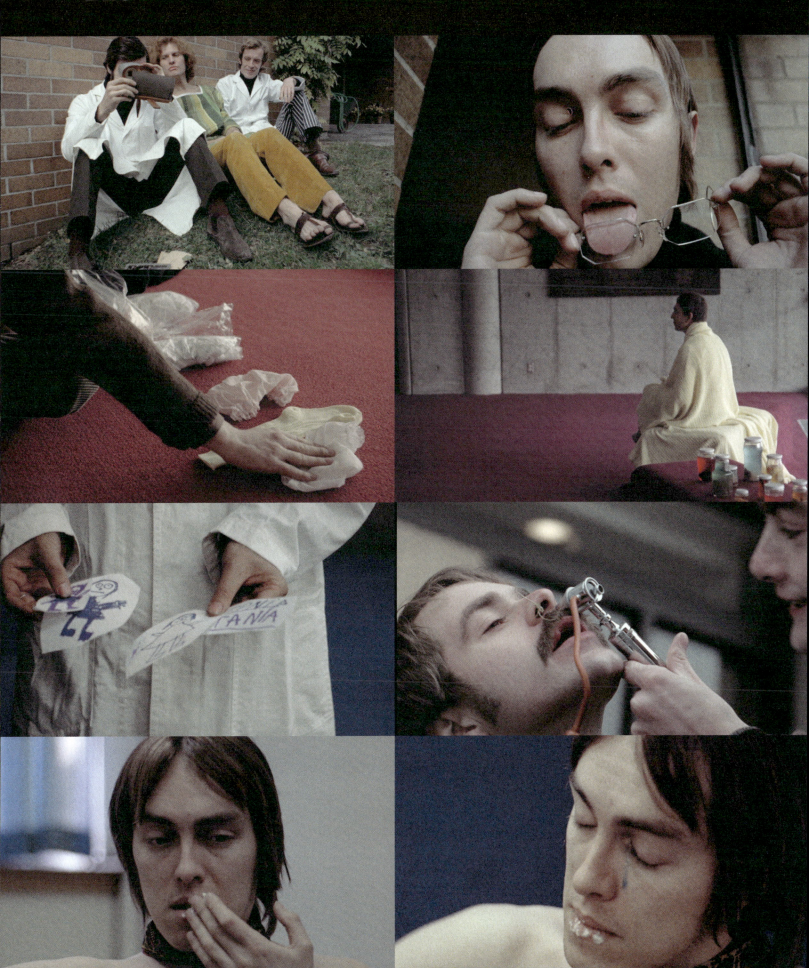
CRIMES OF THE FUTURE (1970)

DAVID CRONENBERG: CLINICAL TRIALS 224

225 SHIVERS

DAVID CRONENBERG: CLINICAL TRIALS

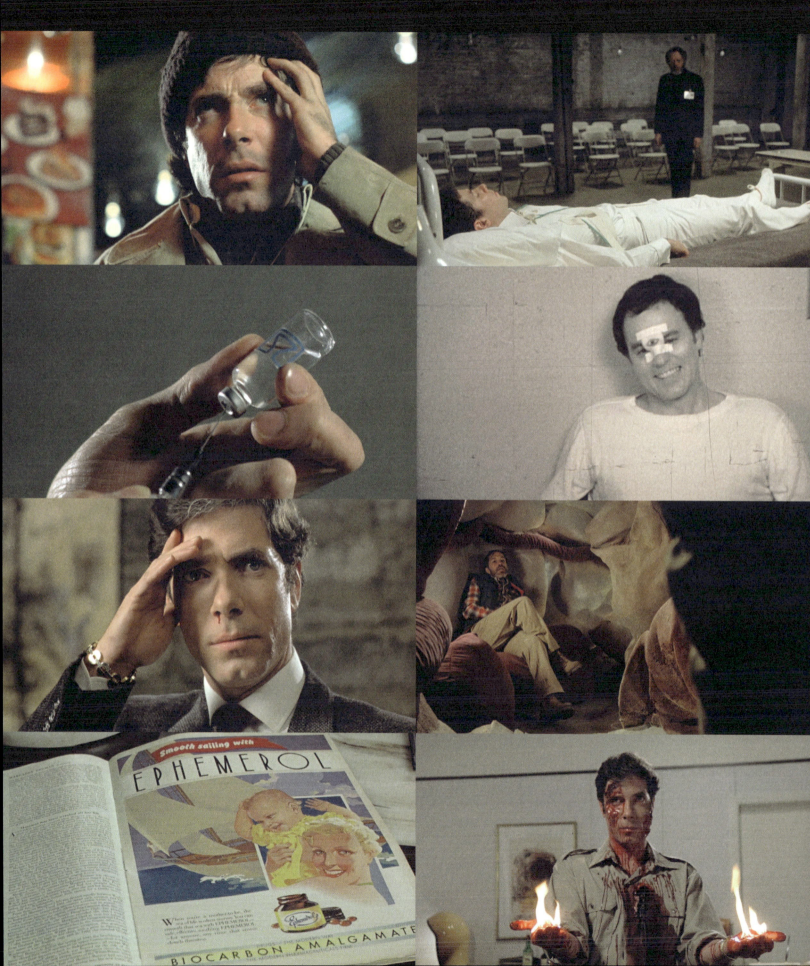

233

SCANNERS

DAVID CRONENBERG: CLINICAL TRIALS

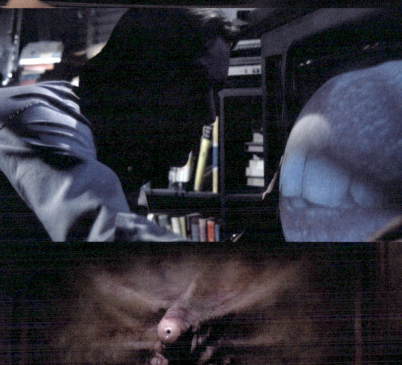

237 THE DEAD ZONE

DAVID CRONENBERG: CLINICAL TRIALS

238

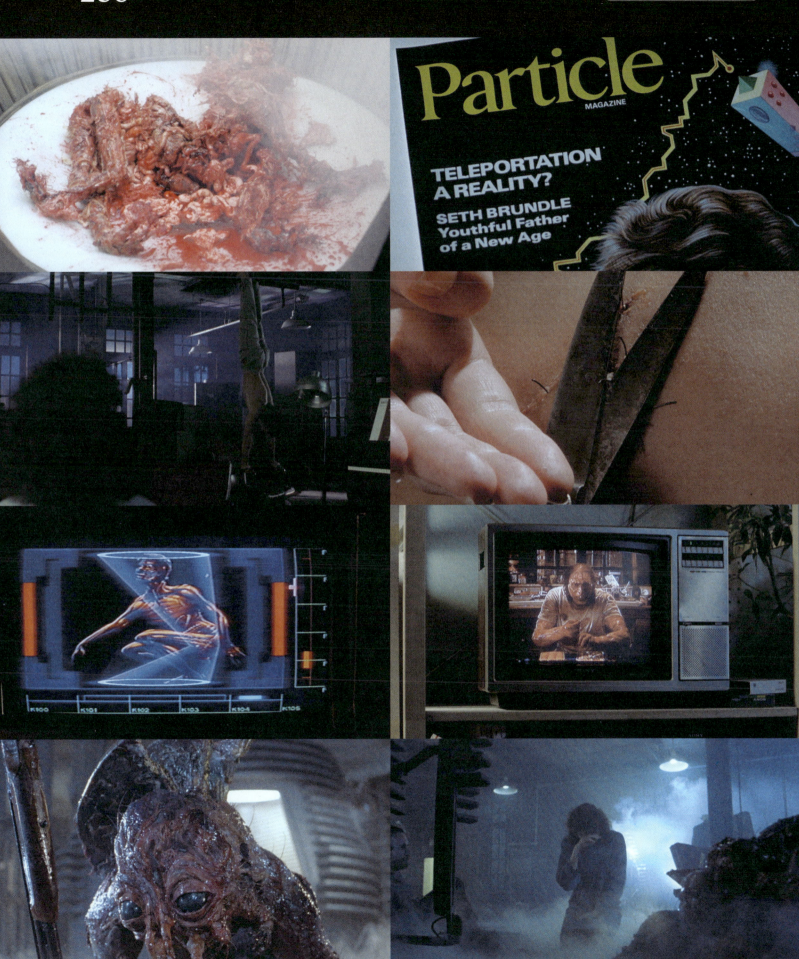

DAVID CRONENBERG: CLINICAL TRIALS

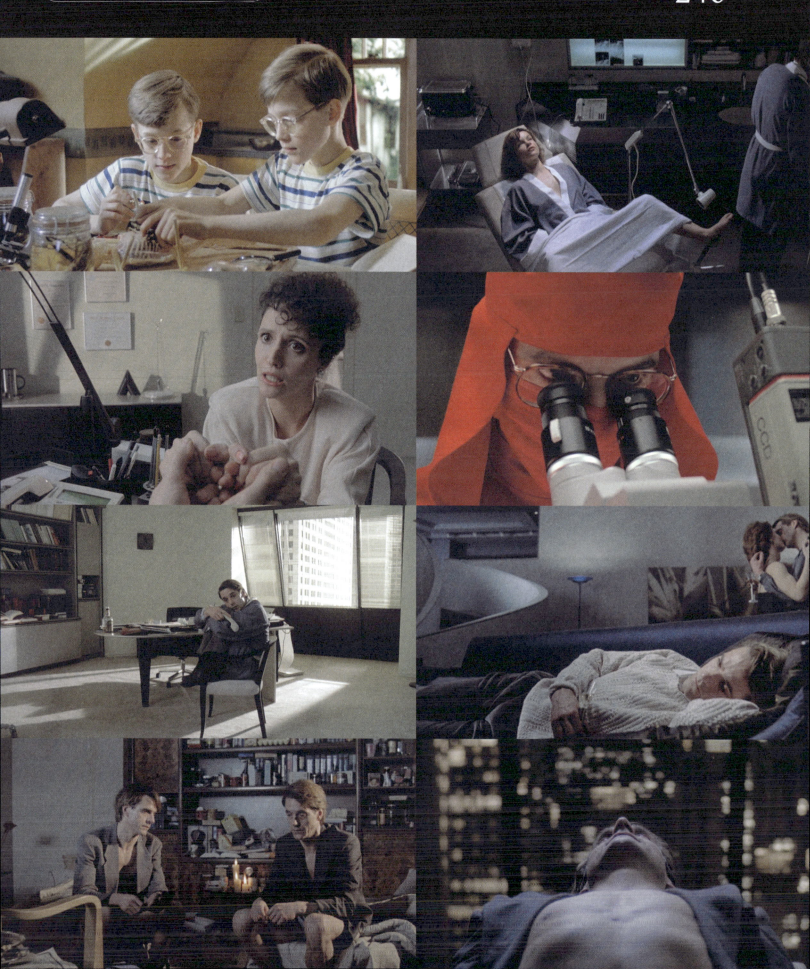

241 DEAD RINGERS

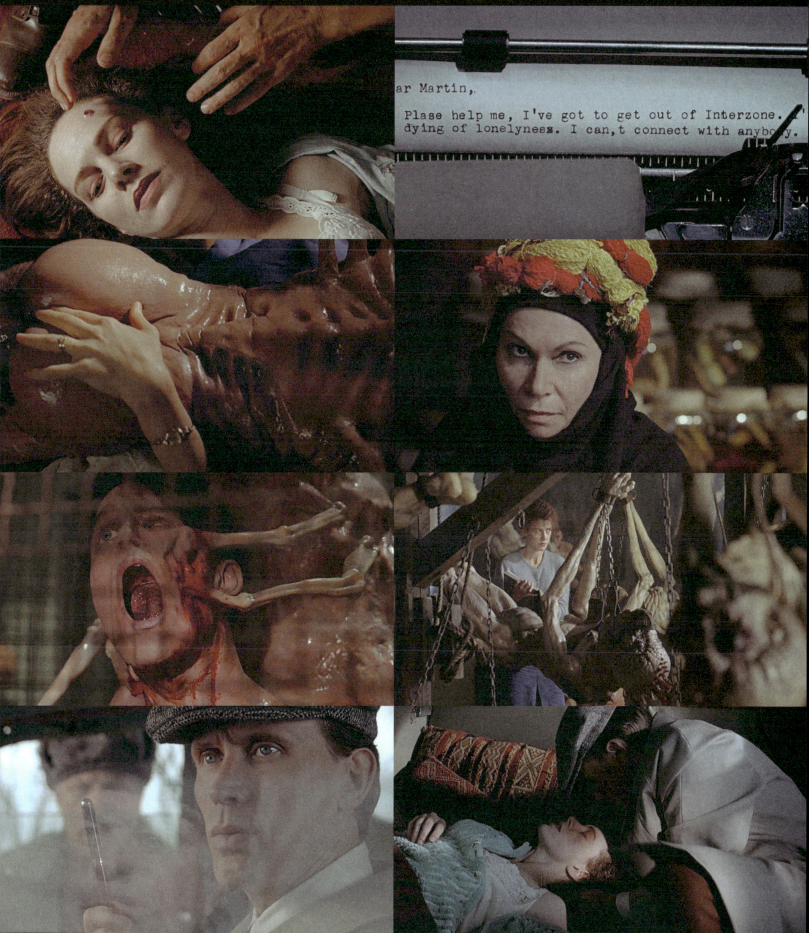

M. BUTTERFLY

247 CRASH

DAVID CRONENBERG: CLINICAL TRIALS

248

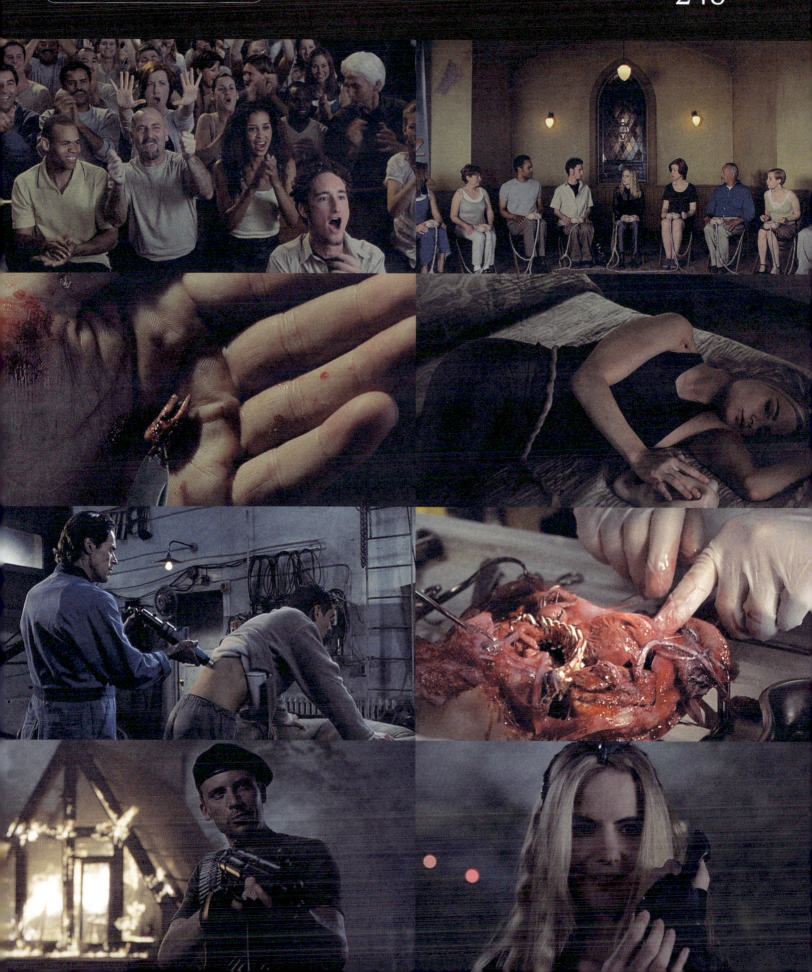

249

EXISTENZ

DAVID CRONENBERG: CLINICAL TRIALS

250

DAVID CRONENBERG: CLINICAL TRIALS

252

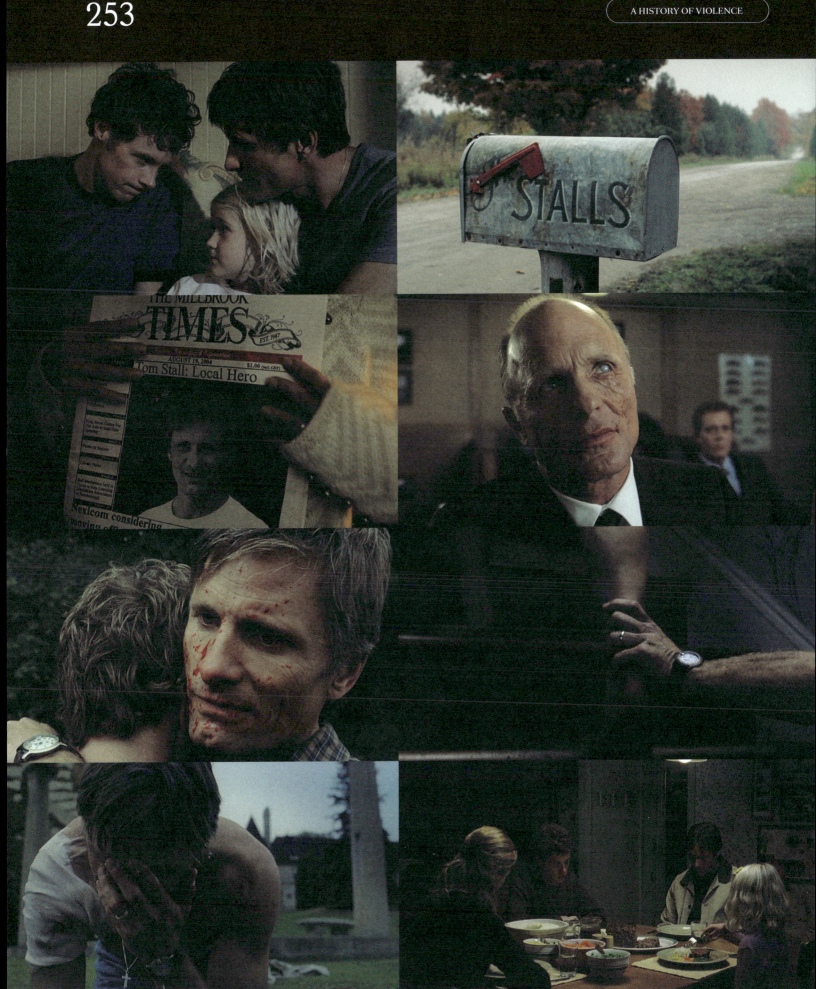

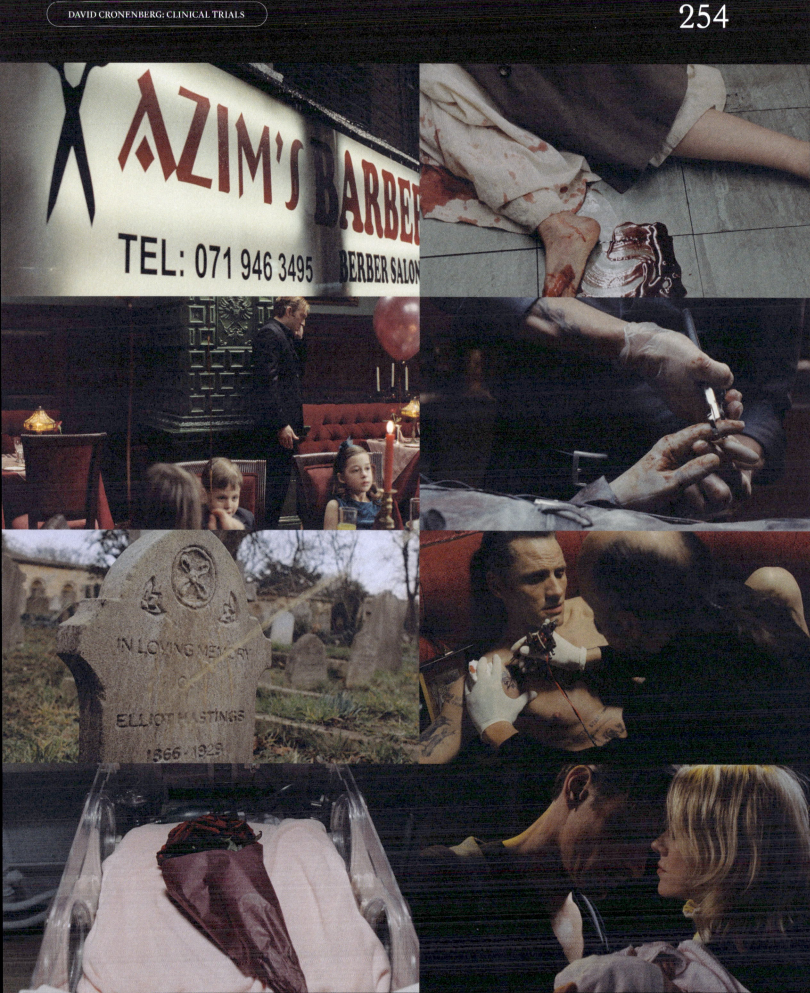

EASTERN PROMISES

DAVID CRONENBERG: CLINICAL TRIALS

257 A DANGEROUS METHOD

DAVID CRONENBERG: CLINICAL TRIALS

DAVID CRONENBERG: CLINICAL TRIALS

CRIMES OF THE FUTURE (2022)

Stereo (63 mins, 1969)
Writer: David Cronenberg
Stars: Ronald Mlodzik, Jack Messinger, Paul Mulholland
Cinematography: David Cronenberg
Editing: David Cronenberg
Country: Canada

Crimes of the Future (63 mins, 1970)
Writer: David Cronenberg
Stars: Ronald Mlodzik, Jon Lidolt, Tania Zolty
Cinematography: David Cronenberg
Editing: David Cronenberg
Country: Canada

Shivers (88 mins, 1975)
Writer: David Cronenberg
Stars: Paul Hampton, Joe Silver, Lynn Lowry, Allan Kolman
Cinematography: Robert Saad
Score: Ivan Reitman
Editing: Patrick Dodd
Country: Canada

Rabid (91 mins, 1977)
Writer: David Cronenberg
Stars: Marilyn Chambers, Frank Moore, Terry Schonblum
Cinematography: René Verzier
Score: Ivan Reitman
Editing: Jean LaFleur
Country: Canada

Fast Company (91 mins, 1979)
Writer: David Cronenberg, Phil Savath, Courtney Smith
Stars: William Smith, Claudia Jennings, John Saxon
Cinematography: Mark Irwin
Score: Fred Mollin
Editing: Ronald Sanders
Country: Canada

The Brood (92 mins, 1979)
Writer: David Cronenberg
Stars: Oliver Reed, Samantha Eggar, Art Hindle
Cinematography: Mark Irwin
Score: Howard Shore
Editing: Alan Collins
Country: Canada

Scanners (103 mins, 1981)
Writer: David Cronenberg
Stars: Jennifer O'Neill, Stephen Lack, Patrick McGoohan, Lawrence Dane, Michael Ironside
Cinematography: Mark Irwin
Score: Howard Shore
Editing: Ronald Sanders
Country: Canada

Videodrome (88 mins, 1983)
Writer: David Cronenberg
Stars: James Woods, Sonja Smits, Debbie Harry, Peter Dvorsky
Cinematography: Mark Irwin
Score: Howard Shore
Editing: Ronald Sanders
Country: Canada

220–221
STEREO

Without the droll, jargon-loving voiceover posing questions like, "Is abstract logical thought even possible without language?" playing over them, the icy formalism and high contrast black-and-white photography of Cronenberg's compositions more clearly announce themselves as the work of a first-time filmmaker. Still, there's something delicious about the banal sensuality and looming disaster in these painfully mid-century arthouse images, like a Victorian poem memorializing the tragedy of beautiful youths. There's truth in the stylization. Pharmacology and free love transpire against the backdrop of the University of Toronto's horrible brutalist architecture (built out of cement!)—just as it did during the sixties.

222–223
CRIMES OF THE FUTURE (1970)

The Internet used to only be stuff like this—obsessives, nerds, and fetishists who seemed to be hard at work, devising new and increasingly strange ways of getting off. ("Roy Orbison wrapped in cling film" is emblematic of this era.) Everything in the nearly empty, post-post-pubescent female world of *Crimes of the Future* is enlisted in the service of potentially getting off: an otoscope, feet, and yes, even a five-year-old girl. Everything is ordered, everything is shameless; everything flows forth from Ronald Mlodik, who plays lead lonely boy genius Adrian Tripod. His regal, scientific, and composed queerness saturates every still.

224–225
SHIVERS

A very different type of laboratory: Starliner Towers, the exclusive high rise on Montreal's Nuns Island that has every amenity—from a doctor's office to a department store—that residents could wish for. (And, like every expensive new condo, there are still plenty of empty units.) But the luxury and seclusion the residents have paid for descend into the violence and blood-soaked sexual frenzy pictured here. Orgies dissolve the barriers between servants and who they serve, between young and old, and even between family members. Everyone's writhing and biting and bleeding together—a fate far beyond their worst fears of city life. John Waters loves this film for a reason.

226–227
RABID

Another plague comes to Montreal—and this time Cronenberg has the budget to show it. The peace and freedom of the open road come with danger, but not as much danger as what's inside the Keloid Clinic, a soon-to-be franchised plastic surgery outfit, whose patients seem to be almost exclusively people with undiagnosed body dysmorphic disorder. It's in this strange, self-hating environment that Rose (Marilyn Chambers) sprouts a penis in her armpit and starts sucking blood. Her life becomes absurd and tragic, but her demise is legitimately upsetting: Rose is thrown into the back of a garbage truck and gets compacted with bags of trash. It's so plainly an atheist's metaphor for burial, but it stings even the true believers.

228–229
FAST COMPANY

Contrary to what *Rabid* or *Crash* posit, you can go as fast as you want on an open road—and even destroy your vehicle in a fiery blaze!—without developing a vampiric sex organ or a paraphilia about car crashes. There are no great lessons about the meaning of speed here; *Fast Company* is just fun races, stupid jokes, and leggy broads in short-shorts. Yet no one is degraded. The villain here—aside from miscalculated torque—is a greedy jerkoff (not pictured) who works for a motor oil company and sponsors races in bad faith. To hell with suits, to hell with money. Just drive and be free.

230–231
THE BROOD

Here, everyone is bitter and can never be healed: Frank resents Nola for being ill, Nola resents her family for fucking her up, and Mike, prone to breaking out in psychoplasmic hives and sobbing, resents Dr. Raglan for abandoning him. They're all justified in their anger and heartbreak. But the true victim isn't the adults: it's Candy, who's not only physically and emotionally abused, but bears witness to three gruesome murders by creatures that look like monstrous versions of her. Like all of life's worst experiences, she's doomed to suffer this one alone—even if she's surrounded by people.

232–233
SCANNERS

Beyond the genre elements (cars that crash and then explode, heads that explode, computers that explode, a gang of shotgun-wielding telepaths) or the critique of the postwar intelligence apparatus (where private companies that specialize in "international security" can do whatever they want), there's the central tragedy of Cameron Vale. Not unlike Dennis "Spider" Clegg, Cameron, as we all are, is born into a confusing world, made to construct an identity based on incomplete or confusing information, and then forced to make moral choices. But, because of his powers and those rough and strange genre elements, Cameron's also nothing like us. If only every coming-of-age movie were this wild and truthful.

234–235
VIDEODROME

What if you took the accusations of your worst haters and embellished them further, making them strange and mystical? Liberate yourself from the fear of being disliked and slide into the new flesh of *Videodrome*. According smiling jackal Barry Convex, Max Renn, who's always on the hunt for something harder, is sentenced to death by *Videodrome* signal. Barry and his colleagues at Spectacular Optical (clearly

The Dead Zone (103 mins, 1983)
Writer: Jeffrey Boam (based on the novel by Stephen King)
Stars: Christopher Walken, Brooke Adams, Tom Skerritt
Cinematography: Mark Irwin
Score: Michael Kamen
Production Design: Carol Spier
Editing: Ronald Sanders
Country: Canada, USA

The Fly (96 mins, 1986)
Writer: David Cronenberg, Charles Edward Pogue
Stars: Jeff Goldblum, Geena Davis, John Getz
Cinematography: Mark Irwin
Score: Howard Shore
Production Design: Carol Spier
Editing: Ronald Sanders
Country: Canada, USA

Dead Ringers (115 mins, 1988)
Writer: David Cronenberg, Norman Snider
Stars: Jeremy Irons, Geneviève Bujold, Heidi von Palleske
Cinematography: Peter Suschitzky
Score: Howard Shore
Production Design: Carol Spier
Editing: Ronald Sanders
Country: Canada

Naked Lunch (115 mins, 1991)
Writer: David Cronenberg
Stars: Peter Weller, Judy Davis, Ian Holm
Cinematography: Peter Suschitzky
Score: Howard Shore, Ornette Coleman
Production Design: Carol Spier
Editing: Ronald Sanders
Country: UK, USA

M. Butterfly (101 mins, 1993)
Writer: David Henry Hwang
Stars: Jeremy Irons, John Lone, Barbara Sukowa, Ian Richardson
Cinematography: Peter Suschitzky
Score: Howard Shore
Production Design: Carol Spier
Editing: Ronald Sanders
Country: USA

Crash (100 mins, 1996)
Writer: David Cronenberg
Stars: James Spader, Holly Hunter, Elias Koteas
Cinematography: Peter Suschitzky
Score: Howard Shore
Production Design: Carol Spier
Editing: Ronald Sanders
Country: Canada, UK

eXistenZ (97 mins, 1999)
Writer: David Cronenberg
Stars: Jennifer Jason Leigh, Jude Law, Ian Holm, Willem Dafoe
Cinematography: Peter Suschitzky
Score: Howard Shore
Production Design: Carol Spier
Editing: Ronald Sanders
Country: Canada, UK

a CIA cutout) want to rid North America of perverts just like Max. But Max seizes control—maybe. Just like *eXistenZ*, technology becomes another erogenous zone, and any space can abruptly turn into a bloodbath. After a certain point, it ceases to matter if it's real or not. After all, Nicki's waiting for you, just off-screen.

236–237
THE DEAD ZONE

This is one of the most successful adaptations of a Stephen King novel because, like its voluminous source material, it has so many conflicting textures that somehow come together: stiff New England religious bullshit infused with camp, unwanted psychic powers, disability, a serial killer, a corrupt politician, WWII, and a tragic love story. Even when Johnny Smith's psychic powers succeed in helping others, he loses something. He's wounded while apprehending the Castle Rock Strangler; he prevents Chris (but not the other boys) from playing hockey that fateful day; and he commits the ultimate act of self-sacrifice, even though no one will understand why.

238–239
THE FLY

Yes, the greatest cinematic expression of the agony and unfairness of death features a man in a silicone fly suit barfing up acid. And why not? By taking on operatic qualities, *The Fly* says what strict naturalism cannot. Bodily decay against clean hospital sheets and beeping machines offers a false sense of control, of mitigation. Death comes for us all, no matter what medical interventions we throw at it. Here, Seth is literally falling apart alone at home, secluded from the rest of the world, and it's Ronnie, his great love, who's forced to serve as euthanizer on top of everything else she's suffered. "Fuck," is what I'm thinking!

240–241
DEAD RINGERS

The Mantle twins have feet in two worlds: their own and the one we live in. Though Beverly is momentarily tantalized by the prospect of intimacy exclusively with Claire, the lure of the familiar is too great, and at the end of the film, he and Elliot have exited our reality. Beverly's abuse of pills exacerbates the path the twins have always been on, pushing and exceeding every privilege afforded to doctors. This culminates in the creation of tools for "mutant women," to make a woman who conforms to Beverly's ideal interiors. The little girl at the beginning was right: "Fuck off, you freaks . . . I know for a fact you don't even know what 'fuck' is!"

242–243
NAKED LUNCH

Junky creativity is unmatched, as the obstacles to getting drugs (money, dealer location/schedule, pain from withdrawal symptoms, etc.) are harder to solve than the difficulties of those who can just drink socially ever have to face. This isn't a romanticization of substance abuse, but a statement of fact, one that's on full display here. The lengths Bill Lee's mind goes to in an attempt to avoid facing the fact he really shot and killed his wife, his homosexuality, and the depths of his addiction are magnificent. Still, reality pokes through: bossy bottom typewriters with talking assholes, a dick-sucking factory that produces drugs, and the repetition of the fatal William Tell routine. Drugs alter our experience of time and reality but can never be used to rewrite either in our favor.

244–245
M. BUTTERFLY

Jeremy Irons plays another character who only thinks he's got everything under control. But whereas the Mantles gradually had their imperiousness worn down by drugs and paranoia, René Gallimard is ready to unleash his unbelievably messy feelings almost immediately. A consummate performer, it's impossible to tell what role Song adopted willingly or had forced upon them. The Cultural Revolution's wanton destruction of China's past—including the "Ning-Xing" (male favorites) of Han emperors—had no room for whatever Song wished to be. The delicate figure of an Air China stewardess follows René's clumsy, offensive attempt to fuse with what he thought Song was—another person forced to perform femininity, regardless of how she feels.

246–247
CRASH

Everything is bruised in *Crash*, which, in Vaughan's formulation, means everything is erotic. Not erotic like a porno, but simply erogenous. So much of this desire is mediated: a magazine about Jayne Mansfield and Polaroids of Colin Seagrave in drag are strewn about the insides of the wreck he so assiduously recreated; Dr. Remington and other members of Vaughan's sect hungrily watch and rewatch slow-motion car crashes on VHS; Vaughan takes pictures of Catherine Ballard standing next to the bloodied remnants of an expressway pileup before ravishing her inside a car wash. The mindlessness of the characters' consumption, fucking, and death lay bare what they are: animals careening around inside two-ton steel boxes with wheels.

248–249
EXISTENZ

Conceived eleven years before the first "gamer chair," *eXistenZ* expresses the liminal state of video games: our bodies are at rest, frozen in the real world, yet simultaneously stimulated. Rather than huffing and getting mad because you lost before you could save, this stimulation is related to sex, digestion, and penetration. Allegra's game pod is her pet, but also her fleshy sex toy; Ted's new port is an anus for the older Allegra to tease; the "special" at the Chinese restaurant is stomach-turning, a type of gore that leads to the discovery of the bone gun, more gore, a "real" gun, and "real" gore.

Spider (98 mins, 2002)
Writer: Patrick McGrath
Stars: Ralph Fiennes,
Miranda Richardson, Gabriel Byrne
Cinematography: Peter Suschitzky
Score: Howard Shore
Production Design: Andrew Sanders
Editing: Ronald Sanders
Country: Canada, France, UK, USA

A History of Violence (96 mins, 2005)
Writer: Josh Olson
Stars: Viggo Mortensen, Maria Bello, Ed Harris, William Hurt
Cinematography: Peter Suschitzky
Score: Howard Shore
Production Design: Carol Spier
Editing: Ronald Sanders
Country: USA

Eastern Promises (100 mins, 2007)
Writer: Steven Knight
Stars: Viggo Mortensen, Naomi Watts, Vincent Cassel
Cinematography: Peter Suschitzky
Score: Howard Shore
Production Design: Carol Spier
Editing: Ronald Sanders
Country: Canada, UK

A Dangerous Method (99 mins, 2011)
Writer: Christopher Hampton
Stars: Keira Knightley, Viggo Mortensen,
Michael Fassbender, Sarah Gadon,
Vincent Cassel
Cinematography: Peter Suschitzky
Score: Howard Shore
Production Design: James McAteer
Editing: Ronald Sanders
Country: Canada, Switzerland, UK, Germany

Cosmopolis (109 mins, 2012)
Writer: David Cronenberg
Stars: Robert Pattinson,
Juliette Binoche, Sarah Gadon
Cinematography: Peter Suschitzky
Score: Howard Shore
Production Design: Arvinder Greywal
Editing: Ronald Sanders
Country: Canada, France

Maps to the Stars (112 mins, 2014)
Writer: Bruce Wagner
Stars: Julianne Moore, Mia Wasikowska,
John Cusack, Evan Bird, Robert Pattinson
Cinematography: Peter Suschitzky
Score: Howard Shore
Production Design: Carol Spier
Editing: Ronald Sanders
Country: Canada, USA, France, Germany

Crimes of the Future (107 mins, 2022)
Writer: David Cronenberg
Stars: Viggo Mortensen, Léa Seydoux, Scott Speedman, Kristen Stewart
Cinematography: Douglas Koch
Score: Howard Shore
Production Design: Carol Spier
Editing: Christopher Donaldson
Country: Canada, UK

250–251
SPIDER

Just as—or perhaps even more—miserabilist than a British director's depiction of life in London's East End, *Spider* unravels the tragedy of a blunted self. Dennis "Spider" Clegg appears as a child and as a mumbling, shabby adult. His adult self sometimes watches his younger self interacting with his parents and takes notes on these vivid ruminations using a cypher in a hidden notebook. As with his childhood love of weaving with twine, time reveals that even Spider's most benign memories and hobbies twist toward something nasty and violent. Sadly, no one seems to have the time to set him straight, so he's just sent away.

252–253
A HISTORY OF VIOLENCE

"Hey, broheem. You're still pretty good with the killing. That's exciting," Ritchie Cusack tells his brother Joey after nearly two decades apart. Their unexpected—and from Joey's side, wholly unwanted—reunion has indeed come after a high body count. Joey left Philly and became Tom Stall, a relentlessly good family man who owns a diner in small-town Indiana. But this fabrication was ruined after two thieves entered Tom's diner. Maybe Tom became Joey again, or maybe Joey never left, because he iced those fuckers. The miracle of Tom's brutality made him famous—and leaves us wondering how much difference there is between a ruthless crime kingpin like Ritchie and the people who cheered Tom on.

254–255
EASTERN PROMISES

Cronenberg's second action film that operates on horror principles typically limited to horror: show more of the violence, not less. In an attempt to do the right thing for a newborn whose mother died in childbirth, Anna, a midwife at Trafalgar Hospital, unwittingly steps into the world of the Russian mafia. There she meets the deceptively cuddly Semyon, the overtly idiotic Kirill, and the exceedingly obedient Nikolai. Despite uncovering information about Semyon's operation that would get her killed, she avoids seeing the worst of what the vor v zakone (and other Eastern European gangs) have to offer, and remains pure. That—and the baby—are the greatest gifts Nikolai could give her.

256–257
A DANGEROUS METHOD

It's impossible to know how much of the world was actually made by those who exist in the periphery of history. Sabina Spielrein's role in the lives of Carl Jung and Sigmund Freud is still debated, but life isn't as simple as fiction—she wasn't performing a role; she was living her life. In this telling, she's the catalyst for some of Sigmund Freud and Carl Jung's most provocative ideas, as well as the disintegration of their bromance. Whereas the homes of Freud and Jung are explored (and sometimes comically compared), Spielrein's remains largely unseen—there are only snippets of her apartment. The film offers us a way to fill that space up.

258–259
COSMOPOLIS

With screens all over his private limo, Eric Packer is never lacking information. Yet he's constantly surprised: the yuan (which he shorted) doesn't fall; his old-money wife actually can see through his bullshit; there are anti-capitalist riots all over the city, and one mutilates his limo; Brutha Fez (one of his favorite musicians) died; and his childhood barber, whose services he's been seeking all day, isn't that great at cutting hair. Eric was once a prince of finance; by the end of this day, he's just another unsightly pile of god-knows-what on a Manhattan sidewalk.

260–261
MAPS TO THE STARS

Toying with our familiarity with the history of Hollywood and the history of how Hollywood self-mythologizes, *Maps to the Stars* naturally covers incest, molestation, drug abuse, hallucinations, spirituality, fate, desire, badly conceived threesomes, celebrity, and moonlike stages of fame (full, waxing, waning, and last quarter). But above all of these blind items, death dominates this tell-all tabloid. Agatha, banished Hollywood royalty, is physically marked by her previous attempt to snuff out her abominable family. She returns to the kingdom to finish the job and succeeds because of her unconventional appearance—in the land of the vapid, the scarred woman is queen.

262–263
CRIMES OF THE FUTURE (2022)

Producing art is often painful, though pain doesn't necessarily produce art. Here, in a world (mostly) without pain, the line is blurred even further. One of Cronenberg's funniest films, this *Crimes of the Future* draws out the lighter side of gaining legendary status in your field—getting worshipped by sycophantic weirdos, watching shitty imitations of your work, and attempting to preserve the integrity and responsibility you initially set out to create with. Though Caprice and Saul fail to valorize Lang's plastic-eater movement in a giant spectacle, they do manage to do it on a smaller, intimate scale—no less revolutionary.

FILMOGRAPHY

DAVID CRONENBERG: CLINICAL TRIALS

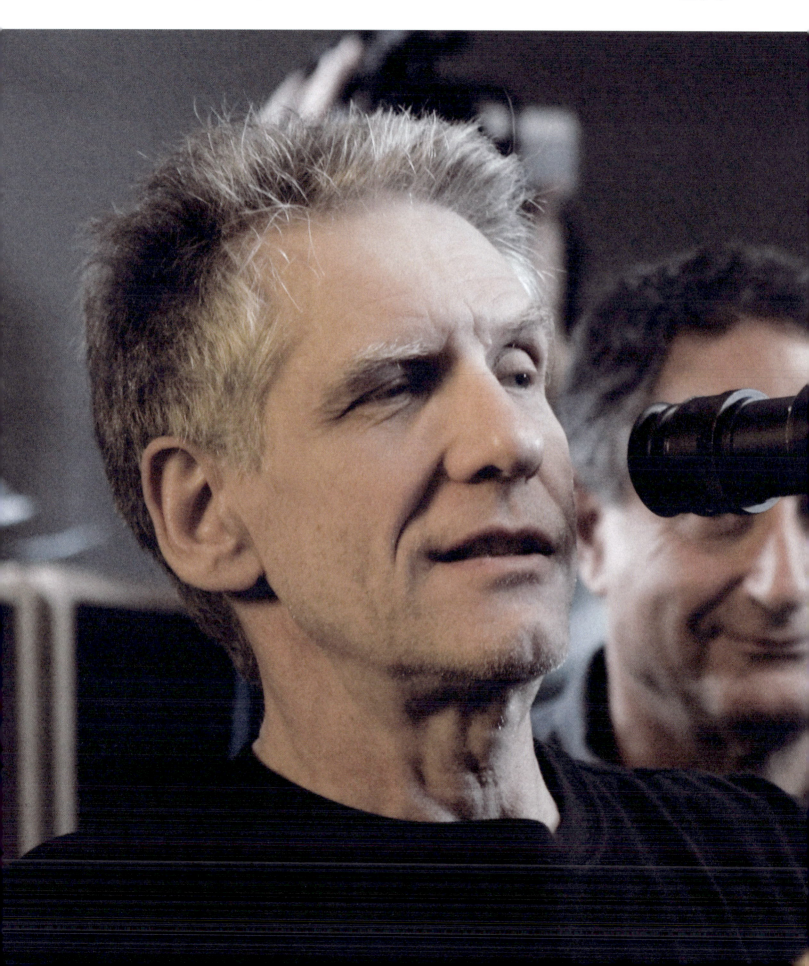

271

DAVID CRONENBERG: CLINICAL TRIALS 272

273

Afterword

THE AUTHOR IN REFLECTION

In these final lines, all I can think about are all the things I could've mentioned in this book but didn't. This is not so much a complaint (or an excuse), but a dose of reality in a text that explores over fifty years of Cronenberg's numinous fictions. There will always be more to say about the films, or things to feel without putting them into words. A definitive statement is impossible. But maybe I've given you a few leads.

Hopefully the notion of using Jung's ideas as a lens to look at a hardcore materialist like Cronenberg seems less heretical now. Like Jung's, Cronenberg's work is largely preoccupied by questions of identity. Both argue that identity is not fixed, but a constant process of creation and recreation that takes place over the course of a lifetime—a process that we have some but not total control over, even though we are often told otherwise. Though they're not the only thinkers/artists who've noted this, they both find ways to break down and make comprehensible the bizarre, amorphous production of identity. Spider's delusions are not the same as the Mantle twins' are not the same as William Lee's are not the same as Benjie Weiss's. They each suffer in their own way: their crises arise from and exist in vastly different conditions, but their struggles with identity and "reality" are, at their heart, universal. Memories are unreliable, and vision even less so. To combat this, humanity devises methods to measure the world that are highly fallible (even though far too many believe them to be perfect). These are, by design, tainted with our own flawed, monkey-brained understanding of the world, which means we only see it as we can imagine seeing it. The reproducibility crisis in all areas of science and medicine, which calls into question many discoveries of the past century, drives home the seriousness of this problem. We don't actually know what we're talking about.

But attempting to understand is better than merely accepting things as they are. One can understand Cronenberg's films as the act of cutting into skin and opening up a body, in which we find not only organs but a host of philosophical quandaries alongside the materialist, empirical facts of their existence. Bringing these together is an alchemical act, which allows us to see a little better, and, more importantly, to feel something valuable. Illness, pain, and death are inescapable, but they too possess numinous characteristics. *The Shrouds*, Cronenberg's latest, longest, and most personal film, probes this sad, terrifying, and enlightening confluence of science and the numinous. Karsh (Vincent Cassel) is the head of GraveTech which makes burial shrouds made up of thousands of tiny cameras that allow the living to monitor and connect with the dead via a smartphone app. However, the technology is highly controversial. A few graves, including that of Karsh's wife, are vandalized—an even greater taboo than penetrating the veil of death. He sets out to find the perpetrators.

Parallels between other Cronenberg films immediately spring to mind from this brief summary—perhaps most strikingly that of the first and second *Crimes of the Future*: both Adrian Tripod and Saul Tenser are men of science who are presented with a mystery and turn themselves into detectives, journeying further and further into increasingly strange niches of society. Like Adrian, Karsh finds death. The inescapable truth, the unbearable unfairness, the beauty of it all. And like Saul, Karsh finds grace. He's one of the lucky ones.

ACKNOWLEDGMENTS

When you write a book, you discover three things:
1. all the books you should've read beforehand and now have no time to read
2. what it's like to go up against yourself
3. and who your best collaborators and moral supporters are.

This latter category is really the only one worth making public. This book wouldn't exist without my incredibly patient editor, David Jenkins, who really is the nicest guy imaginable. Clive Wilson also provided crucial input that always made things better, and Ryan Cahill was invaluable as an arranger of interviews, a transcriptionist, and performer of countless other invisible, invaluable labors. Seeing Tertia Nash's first designs for this book put me in a state of unadulterated bliss and hopefulness that I hadn't felt since Christmas morning 1992, and Moira Letby's contributions have been stunning. It's hard to believe that this was once a blank Word document that I was afraid to look at for too long. Fellow American Lucy Walker provided fantastic boots-on-the-ground research support from Toronto. James D. Perrin, an incredible scholar and just generally awesome person to talk to, provided invaluable insights into Carl Jung and some superb edits in the pre-chapter sections. (If I blew anything about Jung in the chapters themselves, that's all me.) Viggo Mortensen, who not only asked for my input on his superb introduction but also telepathically knew how much I love the band X, is a true renaissance man whom I couldn't be more thrilled to share book space with.

Then there are the friends who believed in me and responded to texts that were either dumb bullshit I'd found online to waste time or horrific bursts of self-doubt and anxiety. Their humor and compassion made this possible: Jocelyn Giannini, Matthew Sherrill, Jad Kamal, Keith Xenos (the best Williams S. Burroughs explainer), Kate Jenkins, Michael Heinz, Aryeh Cohen-Wade, Meredith Slifkin, Laura Kern, Julia Greene, Justin Stewart (Jstew), Bill Akerman, Ian Mantgani, Steve "Movieman" Mears, Ann Neumann, Damon Jablons, Amna Siddiqui, Sherwyn Spencer, and Brian Waite. Thanks to Will Sloan, Justin Decloux, Adam Nayman, and Caden Mark Gardner for reading various chapters and letting me know I was on the right path, and thanks to Will Newman for his support and willingness to use his expensive law degree to look over my book contract several times. Thanks to Connor Leonard and all the editorial and design staff at Abrams. Finally, thanks to Chris Liddell-Westefeld for encouraging me to put more me in the book, Jack for saving Emmylou's life, and Phil, Don, and Anthony.

I also need to assert enormous and unabiding gratitude for my analyst Griffin Hansbury, who is not a Jungian but helped me get through the process of writing and other horrible things that happened while I was putting this thing together.

I owe a tremendous debt to my family—Aunt Susan, Uncle Michael, Grandpa, and Mom—which can't be repaid. Even though half of them are gone, I hope they know how deeply I feel this. Finally I must thank my cats, Emmylou and Perkins, who are the very best companions a writer could have: soft, quiet, emotionally intelligent, cute, not stinky, and not too demanding.

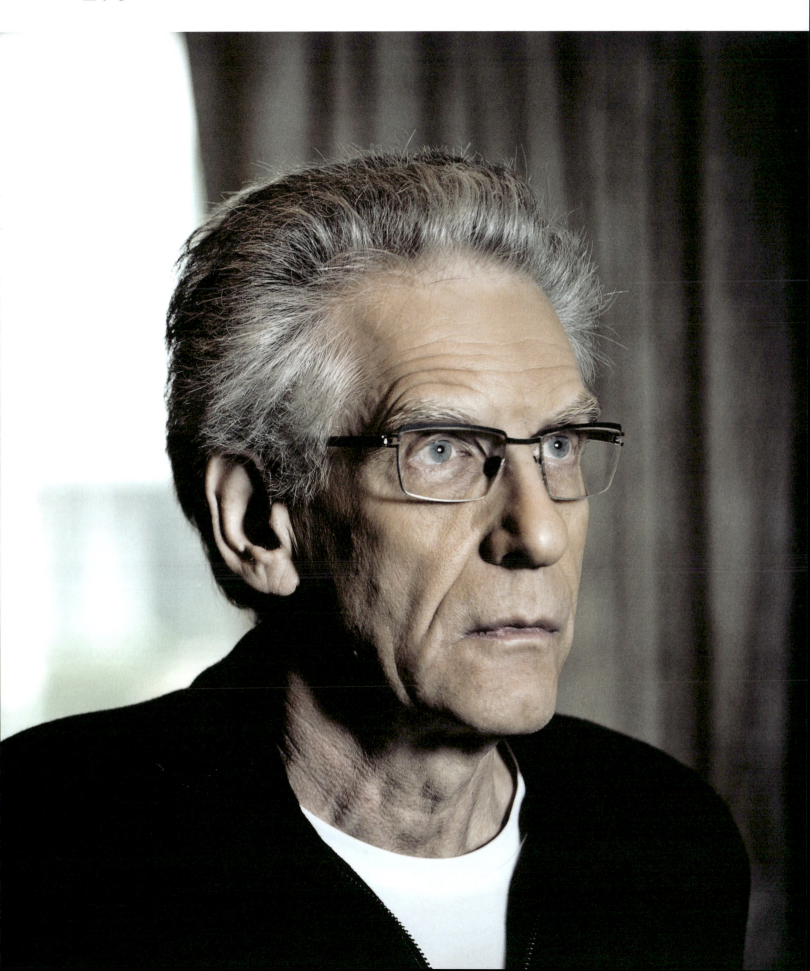

IMAGE CREDITS

6	*Everett Collection Inc / Alamy Stock Photo*	59	*Everett Collection Inc / Alamy Stock Photo*	172	*Maximum Film / Alamy Stock Photo*
8	*Photo 12 / Alamy Stock Photo*	60	*Collection Christophel / Alamy Stock Photo*	174	*TCD/Prod.DB / Alamy Stock Photo*
12	*Album / Alamy Stock Photo*	67	*Associated Press / Alamy Stock Photo*	175	*ScreenProd / Photononstop / Alamy Stock Photo*
24	*Photo 12 / Alamy Stock Photo*	73	*Album / Alamy Stock Photo*	179	*TCD/Prod.DB / Alamy Stock Photo*
29	*ScreenProd / Photononstop / Alamy Stock Photo*	74	*TCD/Prod.DB / Alamy Stock Photo*	180	*TCD/Prod.DB / Alamy Stock Photo*
30	*TCD/Prod.DB / Alamy Stock Photo*	75	*TCD/Prod.DB / Alamy Stock Photo*	182	*Photo 12 / Alamy Stock Photo*
31	*TCD/Prod.DB / Alamy Stock Photo*	78	*LANDMARK MEDIA / Alamy Stock Photo*	184	*ScreenProd / Photononstop / Alamy Stock Photo*
32	*Everett Collection Inc / Alamy Stock Photo*	91	*TCD/Prod.DB / Alamy Stock Photo*	193	*Album / Alamy Stock Photo*
35	*Album / Alamy Stock Photo*	96	*Collection Christophel / Alamy Stock Photo*	198	*ScreenProd / Photononstop / Alamy Stock Photo*
36	*TCD/Prod.DB / Alamy Stock Photo*	102	*TCD/Prod.DB / Alamy Stock Photo*	205	*Everett Collection Inc / Alamy Stock Photo*
38	*TCD/Prod.DB / Alamy Stock Photo*	122	*TCD/Prod.DB / Alamy Stock Photo*	212	*Album / Alamy Stock Photo*
39	*TCD/Prod.DB / Alamy Stock Photo*	124	*TCD/Prod.DB / Alamy Stock Photo*	219	*TCD/Prod.DB / Alamy Stock Photo*
40	*Collection Christophel / Alamy Stock Photo*	130	*ScreenProd / Photononstop / Alamy Stock Photo*	270	*Entertainment Pictures / Alamy Stock Photo*
43	*Everett Collection Inc / Alamy Stock Photo*	149	*Album / Alamy Stock Photo*	272	*Album / Alamy Stock Photo*
44	*Everett Collection Inc / Alamy Stock Photo*	154	*Photo 12 / Alamy Stock Photo*	275	*Abaca Press / Alamy Stock Photo*
50	*TCD/Prod.DB / Alamy Stock Photo*	155	*Album / Alamy Stock Photo*	276	*Moviestore Collection Ltd / Alamy Stock Photo*
51	*ScreenProd / Photononstop / Alamy Stock Photo*	159	*TCD/Prod.DB / Alamy Stock Photo*	278	*Agencja Fotograficzna Caro / Alamy Stock Photo*
53	*Everett Collection Inc / Alamy Stock Photo*	160	*TCD/Prod.DB / Alamy Stock Photo*		
57	*Everett Collection Inc / Alamy Stock Photo*	166	*Album / Alamy Stock Photo*		

Cover *TCD/Prod.DB / Alamy Stock Photo*
Illustration *Sophy Hollington*
Vito Boox

Every effort has been made to identify copyright holders and obtain their permission for the use of copyrighted material. The publisher apologizes for any errors or omissions and would be grateful if notified of any corrections that should be incorporated in future reprints or editions of this book.

INDEX

A

Acts of Violence (documentary), 67
Adler, Alfred, 150
alchemy, 129, 132, 168, 171, 178
allegory, 142
animus/anima/animum, 92, 94–114, 129
  background, 92, 94
  in *Crash*, 95, 108–114
  in *Dead Ringers*, 95–99, 168
  in *M. Butterfly*, 95, 105–108
  in *Naked Lunch*, 95, 99–105
  in psychotherapy, 140
archetypes
  animum and, 94
  artist archetype, 163
  car archetype, 110–111
  child archetype, 143, 146, 148–150
  in *Cosmopolis*, 143, 146
  in *Crash*, 110–111
  in *The Fly*, 121
  madwoman/outcast archetype, 150
  in *Maps to the Stars*, 148–150
  in *Naked Lunch*, 101–102, 105
  in psychotherapy, 129
  in *Spider*, 150, 163
  trickster archetype, 101–102, 105
  artist archetype, 163
At the Suicide of the Last Jew in the World in the Last Cinema in the World (film short), 31
auteur theory, 22

B

Ballard, J.G.
  "The Car, the Future," 110
  Crash (book), 59, 60, 109, 110–111, 114, 208
  Crash film adaptation and, 208. *See also Crash* (film)
  friendship with Cronenberg, 60, 61
  High-Rise, 37
  influence on Cronenberg, 30, 37, 59
Basic Instinct 2 cancellation, 64
Baum, Carol, 48, 54
Beaty, Bart, 137
Becker, Ernest, 84
Behaviorism, 87
body horror, 129, 165
Boursicot, Bernard, 58, 105
Bowles, Jane, 100
Bowles, Paul, 54, 57, 100
Branco, Juan Paulo, 73
Branco, Paulo, 73
The Brood (film)
  critical and commercial success, 42
  The Dead Zone comparison, 49
  filmographic details, 264, 265
  film production, 40, 41–42, 192
  film production attempt, 38
  "More blood! More blood!" catchphrase from, 42
  self in, 117, 120–121
  Shore's work on, 42, 192
  socially acceptable madness in, 21
  still frames, 230–231
Brooks, Conrad, 56
Brooks, Mel, 52, 53–54
Burroughs, William S.
  background, 55–57, 100–102
  influence on Cronenberg, 30, 33, 52
  on drug use, 28
  Naked Lunch (book), 45, 55–57, 99, 100, 101, 194, 205
  Naked Lunch film production and, 57–58, 189, 194, 207, 211
  on Rushdie, 62

C

Cameron, Ewen, 89–90, 92
Canadian Broadcasting Company, 29, 34, 38
Canadian Film Awards, 28–29, 38
Canadian Film Development Corporation (CFDC), 35, 37, 38. *See also* Telefilm Canada
Canadian Film-makers Distribution Centre, 32
car archetype, 111, 114
catharsis. *See* confession
cave drawings, 176
Chambers, Marilyn, 38, 39, 118, 264–265
child archetype, 143, 146, 148–150
CIA, 85–89
cinematography process. *See* Suschitzky, Peter
Cinépix, 35–37
coincidence (synchronicity), 122–123, 156
Cold War era, 85–88
Coleman, Ornette, 57, 194–195, 199, 266
collective unconscious, theories of, 17–18
confession, 132–140
  background, 129, 132–134, 150
  in *Eastern Promises*, 134, 138–140
  in *A History of Violence*, 134, 135–137
consciousness, 114, 143, 168, 170–171, 176
Consumed (Cronenberg), 67, 77
Coppola, Francis Ford, 61, 209
Cosmopolis (book by DeLillo), 73
Cosmopolis (film)
  archetypes in, 142–143, 146
  critical and commercial success, 65–66, 76
  elucidation in, 142–146
  filmographic details, 268, 269
  film production, 72–76, 218
  premiere of, 78
  score for, 192, 199
  still frames, 258–259
  costumes. *See* Cronenberg, Denise
  countertransference, 132, 142
Crash (book by Ballard), 59, 60, 109, 110–111, 208
Crash (film)
  animus/anima/animum in, 94, 108–114
  archetypes in, 110–111
  critical and commercial success, 60–61, 208, 209
  filmographic details, 266, 267
  film production, 59–60, 205, 208, 218
  premiere of, 60, 208
  Shore's score for, 59–60, 197
  still frames, 246–247
Crimes of the Future (1970 film)
  connection to 2022 film, 34
  critical and commercial success, 34
  filmographic details, 264, 265
  film production, 33, 34
  shadow in, 84, 85, 88
  socially acceptable madness in, 21
  still frames, 222–223, 265
Crimes of the Future (2022 film)
  connections to 1970 film, 34
  critical and commercial success, 81–82
  Dead Ringers elements in, 81, 165
  Eastern Promises elements in, 165
  education in, 152, 164–167
  filmographic details, 268, 269
  film production, 80–81
  Naked Lunch elements in, 81
  numinous quality of, 22
  premiere of, 81–82
  Spider elements in, 81
  still frames, 256–257, 271
  streaming possibilities, 77
Cronenberg, David
  background, 21, 210
  daughter (Caitlin), 80
  daughter (Cassandra), 34, 41, 57
  death of father, 82
  on film length, 213
  filmography overview, 264–271, 275. *See also specific films*
  Hampton on collaborating with, 201–203
  Jungian concepts in. *See* animus/anima/animum; confession; education; elucidation; persona; self; shadow; transformation
  legacy of, 9–11, 210
  marriage to Carolyn, 41, 67, 79, 80
  marriage to Margaret, 41
  Mortensen on, 9–11
  Shore's collaborations with, 195
  son (Brandon), 68
  Suschitzky's collaborations with, 213, 215, 216, 218
  Thomas's collaborations with, 206
Cronenberg, Denise (sister)
  childhood, 30
  Cosmopolis and, 76
  Crash and, 59
  A Dangerous Method and, 71
  Dead Ringers and, 31, 55
  death of, 78
  The Fly and, 53
  M. Butterfly and, 58
  Naked Lunch and, 57
  Spider and, 65
Spier on, 191

D

Dangerous Liaisons (film), 200
Dangerous Liaisons (play by Hampton), 200
A Dangerous Method (film)
  author's familiarity with, 17
  critical and commercial success, 72
  education in, 152–157
  filmographic details, 268, 269
  film production, 71–72, 198, 199, 208, 209, 210
  premiere of, 72
  still frames, 256–257
David, Pierre, 41, 42, 46–47
The Day of the Locust (West), 147
Dead Ringers (film)
  animus/anima/animum in, 94–99
  Crimes of the Future (2022) with elements from, 81, 165
  critical and commercial success, 55
  filmographic details, 266, 267
  film production, 31, 34, 55, 188, 195, 212, 216
  A History of Violence comparison, 66, 67
  remake of, 79
  self in, 168
  series speculations, 77
  socially acceptable madness in, 21
  still frames, 240–241
The Dead Zone (book by King), 48, 49, 152
The Dead Zone (film)
  critical and commercial success, 49
  education in, 152, 157–161
  filmographic details, 266, 267
  film production, 48–49
  shadow in, 85
  still frames, 236–237
death, life after, 10, 143, 170
death drive, 111, 152
The Death of David Cronenberg (film), 80
Delaney, Marshall, 37–38
De Laurentiis, Dino, 48–49, 52, 55
De Laurentiis Entertainment Group (DEG), 48–49, 54–55
DeLillo, Don, 73
The Denial of Death (Becker), 84
Dick, Philip K., 30, 49, 63
Dolan, James, 80
Donaldson, Christopher, 82, 194, 268
doppelgangers, 96, 99, 173
Dreyer, Carl, 9, 167
Dunning, John, 35–37, 38

E

Eastern Promises (film)
  confession in, 134, 138–140
  Crimes of the Future (2022) with elements from, 165

Eastern Promises (film) (cont.)
    critical and commercial success, 65–66, 70
    filmographic details, 268
    film production, 68–70, 188
    premiere of, 66
    shadow in, 134, 138
    still frames, 254–255
education, 150–167
    background, 129, 150–152
    in *Crimes of the Future* (2022), 152, 164–167
    in *A Dangerous Method*, 152–157
    in *The Dead Zone*, 152, 157–161
    in *Spider*, 152, 161–163
elucidation, 140–150
    background, 129, 140–142, 150
    in *Cosmopolis*, 142–146
    in *Maps to the Stars*, 142, 147–150
Emergent Films, 32, 34
Ewing, Ian, 32
eXistenZ (film)
    critical and commercial success, 64
    filmographic details, 266, 267
    film production, 62–64
    numinous quality of, 22
    premiere of, 64
    still frames, 248–249
    transformation in, 170, 173–181
    Videodrome comparison, 177–178

F
Fassbender, Michael, 72
Fast Company (film)
    filmographic details, 264, 265
    film production, 40–41
    still frames, 228–229
Fiennes, Ralph, 65, 71, 152, 200
The Fifth Estate (news magazine program), 89
film scores. *See* Shore, Howard
The Fly (film)
    archetypes in, 121
    critical and commercial success, 54
    filmographic details, 266, 267
    film production, 52–54
    self in, 116, 119, 121–125
    Shore's score for, 196, 197
    still frames, 50–51, 238–239
    transformation in, 170
Fothergill, Robert, 32
Frankenstein film adaptation, 42, 45
Freud, Sigmund
    Cronenberg on, 31

in *A Dangerous Method*, 71–72, 152–153, 156–157, 199
on death drive, 111, 152
Hampton on, 200, 201
on narcissism, 99
on psychotherapy process, 132, 201
on psychotherapy termination, 129
on self, 116
From the Drain (film), 33
Fulford, Robert (publishing as Delaney), 37–38, 61

G
Gadon, Sarah, 72
gender and sexuality. *See* animus/anima/animum
Ginsberg, Allen, 101, 105
Gottlieb, Sidney, 87
Greenwell, Garth, 109
Gross, Otto, 156, 202

H
Hampton, Christopher
    background, 200
    on being on set, 204
    A Dangerous Method collaboration by, 71, 72, 200–204
    play by, 71, 72, 200
    screenplay process, 200–204
    Thomas on, 209
Harding, M. Esther, 168
HBO, 52
Hindson, Margaret, 41
A History of Violence (book by Wagner and Locke), 66
A History of Violence (film)
    confession in, 134, 135–137
    critical and commercial success, 65–66, 68
    Dead Ringer comparison, 66, 67
    filmographic details, 268, 269
    film production, 66–67
    premiere of, 67–68
    shadow in, 134, 137
    still frames, 252–253
Hitchcock, Alfred, 114
Hofsess, John, 32
Hwang, David Henry, 58, 105, 197. *See also Madame Butterfly*

I
identity. *See* persona; self
individuation, 23, 129, 168, 199. *See also* animus/anima/animum; persona; self; shadow
"influencing machines," 173
Irons, Jeremy, 54, 55, 58, 95, 106, 267
Irwin, Mark, 40, 55, 187

The Italian Machine (*Teleplay* episode), 39–40

J
Jung, Carl
    on alchemy, 132, 168–170
    on animus/anima/animum, 92–94
    on child archetype, 143, 146
    in *A Dangerous Method*, 17, 71–72, 152–153, 156–157, 199, 200. *See also A Dangerous Method*
    on education, 152
    Hampton on, 200, 201
    on individuation process, 23, 168
    on libido, 111
    on life after death, 170
    on masculinity, 107–108
    on mental illness, 17–18, 20, 116
    on numinous, 22–23
    on psychotherapy process, 23, 129, 132–134, 150, 200, 201
    on self, 116, 143
    on shadow projection, 84
    Spielrein's records and, 200
    on tricksters, 101
Jung, Emma, 72, 152, 157
Jungian concepts. *See* animus/anima/animum; confession; education; elucidation; persona; self; shadow; transformation

K
Kerr, John, 71, 200, 201
King, Stephen, 48–49, 54, 152
Knight, Steven, 70
Knightley, Keira, 72, 152, 209
Koch, Douglas, 80, 81, 82, 187

L
Lantos, Robert, 80
life after death, 10, 143, 170
Link, André, 35
Liston, Robert, 98
Litvinenko, Alexander, 70
location decisions. *See* Spier, Carol
Locke, Vince, 66
Lom, Herbert, 49, 158

M
Madama Butterfly (opera by Puccini), 105, 108, 196
Madame Butterfly (play by Hwang), 58, 105, 106
madwoman archetype, 150
Maps to the Stars (book by Wagner), 77
Maps to the Stars (film)
    archetypes in, 148–150
    critical and commercial success, 65–66, 79
    elucidation in, 142, 147–150
    filmographic details, 268, 269
    film production, 77–78, 212, 218
    still frames, 260–261
Matejko, Jan, 165
M. Butterfly (film)
    animus/anima/animum in, 94, 105–108
    critical and commercial success, 59
    filmographic details, 266, 267
    film production, 58–59, 191, 192, 195
    still frames, 244–245
    transformation in, 173
McAteer, James, 189
McGrath, Patrick, 65
McLuhan, Marshall, 47, 172, 176
McMaster Film Board (MFB), 32
meaningful coincidence (synchronicity), 121–122, 156
Metric, 199
Michaels, Lorne, 32
Miramax, 64
MK-ULTRA, 87, 89
Mlodzik, Ronald
    Crimes of the Future (1970) and, 34
    M. Butterfly and, 58
    Secret Weapons and, 34–35
    Shivers and, 117
    Stereo and, 33, 87
Modern Man in Search of a Soul (Jung), 152
Morbid Anatomy, 17
"More blood! More blood!" catchphrase, 26, 38–40, 41
Mortensen, Viggo
    almost respectable, 48–54
    background, 23, 26
    beyond bounds of depravity, 59–62
    car trouble, 72–77
    Cronenberg's persona, 26–33
    in dreams, 71–72
    get in loser, 40–42
    high culture for lowbrows, 34–38
    Hollywood or bust, 77–78
    independent mutations, 64–66
    long live new flesh, 80–82
    lost years, 79–80

N
Naked Lunch (book by Burroughs), 45, 55–57, 99, 100, 101, 194, 205
Naked Lunch (film)
    animus/anima/animum in, 94, 99–105
    archetypes in, 101–102, 105
    on Burroughs and, 62
    Crimes of the Future (2022) with elements from, 81
    critical and commercial success, 56–57, 58, 205, 208, 209
    filmographic details, 264
    film production, 55–58, 189, 205, 207, 210, 218
    Shore's score for, 58, 192, 194, 196
    still frames, 228–229, 265
narcissism, 98–99, 149, 173
National Film Board, 29, 35
National Film Commission, 29
Neely, Jordan, 20
Netflix, 77, 79
New Line Pictures, 66
Niveau, Claire, 54, 95–96
numinous, 22–23

O
Olson, Josh, 66
Other, 84, 94
Otto, Rudolf, 21
outcast archetype, 150

P
paranoid delusions, 173
Parker, Charlie, 194
The Passion of Joan of Arc (Dreyer), 10, 167
Pasulka, Diana, 17
Pattinson, Robert, 72–73, 76, 77, 78, 142, 147
Paxton, Jim, 32
Pei Pu, Shi, 58, 105, 106
Perrin, James, 94
persona, 24–82. *See also* self

mind control, 42–48
"More blood! More blood!" catchphrase, 38–40
new sex, 58–59
notes from underground, 68–71
plug and play, 62–64
post-pinnacle of *The Fly*'s success, 54–58
preliminary experiments, 33–34
in psychotherapy, 140, 152. *See also* education
quiet American, 66–68
"psychic driving," 89
psychological experiments (unethical), 85–89, 90
psychotherapy
    animus/anima/animum in, 140
    background, 23, 129
    countertransference, 132, 142
    Hampton on, 200
    history of, 152–157
    persona in, 140, 152
    self in, 140, 142
    shadow in, 134, 140
    stages of, 132–134. *See also* confession; education; elucidation; transformation
    transference, 132, 140–142, 153

Q
Queer (Burroughs), 101, 102

R
Rabid (film)
    critical and commercial success, 39
    filmographic details, 264, 265
    film production, 38–39
    remake of, 79
    self in, 116, 118–120
    Shivers as "companion piece" to, 118
    socially acceptable madness in, 21
    still frames, 226–227
Rank, Otto, 84, 99
Rauschenbach, Emma (Jung's wife), 72, 152, 157
Rear Window (film), 114
Reitman, Ivan, 32, 35, 38, 48, 52, 54
"re-patterning" therapy, 89
Ritts, Morton, 31, 32–33
Roberts, Julia, 71, 200
Rodley, Christopher, 46, 62, 206
Rushdie, Salman, 61, 62
Russian Criminal Tattoo Encyclopedia, 70

INDEX

S
Sanders, Ronald
    Crimes of the Future and, 80
    Dead Ringers and, 55
    The Dead Zone and, 49
    Fast Company and, 41
    The Fly and, 53
    Naked Lunch and, 57, 58
    Scanners and, 45
    Shore on collaborations with, 193
    Spider and, 65
    Videodrome and, 47
The Satanic Verses (Rushdie), 62
Scanners (film)
    critical and commercial success, 46
    The Dead Zone comparison, 49
    filmographic details, 264, 265
    film production, 41, 45–46
    A History of Violence comparison, 66
    self in, 168
    series speculations, 76
    shadow in, 84, 85, 86, 89–91
    Shore's score for, 192, 195
    socially acceptable madness in, 21
    still frames, 232–233
schizophrenia, 17–21, 65, 173
scores. *See* Shore, Howard
Scorsese, Cathy, 49
Scorsese, Martin, 49
Secret Weapons (film), 34–35
Secter, David, 31, 32
self, 114–125
    background, 114–116
    in *The Brood*, 116, 120–121
    child archetype and, 143, 146
    in *Dead Ringers*, 168
    in *The Fly*, 116, 119, 121–125
    in psychotherapy, 140, 142
    in *Rabid*, 116, 118–120
    in *Scanners*, 168
    in *Shivers*, 116, 117–118
    transformation and, 168
self-improvement, 168
sexuality and gender. *See* animus/anima/animum
shadow, 82–91
    Cold War era and, 85–88
    in *Crimes of the Future* (1970 film), 84, 85, 88
    Cronenberg on, 82
    in *The Dead Zone* (film), 85
    defined, 82–84
    in *Eastern Promises*, 134, 138
    in *A History of Violence*, 134, 137
    in psychotherapy, 134, 140
    in *Scanners*, 84, 85, 86, 89–91
    in *Stereo*, 84, 87–88
    in *Videodrome*, 85
shadow projection, 85
shadow work, 84
shamanism, 101
Shivers (film)
    critical and commercial success, 37–38
    filmographic details, 264, 265
    film production, 35–37
    The Italian Machine elements from, 40
    Rabid as "companion piece" to, 118
    self in, 116, 117–118
    socially acceptable madness in, 21
    still frames, 224–225
Shore, Howard
    background, 192
    The Brood and, 42, 192
    Cosmopolis and, 192, 199
    Crash and, 59–60, 197
    Crimes of the Future (2022) and, 80, 81
    Dead Ringers and, 55, 196
    The Dead Zone and, 53
    eXistenZ and, 63
    The Fly and, 196—197
    M. Butterfly and, 58, 192, 195
    Naked Lunch and, 57, 192, 194–196
    Scanners and, 90, 192, 196
    on score development, 192–199
    The Shrouds and, 82, 192
    Spider and, 65
    Videodrome and, 196
The Shrouds (film), 77, 82, 192, 275
Sims, J. Marion, 98
Snider, Norman, 34, 54
Spider (book by McGrath), 65
Spider (film)
    archetypes in, 150, 163
    Crimes of the Future elements from, 81
    critical and commercial success, 65–66
    Cronenberg on, 163
    education in, 152, 161–163
    filmographic details, 268, 269
    film production, 65
    still frames, 250–251
Spielrein, Sabina, 71–72, 111, 152–157, 200–202, 269
Spier, Carol
    background, 186
    on character development, 186
    cinematography collaborations, 187
    Crash and, 59
    Crimes of the Future and, 80, 81
    Dead Ringers and, 55, 188
    The Dead Zone and, 49
    on Denise Cronenberg, 191
    Eastern Promises and, 70, 187
    Eastern Promises II and, 191
    Fast Company and, 41
    The Fly and, 53–54
    A History of Violence and, 67
    location decisions by, 187, 188, 189
    M. Butterfly and, 58, 190
    Naked Lunch and, 57, 189, 190
    on production design, 186–191
    Scanners and, 45
    Spider and her absence from, 65
    Videodrome and, 47, 189
Stereo (film)
    critical and commercial success, 33–34
    filmographic details, 264, 265
    film production, 33–34
    shadow in, 84, 87–88
    socially acceptable madness in, 21
    still frames, 220–221
Stevens, Anthony, 116
streaming services, 77, 79–80
Subotnick, Morton, 196
Surgical Instrument for Operating on Mutants (documentary), 34
Suschitzky, Peter
    Acts of Violence and, 67
    background, 213, 214
    on cinematography process, 213–218
    citizenship status, 80
    Cosmopolis and, 217
    Crash and, 59, 217
    Dead Ringers and, 55, 213, 215
    eXistenZ and, 63
    on film production, 188, 213
    Maps to the Stars and, 213, 217
    M. Butterfly and, 58
    Naked Lunch and, 57, 217
    Spider and, 65
synchronicity, 121–122, 156

T
Takemitsu, Toru, 196
The Talking Cure (Hampton), 71, 72, 198, 199, 203
talk therapy. *See* psychotherapy
Tausk, Victor, 173
Telefilm Canada, 55, 79, 165, 208
"The Car, the Future" (Ballard), 111
therapy. *See* psychotherapy
Thomas, Jeremy
    background, 55–56, 206, 209, 210
    on Coppola, 61
    Crash and, 59, 61, 206, 207, 208, 209
    on Cronenberg's legacy, 210
    A Dangerous Method and, 71, 199, 206, 208, 210, 211
    on film production, 204–210
    Naked Lunch and, 55, 57, 206, 207, 208, 209, 210, 211
    on national incentives for films, 207
The Three Stigmata of Palmer Eldritch (Dick), 63
TikTok, 173
Toronto Film Co-op, 32
Total Recall (film), 49
A Touch of Evil (film), 137
Transfer (film short), 31–32
transference, 132, 140–142, 153
transformation, 168–181
    background, 129, 168–170
    in *eXistenZ*, 170, 173–181
    in *The Fly*, 170
    in *M. Butterfly*, 173
    self and, 168
    in *Videodrome*, 171–174
trickster archetype, 101–102, 105
Turner, Ted, 61, 66, 210
Twins (novel), 48, 54–55

U
unconscious, 17–18, 140, 150. *See also* confession; elucidation; shadow
unethical psychological experiments, 85–89, 90
unknown maiden archetype, 150

V
Vertigo (film), 114
Videodrome (film)
    critical and commercial success, 48
    eXistenZ comparison, 177–178
    filmographic details, 270
    film production, 41, 47–48
    numinous quality of, 22
    shadow in, 85
    Shore's score for, 196
    Spier on set creation, 189
    still frames, 234–235
    transformation in, 171–174
Vollmer, Joan, 56, 100–101
von Franz, Marie-Louise, 116

W
Wagner, Bruce, 68, 77
Wagner, John, 66
Walken, Christopher, 157–158
Watkins, Peter, 28–29
Weinstein family, 64
Welles, Orson, 77, 137
West, Nathanael, 147
"William Tell routine," 56, 101, 105, 267
Winstanley, Nicole, 77
Winter Kept Us Warm (film), 31
Wong, B. D., 106

Z
Zeifman, Carolyn, 41, 67, 79, 80

BIBLIOGRAPHY

ACADEMY OF CANADIAN CINEMA. *The Shape of Rage: the Films of David Cronenberg.* Edited by Piers Handling. General Publishing Group, 1983.

ADILMAN, SID. "Japanese style strange objects from Toronto filmmaker's movies, TV shows and commercials have been taken to Tokyo for the largest retrospective ever for his work, which is revered in Japan." *Toronto Star*, March 14, 1993.

AISENBERG, LINDA AND LEORA EISEN. "Seeing doubles on the set of David Cronenberg's Twins." *Toronto Star*, April 16, 1988.

ALS, HILTON. "Double-Talk." *The New Yorker*, October 31, 2011.

AMERICAN FILM INSTITUTE. "Peter Weller on Naked Lunch." Dec 20, 2011.

AMERICAN THEATRE WING. *Working in the Theater.* Episode 133, "Production: "M. Butterfly."" CUNY-TV, April 1988.

ANDERSON, ARISTON. "Spike Lee, David Cronenberg Debate Future of Cinema, How Netflix Tracks Bathroom Breaks." *Hollywood Reporter*, September 3, 2018.

"A scarey-movies man is at the crossroads." *Windsor Star*, February 7, 1979.

BALFOUR, BRAD. "David Cronenberg: A Director Looks At Violent America." *PopEntertainment*, Nov 3, 2005.

"Basic Instinct 2: R.I.P." *IGN*, June 8, 2001.

BEARD, WILLIAM. *The Artist As Monster: The Cinema of David Cronenberg.* University of Toronto Press, 2001.

BEATY, BART. *David Cronenberg's A History of Violence.* University of Toronto Press, 2008.

BEKER, MARILYN. "Young movie-makers popping up all over the Toronto scene." *Toronto Daily Star*, June 10, 1967.

BERGESON, SAMANTHAN. "David Cronenberg's 'Eastern Promises' Sequel Is Dead, Says Vincent Cassel." *Indiewire*, Feb 27, 2023.

BOKYO, JOHN. *Cold Fire: Kennedy's Northern Front.* Knopf Canada, 2016.

BOUZEREAU, LAURENT, dir. "David Cronenberg Discusses M. Butterfly." *M. Butterfly*, DVD. Warner Home Video, 2009.

BRAMESCO, CHARLES. "David Cronenberg: 'Movies were made for sex.'" *Guardian*, February 27, 2020.

BROWNING, MARK. ""THOU, THE PLAYER OF THE GAME, ART GOD": Nabokovian Game-playing in Cronenberg's "eXistenZ."" *Canadian Journal of Film Studies*, Spring 2003.

BUCHANAN, KYLE. "Cannes 2022: David Cronenberg Is Practically Bionic Now." *New York Times*, May 26, 2022.

BURR, TY. "'History' Lessons." *Boston Globe*, September 18, 2005.

BURROUGHS, WILLIAM S. *Burroughs Live: The Collected Interviews of William S. Burroughs, 1960-1997.* Edited by Sylvère Lotringer. Semiotext(e), 2000.

BURROUGHS, WILLIAM S. *Junky: The Definitive Text of "Junk."* Grove Press, 2012.

BURROUGHS, WILLIAM S. *Naked Lunch: The Restored Text.* Edited by James Grauerholz and Barry Miles. Grove Press, 2014.

BURROUGHS, WILLIAM S. *Word Virus: the William S. Burroughs Reader.* Edited by James Grauerholz and Ira Silverberg. Grove Press, 2000.

"Canada's Role in the Cuban Missile Crisis." *Diefenbaker Canada Centre.*

CANFIELD, KEVIN. "David Cronenberg Bloody and Unbowed." *Boston Globe*, September 16, 2007.

CARAMAZZA, ELENA. *The Absolute Shadow: Destiny, Fate, and Intergenerational Processes in Analytical Psychology.* Translated by Susan Ann White. Routledge, 2023.

CARREYROU, JOHN. "The Strange $55 Million Saga of a Netflix Series You'll Never See." *New York Times*, November 22, 2023.

CARTY-WILLIAMS, CANDICE. "An interview with writer and director David Cronenberg." *4th Estate*, October 1, 2014.

"Censors won't allow Cronenberg movie to be shown uncut." *Globe and Mail*, September 13, 1983.

CHELSEY, STEPHEN. "It'll bug you." *Cinema Canada*, September 19, 1975.

CHONG, BARRY. "Avro Arrow." *Canadian Encyclopedia*, November 10, 2022.

CHUTE, DAVID. "David Cronenberg's "gore-tech visions."" *Rolling Stone*, March 17, 1983.

CHUTE, DAVID. "He Came from Within." *Film Comment*, March/April 1980.

CHUTE, DAVID. "Journal: David Chute from Los Angeles." *Film Comment*, January/February 1982.

CINEMATOGRAPHERS ON CINEMATOGRAPHY. "Peter Suschitzky on Dead Ringers (David Cronenberg,1988)." Oct 26, 2022.

CLEMONS, WALTER. "The Imaginary Woman." *New York Times*, October 31, 1993.

COLE, STEPHEN. "David Cronenberg's crash course in existentialism." *National Post*, April 23, 1999.

CONDON, SÉAN FRANCIS. "David Cronenberg's Cosmopolis takes Robert Pattinson to the fringe." *Georgia Straight*, June 6, 2012.

COVERT, COLIN. "A history of collaboration." *Minneapolis Star Tribune*, September 16, 2007.

"Crimes of the Future Press Notes." May 2022.

CRONENBERG, DAVID. "Canadian films." *Globe and Mail*, June 8, 1978.

CRONENBERG, DAVID. "Cronenberg meets Rushdie." *Shift Magazine*, June/July 1995.

CRONENBERG, DAVID. "David Cronenberg: I would like to make the case for the crime of art." *Globe and Mail*, June 22, 2018.

CRONENBERG, DAVID. "Letter in support of not cutting Catherine Breillat's A Ma Soeur." *Toronto Star*, November 23, 2001.

CRONENBERG, DAVID. "Letter to the Editor." *Globe and Mail*, September 19, 1975.

CRONENBERG, DAVID. "Letter to the Editor." *Saturday Night*, November 1975.

CRONENBERG, DAVID. "The night Attila met the anti-Christ she was shocked and he was outraged." *Globe and Mail*, May 14, 1977.

CRONENBERG, DAVID AND J.G. BALLARD. "Set for Collision." *Index on Censorship*, May 1997.

"Cronenberg leaving Basic Instinct II?" *Globe and Mail*, January 31, 2001.

"Cronenberg renonce à « Basic Instinct 2 »." *Le Parisien*, February 1, 2001.

"Cronenberg signed to write, direct Filmplan's 'Video.'" *Hollywood Reporter*, February 24, 1981.

CROW, JONATHAN. "David Cronenberg Talks About Freud, Keira Knightley, and a Dangerous Method." *Yahoo Entertainment*, November 22, 2011.

CUFF, JOHN HASLETT. "TV documentary explores the macabre imagination of a unique Canadian filmmaker." *Globe and Mail*, June 5, 1987.

CZARNECKI, MARK. "A vivid obsession with sex and death." *Maclean's*, February 14, 1983.

DALTON, STEPHEN. "You're Hung Up About a Lot in Britain: David Cronenberg Interviewed." *Quietus*, January 27, 2012.

"David Cronenberg Claims He's Producing The Most 'Controversial' Film In Canada." *Herald*, September 18 1969.

"David Cronenberg Is Developing a TV Series." *Variety.* Sep 1, 2018.

"David Cronenberg on Spider: Reality Is What You Make of It." *Indiewire*, February 28, 2001.

"David Cronenberg: Tapping basic instincts?" *Globe and Mail*, December 29, 2000.

BIBLIOGRAPHY

"Dead Ringers Press Notes." *Astral Films*, 1988.

DEE, JONATHAN. "David Cronenberg's Body Language." *New York Times*, September 18, 2005.

DELANEY, MARSHALL. "You should know how bad this film is. After all, you paid for it." *Saturday Night*, September 1975.

DEXTER, STEVEN. "M Butterfly Channel 4 News Report." YouTube video, 7:07, May 17, 2020.

DICKER, RON. "Old Blood and Guts." *Hartford Courant*, September 23, 2007.

DIECKMANN, KATHERINE. "Off-Screen: Cronenberg's Inside Movies." *Village Voice*, September 28, 1989.

DITZIAN, ERIC. "David Cronenberg Looks To Lock In His Denzel/Cruise Spy Thriller 'The Matarese Circle'." *MTV.com*, April 2, 2009.

DOWNING, DAVID AND KIM KERBIS. "Exterminate All Rational Thought." *Psychoanalytic Review*, October 1998.

DUNPHY, CATHERINE. "The crew: Behind every director is a film crew and David Cronenberg has used the same core group to make his magic in 12 films." *Toronto Star*, May 23, 1997.

DVDGUY2012. "David Cronenberg: Lifetime Interview 1986 (The Fly)." Youtube video, 8:23, February 25, 2011.

ELLIOTT, LOIS. "Good riddance David Cronenberg." *Toronto Star*, May 22, 1987.

EVERITT, DAVID. "David Cronenberg Talks About His Latest and Most Bizarre Feature." *Fangoria*. May 1983.

FLEMING, MIKE JR. "David Cronenberg Sets Viggo Mortensen, Léa Seydoux, Kristen Stewart For 'Crimes Of The Future'; Neon, Serendipity Point Firm Summer Start In Greece." *Deadline*. Apr 29, 2021.

FORD, REBECCA. "Cannes 2012: Robert Pattinson Says He Spent Two Weeks in His Hotel Room Worrying About 'Cosmopolis.'" *Hollywood Reporter*, May 25, 2012.

FOUTCH, HALEIGH. "David Cronenberg Talks MAPS TO THE STARS." *Collider*, February 27, 2015.

FRANCIS, DIANE. "Fun and games on the terror set." *Maclean's*, July 9, 1979.

GALLAGHER, BRIAN. "David Cronenberg Talks A Dangerous Method [Exclusive]." *Movieweb*, November 21, 2011.

GALLOWAY, STEPHEN. "'A Dangerous Method': David Cronenberg's Mild Manner and Outrageous Movies." *Hollywood Reporter*, September 7, 2011.

GALLOWAY, STEPHEN. "David Cronenberg: A Director, Now Less Dangerous." *Hollywood Reporter*, September 6, 2011.

GARRIS, MICK. *The Making of David Cronenberg's VIDEODROME*, 1982.

GRANATSTEIN, J.I. "NORAD." *Canadian Encyclopedia*, January 14, 2021.

GRITTEN, DAVID. "A Dangerous Method: on the set of David Cronenberg's new film." *Telegraph*, January 28, 2012.

GROSS, TERRY. "David Cronenberg on 'A History of Violence.'" *Fresh Air*, October 3, 2005.

GROVE, LLOYD. "Film's Shockmeister: David Cronenberg, the Man Behind 'The Fly.'" *Washington Post*, September 2, 1986.

GRÜNBERG, SERGE. *David Cronenberg: Interviews with Serge Grünberg*. Plexus Publishing Ltd, 2005.

GRUNDMANN, ROY. "Plight of the crash fest mummies: David Cronenberg's Crash." *Cineaste*, January 1997.

HAITHMAN, DIANE. "A director who specializes in horror." *Sun*, February 8, 1981.

HALLIGAN, FIONNUALA. "Head-on collision with controversy." *South China Morning Post*, July 27, 1996.

HANDLER, RACHEL. "David Cronenberg Explains Himself." *Vulture/New York Magazine*, June 3, 2022.

"Happy film images and money to boot." *Globe and Mail*, October 18, 1969.

HARDING, M. *Psychic Energy: Its Source and Its Transformation*. Princeton University Press, 1973.

"He'll hold a 'grudge' screening." *Toronto Daily Star*, September 30, 1969.

HELLMAN, PETER. "Thesis to Conclusion in 23 Years." *Forward*, January 14, 2012.

HERD, ALEX. "Canada and the Cold War." *Canadian Encyclopedia*, January 21, 2021.

HERTZ, BARRY. "TIFF 2019: 'If this is it for the so-called Cronenberg canon, then so be it': David Cronenberg on acting, streaming and his cinematic legacy." *Globe and Mail*, August 26, 2019.

HOFSESS, JOHN. "Quick Ma, the penicillin!" *Maclean's*, October 6, 1975.

HOFSESS, JOHN. "Shivers.'" *Globe and Mail*, June 8, 1978.

HOOPER, BEVERLEY. *Foreigners Under Mao: Western Lives in China, 1949–1976*. Hong Kong University Press, 2016.

HOPPER, TRISTIN. "'From Canada's point of view, (Kennedy) was an absolute bully': Book blasts JFK legacy north of 49." *National Post*, March 6, 2016.

HORTON, MARC. "Butterfly's metamorphosis: Horror master David Cronenberg reshapes a tale of love, sex and romance in M. Butterfly." *Edmonton Journal*, September 10, 1993.

HOWELL, PETER. "He still has his chops; David Cronenberg says it's the emotional pain that counts, as he brings Eastern Promises to TIFF." *Toronto Star*, September 5, 2007.

HUSKINSON, LUCY. "The Self as violent Other: The problem of defining the self." *Journal of Analytical Psychology*, August 2002.

JAEHNE, KAREN. "Cronenberg's Chronic Case: Double Trouble." *Film Comment*, September/October 1988.

JAEHNE, KAREN. "David Cronenberg on William Burroughs: Dead Ringers Do 'Naked Lunch.'" *Film Quarterly*, Spring 1992.

JAMES, NOAH. "The horrifying David Cronenberg." *Maclean's*, July 9, 1979.

JEANS, KATHERINE A. *The Secret World of Carol Spier*. 1999.

JOHNSON, BRIAN D. "A Fatal Obsession." *Maclean's*, September 19, 1988.

JOHNSON, BRIAN D. "Macleans.ca Interview: David Cronenberg." *Maclean's*, April 2, 2009.

JOHNSON, DEIRDRE. "Models of the 'Self': gendered, nongendered and transgendered." *Self & Society* 43, no. 3. (2015).

JONES, WILL. "Cosmopolis Interview with Robert Pattinson and David Cronenberg." *HeyUGuys*, June 11, 2012.

JUNG, C. G. *Aion: Researches into the Phenomenology of the Self*. Translated by Gerhard Adler and R.F.C. Hull. Princeton University Press, 2012.

JUNG, C. G. *Analytical Psychology: Its Theory and Practice*. Translated by Gerhard Adler and R.F.C. Hull. Princeton University Press, 1986.

JUNG, C. G. *Introduction to Jungian Psychology: Notes of the Seminar on Analytical Psychology Given in 1925*. Edited by Sonu Shamdasani and William McGuire. Princeton University Press, 2012.

JUNG, C. G. *Jung on Active Imagination*. Edited by Joan Chodorow. Princeton University Press, 1997.

JUNG, C. G. "On the Psychology of the Trickster Figure." *The Trickster: A Study in American Indian Mythology*. Schocken, 1988.

JUNG, C. G. *Memories, Dreams, Reflections*. Translated by Richard and Clara Winston. Vintage, 1989.

JUNG, C. G. *The Collected Works of C. G. Jung, Vol. 7: Two Essays in Analytical Psychology*. Edited and translated by Gerhard Adler and R.F.C. Hull. Princeton University Press, 2012.

JUNG, C. G., Marie-Louise von Franz, Joseph L. Henderson, Jolande Jacobi, and Aniela Jaffé. *Man and His Symbols*. Dell Publishing, 1968.

KAMINSKY, ILYA. "Promiscuity Is a Virtue: An Interview with Garth Greenwell". *Paris Review*, January 14, 2020.

KANTE, KATHY. "Lights! Camera! Action!" *Globe and Mail*, September 29, 1979.

KEEN, SAM. "The Heroics of Everyday Life: A Theorist of Death Confronts His Own End." *Psychology Today*, April 1974.

"Keira Knightley details her hysteria in "Dangerous Method.'" *Reuters*. November 22, 2011.

KELLNER, HANS. "Dynamic Duo." *Philadelphia Inquirer*, April 13, 1989.

KELLY, BRENDAN. "Bathed in blood." *Montreal Gazette*, September 11, 2007.

KEMPLEY, RITA. "What's Bugging David Cronenberg." *Washington Post*, March 9, 2003.

KING, SUSAN. "'Eastern Promises.'" *Los Angeles Times*, Sep 9, 2007.

KINZER, STEPHEN. *Poisoner in Chief: Sidney Gottlieb and the CIA Search for Mind Control*. Henry Holt and Co., 2019.

KNELMAN, MARTIN. "Instinct sequel shaky; David Cronenberg backs out on making Basic Instinct 2." *Toronto Star*, January 31, 2001.

KNELMAN, MARTIN. "Rocky Horror Picture Show a cheerful decadent mess." *Globe and Mail*, September 27, 1975.

LACEY, LIAM. "Down 'n' dirty at Cronenberg's Crash site." *Globe and Mail*, May 20, 1996.

LANKEN, DANE. "The Parasite Murders is horrible." *Montreal Gazette*, October 11, 1975.

LANKEN, DANE. "Writer-director Cronenberg protests the maniac tag." *Montreal Gazette*, October 11. 1975.

LATTANZIO, RYAN. "'Maps to the Stars' Writer Bruce Wagner on Raising Hell with David Cronenberg." *Indiewire*, February 27, 2015.

LEE, MICHAEL J. "Maria Bello." *Radio Free Entertainment*, September 22, 2005.

LENNICK, MICHAEL. "The Scanners Way: Creating the Special Effects in Scanners." *Scanners*, DVD. Criterion Collection, 2014.

LENNICK, MICHAEL. "Videodrome: Forging the New Flesh." *Videodrome*, DVD. Criterion Collection, 2004.

LEVIN, CHARLES. "The Body of the Imagination in David Cronenberg's Naked Lunch." *Canadian Journal of Psychoanalysis* 11, no. 2 (Fall 2003).

LEVY, EMANUEL. "History of Violence: Interview with Director Cronenberg." October 30, 2005.

LEWIS, TIM. "David Cronenberg: 'My imagination is not a place of horror.'" *Guardian*, September 13, 2014.

LIAM, LACEY. "David delivers, again." *Globe and Mail*, August 15, 2007.

LINK, ANDRÉ. "Delaney's Dreary Denigration." *Cinema Canada*, October 1975.

LUCAS, TIM. "Medium Cruel: Reflections on Videodrome." *Criterion Current*, December 7, 2010.

LUCAS, TIM. "Moving Images: David Cronenberg's Dead Ringers." *Spin*, November 1988.

LUCAS, TIM. "Videodrome." *Cinefantastique*, July/August 1982.

MACAULAY, SCOTT. "Braking and Entering." *Filmmaker Magazine*, Winter 1997.

MACDONALD, GAYLE. "Joy in the midst of A History of Violence." *Globe and Mail*, March 14, 2006.

MACINNIS, CRAIG. "A Stinker?: Jeers followed the screening of David Cronenberg's film Crash at Cannes." *Calgary Herald*, May 18, 1996.

MADWAR, SAMIA. "Inuit High Arctic Relocations in Canada." *Canadian Encyclopedia*, July 25, 2018.

MALCOLM, DEREK. "The gorge also rises." *Guardian*, April 21, 1981.

MALINA, MARTIN. "Plagued by parasites." *Montreal Star*, November 1975.

MARKFIELD, ALAN. "A Director with a High Blood Count." *Los Angeles Times*, February 28, 1982.

MARSHALL, DOUGLAS. "The Great Canadian Film Saga (Take 144)." *Maclean's*, April 1, 1968.

MARTIN, BOB. "David Cronenberg's Scanners." *Fangoria*, January 1981.

MARTIN, BOB. "On The Set of The Dead Zone Part One." *Fangoria*, July 1983.

MARTIN, BOB. "On The Set of The Dead Zone Part Two." *Fangoria*, September 1983.

MASTERS, TIM. "David Cronenberg says Cosmopolis 'was like making a documentary.'" *BBC*, June 14, 2012.

McCRACKEN, MELINDA. "...while Cronenberg takes a weird look at life." *Globe and Mail*, March 1, 1969.

McDONALD, MARCI. "A visitor asks 'Why no Canadian film industry?'" *Toronto Daily Star*, September 30, 1969.

MECCA, DAN. "Farrell, Cotillard To Enter Cronenberg's 'Cosmopolis.'" *Film Stage*, May 11, 2010.

MICHAEL, PATRICIA. "Cronenberg hits out at 'Brood' cuts." *Screen International*, July 7, 1979.

MICHAEL, PATRICIA. "Dateline Canada." *Screen International*, January 6, 1979.

MIETKIEWICZ, HENRY. "Film makes David Cronenberg 'worried about getting too lovable.'" *Toronto Star*, September 4, 1988.

MIKULEC, SVEN. "'A History of Violence': David Cronenberg's Superb Study of the Basic Impulses that Drive Humanity." *Cinephilia & Beyond*.

MILLER, JENNI. "On the Analyst's Couch with David Cronenberg." *GQ*, November 21, 2011.

MILLER, PRAIRIE. "eXistenZ: David Cronenberg Interview." *Rye Star Interviews*, May 10, 1999.

"MK Ultra: CIA mind control program in Canada." *Fifth Estate*, March 11, 1980.

MONK, KATHERINE. "David Cronenberg's history of genius." *Kingston Whig-Standard*, March 18, 2006.

MONK, KATHERINE. "From Russia with Lots of Creepy Sex." *National Post*, September 7, 2007.

MONROE, JUSTIN. "Interview: David Cronenberg Talks Hollywood's Repulsiveness and Why He's Excited About Filmmaking's Future." *Complex*, February 28, 2015.

MOTTRAM, JAMES. "David Cronenberg: 'I'm not ready to embrace Hollywood respectability quite yet.'" *Independent*, October 21, 2007.

MOVIE TELEVISION. "David Cronenberg Naked Lunch interview 1992 (Movie Television)." YouTube video, 6:02, June 4, 2015.

MYERS, EMMA. "Interview: Stephen Lack." *Film Comment*, September 5, 2014.

"New York firm buys Toronto man's film." *Globe and Mail*, August 9, 1969.

NG, JULIE. "Citizens of Cosmopolis." *Cosmopolis*, DVD. Entertainment One, 2012.

O'HARA, KATHLEEN. "David Cronenberg's A History of Violence shows at Cannes festival." *Whitehorse Star*, May 16, 2005.

PAPADOPOULOS, RENOS K. *The Handbook of Jungian Psychology: Theory, Practice, and Applications*. Routledge, 2006.

PERRIN, JAMES. "The Animum: Queering Jungian and Post-Jungian Anima / Animus Theories." 2021.

PETERSEIM, LOCKE. "Interview - Maps to the Stars screenwriter Bruce Wagner." *Open Letters Monthly Archive*.

PEVERE, GEOFF. "Deep inside David Cronenberg's Videodrome." *Toronto Star*, March 22, 2002.

PEVERE, GEOFF. "Our Spider man off to Cannes; David Cronenberg quits Hollywood project to make own movie for world stage." *Toronto Star*, May 10, 2002.

PICCALO, GINA. "Their history of violence." *Los Angeles Times*, September 11, 2007.

PIEPENBURG, ERIK. "Even for David Cronenberg, 'Slasher' Felt Like Something 'Different.'" *New York Times*, August 11, 2021.

PIZZELLO, STEPHEN. "Driver's Side: Director David Cronenberg pulls over to answer AC's questions about Crash." *American Cinematographer*, April 1997.

ÞÓRSSON, MARTEINN. "A masterclass with David Cronenberg." *Reykjavik International Film Festival*, October 7, 2015.

PORTMAN, JAMIE. "Shivers is making Canadians tremble—with anger." *Calgary Herald*, March 20 1976.

PRESS, JOY AND NATALIE JARVEY. "TV's Streaming Bubble Has Burst, Writers Are Striking, and "Everybody Is Freaking Out."" *Vanity Fair*, May 1, 2023.

PRIOR, DAVID. "Fear of the Flesh: the Making of The Fly." *The Fly*, DVD. Criterion Collection, 2005.

Q WITH TOM POWER. "David Cronenberg on Crimes of the Future and why he sees body horror as "the body beautiful."" YouTube video, June 3, 2022.

RAUGER, JEAN FRANÇOIS. "Cannes 2014 - David Cronenberg : « Je ne déteste pas Hollywood »." *Le Monde*, May 7, 2014.

REID, MICHAEL D. "David Cronenberg puts a new spin on creepy." *Times-Colonist*, March 11, 2003.

RETRONTARIO. "CFTO People to People David Cronenberg (1988)." YouTube video, 20:54, May 17, 2012.

REVOKCOM. "DEAD RINGERS (1988) Behind the scenes and interviews with Cronenberg, Jeremy Irons, and more." YouTube video, 7:08, May 19, 2010.

RICKEY, CARRIE. "Look: sex and violence." *Philadelphia Inquirer*, September 22, 2005.

RICKEY, CARRIE. "Seeing Double Intrigues Director: Filmmaker David Cronenberg's Fascination With Twins Comes Through In "Dead Ringers."" *Philadelphia Inquirer*, October 2, 1988.

RICKEY, CARRIE. "Shocker of a Different Sort: David Cronenberg Says "M. Butterfly" Is Consistent with his Moviemaking Repertoire." *Philadelphia Inquirer*, October 7, 1993.

RINGEL, ELEANOR. "Captured nightmares: 'Dead Zone' director David Cronenberg thinks movies should cause catharsis for audiences." *Atlanta Constitution*, November 6, 1983.

RITCHIE, KEVIN. "A chat about death with director David Cronenberg." *NOW Toronto*, October 2, 2021.

"Robert Pattinson Cosmopolis Interview – Sex Scenes, Cronenberg & Cannes." *Red Carpet News TV*. June 2, 2012.

RODLEY, CHRISTOPHER. *Cronenberg on Cronenberg*. 1st ed. Faber & Faber, 1992.

RODLEY, CHRISTOPHER. *Cronenberg on Cronenberg*. 2nd ed. Faber & Faber, 1997.

RODLEY, CHRISTOPHER. "Making Naked Lunch." *Naked Lunch*, DVD. Criterion Collection, 1992.

ROESLER, CHRISTIAN. "Contemporary Psychotherapy Research, Psychodynamic Psychotherapy and Jungian Analysis." *Psychologia* 62, no. 2 (February 2021).

ROMNEY, JONATHAN. "Split Personality." *Independent on Sunday*. January 12, 2003.

ROTHWELL, GREG. "David Cronenberg may redeem himself with 'Spiders.'" *Guelph Mercury*, July 6, 2002.

BIBLIOGRAPHY

ROY, JONATHAN D. "David Cronenberg: Director explores 'creation of identity.'" *Atlanta Journal-Constitution*, October 2, 2005.

RYZIK, MELENA. "Surprise Winners and Choice Quotes." *Carpetbagger/New York Times*, November 29, 2011.

RYZIK, MELENA. "Viggo Mortensen and 'Dangerous Method's' Fate." *Carpetbagger/New York Times*, December 15, 2011.

SAID, S. F. "High-flown ideas underpin movies of David Cronenberg." *Ottawa Citizen*, January 4, 2003.

SAMMON, PAUL M. "David Cronenberg." *Cinefantastique*, Spring 1981.

SCHWARTZ, DAVID. *David Cronenberg: Interviews*. University Press of Mississippi, 2021.

SCOTT, JAY. "Cronenberg bright, gentle, a master of gore." *Globe and Mail*, February 1, 1983.

SCOTT, JAY. "Cronenberg caters to Dolby fans." *Globe and Mail*, October 18, 1983.

SCOTT, JAY. "Cronenberg's filmmaking comes of age." *Globe and Mail*. September 9, 1988.

SCOTT, JAY. "Perfecting horror with teamwork: King, Cronenberg a killer combo in The Dead Zone." *Globe and Mail*, October 21, 1983.

SEYMOUR, GENE. "Out to Lunch With the Guru of Gross-Out." *Los Angeles Times*, January 5, 1992.

SIMON, ALEX. "David Cronenberg: The Hollywood Interview." *Hollywood Interview*.

SMITH, GAVIN. "Cronenberg: Mind Over Matter." *Film Comment*, March/April 1997.

SNOWDEN, LYNN. "Fifty ways to kill an insect by an ex-junkie exterminator." *Guardian*, April 25, 1992.

SOLOMONS, JASON. "An Interview with Jeremy Thomas." Criterion Collection, 2004.

SO'S REEL THOUGHTS. "Scanners Q&A with Michael Ironside | David Cronenberg Retrospective @ Beyond Fest '18." YouTube video, 18:02, September 30, 2018.

SO'S REEL THOUGHTS. "The Fly Q&A with David Cronenberg, Geena Davis, Howard Shore @ Beyond Fest '18." YouTube video, 32:36, October 1, 2018.

STEVENS, ANTHONY. *Jung: A Very Short Introduction*. Oxford University Press, 1994.

STEVENS, MATTHEW L. *The Magical Universe of William S. Burroughs*. Mandrake of Oxford, 2014.

STONE, ALAN A., MD. "A Dangerous Method." *Psychiatric Times*, April 3, 2012.

STONE, JAY. "David Cronenberg's With Reality Crash." *Ottawa Citizen*, October 4, 1996.

STONE, JAY. "The evolution of David Cronenberg." *Ottawa Citizen*, November 6, 1999.

STONE, JAY. "The monster maker." *Ottowa Citizen*, September 9, 2005.

"Stone's basic instincts scare off Cronenberg." *Guardian*, January 31, 2001.

SWEETAPPLE, CHRISTOPHER. "Revelations and Resurrections: David Cronenberg on A Dangerous Method." *PopMatters*, November 18, 2011.

TANEJA, NIKHIL. "2012 in Indie cinema: David Cronenberg on Cosmopolis." *Firstpost*, December 21, 2012.

TAUBIN, AMY. "Body Double." *Village Voice*, September 28, 1988.

TAUBIN, AMY. "Interview: David Cronenberg." *Film Comment*, August 23, 2012.

TAUBIN, AMY. "Maps to the Stars Q&A Panel with David Cronenberg and Julianne Moore and others at NYFF." *Film at Lincoln Center*, September 27, 2014.

TAUSK, VICTOR. "On the Origin of the 'Influencing Machine' in Schizophrenia." Translated by Dorian Feigenbaum. *Psychoanalytic Quarterly* 2, 1933.

TEODORO, JOSÉ. "The Fly Q&A." *Reykjavik International Film Festival*, October 7, 2015.

TESTA, BART. "The King of Blood." *Globe and Mail*, May 31, 1978.

"Thirty million dollars of production from Filmplan." *Screen International*, April 7, 1979.

THOMAS, BOB. "David Cronenberg likes making scary movies." *Atlanta Constitution*, February 8, 1981.

THOMSON, DESSON. "David Cronenberg, Dead Serious." *Washington Post*, September 17, 2007.

THORNE, MATT. "Bruce Wagner in Hollywood." *Los Angeles Review of Books*, March 9, 2014.

THRIFT, MATTHEW. "Beyond the bounds of depravity: an oral history of David Cronenberg's Crash." *Sight & Sound*, September 5, 2019.

TIFF ORIGINALS. "CAROL SPIER | NAKED LUNCH | David Cronenberg: Virtual Exhibition." YouTube video, 2:32, March 4, 2016.

TIFF ORIGINALS. "CRAFT: Costumes & Location | M. BUTTERFLY | David Cronenberg: Virtual Exhibition." YouTube video, 2:16, March 4, 2016.

TIFF ORIGINALS. "DAVID CRONENBERG & COLLABORATORS | Higher Learning." YouTube video, 1:09:18, March 10, 2014.

TIFF ORIGINALS. "Viggo Mortenson and David Cronenberg on CRASH." YouTube video, 52:14, March 30, 2019.

TIMPONE, ANTHONY. "David Cronenberg: Lord of The Fly Part One." *Fangoria*, August 1986.

TIMPONE, ANTHONY. "David Cronenberg: Lord of The Fly Part Two." *Fangoria*, September 1986.

TISDALE, SALLIE. "Just What Is the Film 'Crash' Driving At?" *Los Angeles Times*, April 5, 1997.

TONG, ALLAN. ""These Movies Work Better If You're Really Stoned:" David Cronenberg on Architecture and His Early Work." *Filmmaker Magazine*, January 24, 2014.

TRESIDDER, JACK. *The Complete Dictionary of Symbols*. Chronicle Books, 2005.

TUCHMAN, MITCH. "Too Extreme . . . Until Now: The 1959 novel 'Naked Lunch'—labeled 'literary sewage' by a Supreme Court justice—has a champion in David Cronenberg." *Los Angeles Times*, May 12, 1991.

VAN GELDER, LAWRENCE. "At the Movies: The dark side of twinhood in Toronto." *New York Times*, September 23, 1988.

VAN GELDER, LAWRENCE. "Director Cronenberg explores his twin fascinations in 'Dead Ringers.'" *Chicago Tribune*, September 30, 1988.

VATNSDAL, CAELUM. *They Came From Within: A History Of Canadian Horror Cinema*. ARP Books, 2014.

VLESSING, ETAN. "Carolyn Cronenberg, Film Editor and Wife of David Cronenberg, Dies at 66." *Hollywood Reporter*, July 5, 2017.

VLESSING, ETAN. "David Cronenberg on his existence in film." *Hollywood Reporter*, May 13, 1999.

VOGEL, JUDY. "Deadly Narcissism in Cronenberg's Dead Ringers." *Canadian Journal of Psychoanalysis* 11, no. 2 (Fall 2003).

WADLER, JOYCE. "The Spy Who Fell in Love with a Shadow." *New York Times*, August 15, 1993.

WAGNER, BRUCE. "Maps to the Stars: my film about the dark side of Hollywood." *Guardian*, September 18, 2014.

WALLACE, AMY. "The Jury's In for the Next 10 Days." *Los Angeles Times*, May 13, 1999.

WARREN, INA. "Film Notes: Dead Ringers creeps its way to success in U.S. cinemas." *Globe and Mail*, November 1, 1988.

WILLIAMS, RUTH. "Jung: Politics, Problems in the World." *C.G. Jung: The Basics*. Routledge, 2019.

WINTER, JESSICA. "Robert Pattinson and Director David Cronenberg on Cars, Cosmopolis and Fans Who Care." *Time* magazine, August 14, 2012.

WISE, WYNDHAM. "David Cronenberg talks about "Existenz" and reality." *Take One*, Spring 1999.

WOLFE, LINDA. "Film makes David Cronenberg 'worried about getting too lovable.'" *New York Magazine*, September 8, 1975.

YAKIR, DAN. "David Cronenberg: 'I push things to an extreme.'" *Boston Globe*, September 19, 1988.

YOSHIDA, EMILY. "Q&A: David Cronenberg on Maps to the Stars and his 'cathartic' first US shoot." *Verge*, February 24, 2015.

YUAN, JADA. David Cronenberg on A Dangerous Method, His 'Falling Off' Body Parts, and Why You Should Never Call His Work 'Cronenbergian.' *Vulture/New York Magazine*, December 2, 2011.

YUAN, JADA. "David Cronenberg on Donating His Weird Movie Memorabilia to the Toronto Film Festival." *Vulture/New York Magazine*, September 10, 2013.

ZEIFMAN, CAROLYN. "A History of Violence." *A History of Violence*, DVD. New Line Cinema, 2006.

ZOLLER, STEPHEN. *Mediascene Prevue*, March/April 1983.

ABOUT THE AUTHOR

Violet Lucca's writing has appeared in the *New York Times*, *Art in America*, *Criterion Current*, *Sight and Sound*, the *Village Voice*, *Bust*, *Reverse Shot*, and elsewhere. She served as Vice President of Digital at *Harper's Magazine*, where she hosted its podcast, and Digital Producer at *Film Comment*, where she hosted its podcast. She lives in Brooklyn, but not in an annoying way, and has a non-negligible psychic connection with her two cats.

FOR LITTLE WHITE LIES

Editor David Jenkins
Art Director & Designer Tertia Nash
Designer Moira Letby
Head of Books Clive Wilson
Editorial Project Manager Ryan Cahill
Research Lucy Walker, Hamza Shehryar
Publisher Vince Medeiros

FOR ABRAMS

Editor Connor Leonard
Managing Editor Krista Keplinger
Design Manager Danielle Youngsmith
Production Manager Denise LaCongo

Library of Congress Control Number: 2024939708

ISBN: 978-1-4197-7191-0
eISBN: 979-8-88707-505-1

Text copyright © 2024 Violet Lucca and Little White Lies
Illustrations copyright © 2024 TCO

Cover © 2024 Abrams

Published in 2024 by Abrams, an imprint of ABRAMS. All rights reserved. No portion of this book may be reproduced, stored in a retrieval system, or transmitted in any form or by any means, mechanical, electronic, photocopying, recording, or otherwise, without written permission from the publisher.

Printed and bound in China
10 9 8 7 6 5 4 3 2 1

Abrams books are available at special discounts when purchased in quantity for premiums and promotions as well as fundraising or educational use. Special editions can also be created to specification. For details, contact specialsales@abramsbooks.com or the address below.

Abrams® is a registered trademark of Harry N. Abrams, Inc.

ABRAMS The Art of Books
abramsbooks.com

195 Broadway
New York, NY 10007
abramsbooks.com